THE MIDRASH PESHER OF HABAKKUK

PAUL D. SANSONE, O.F.M.

SOCIETY OF BIBLICAL LITERATURE
————MONOGRAPH SERIES————

editor
Leander E. Keck

associate editor
James L. Crenshaw

NUMBER 24

THE MIDRASH PESHER OF HABAKKUK
Text, Translation, Exposition
with an Introduction
by
William H. Brownlee

_____WILLIAM H. BROWNLEE

THE MIDRASH PESHER OF
HABAKKUK

_____SCHOLARS PRESS_____

Distributed by
Scholars Press
PO Box 5207
Missoula, Montana 59806

THE MIDRASH PESHER OF HABAKKUK
Text, Translation, Exposition
with an Introduction
by
William H. Brownlee

Library of Congress Cataloging in Publication Data

Habakkuk commentary. English & Hebrew.
  The Midrash Pesher of Habakkuk.

  (Monograph series-Society of Biblical Literature ; no.24)
  Bibliography: p.
  Includes index.
  1. Habakkuk commentary—Criticism, interpretation,
etc.   2. Bible.   O.T.   Habakkuk—Commentaries.
I. Brownlee, William Hugh. II. Title. III. Series: Society
of Biblical Literature. Monograph series ; no. 24.
BS1635.H28 1977   224'.95'06   76-30560
ISBN 0-89130-096-1

Printed in the United States of America
1   2   3   4   5
Edwards Brothers, Inc.
Ann Arbor, Michigan 48104

TABLE OF CONTENTS

Preface vii

Acknowledgements ix

Abbreviations 1

Bibliography and Methods of Citation 4

    Texts and Primary Sources 5

    Works on Qumrân Literature 6

    Miscellaneous Works 13

Transliterations and Vocalizations 16

Introduction 19

    The Qumrân Manuscripts 19

    Translating the Habakkuk Pesher 20

    Relation of This to Other Studies 21

    What is a Pesher? 23

    The Place of *Pēšer* in Interpretative Tradition 28

    The Purpose of Pesher 35

The Midrash Pesher of Habakkuk 37

    Text, Translation, Exposition

An Historical Excursus 95

An Excursus on משל 143

Excursus on the Omission of Chapter Three 218

Index to Commentary (the Pericopes) 220

PREFACE

Here is the fruitage of more than twenty-five years of labor at the task of understanding and explaining an important Dead Sea Scroll – the ancient commentary (or midrash) on Habakkuk which first came to my attention in February, 1948. To grasp most quickly the significance and purpose of the present study, one may do well to read the Introduction first.

Yet, for the convenience of those using this book, I have placed ahead of the Introduction a list of Abbreviations, followed by the Bibliography, for which the Abbreviations are important. Next follows a discussion of Transliterations and Vocalizations. At the very end of this book, one will find an Index to the passages of the ancient Habakkuk Pesher which are treated *ad seriatim* in the body of the work.

Each major passage (or pericope) is presented first in pointed Hebrew, next in translation, and is then explained in an Exposition which shows (among other things) the relationship of the ancient commentary to the Biblical text on which it is based.

An estimated 85% of the text is preserved in the Qumrân manuscript. Much of the missing material can be restored. The simplest and most certain restorations are translated within single brackets, [ ]; but where the restorations are less certain (often by reason of their length) and where they serve largely to set forth the general nature of the probable contents (or to test whether such contents can fit the available space), they are enclosed within double brackets, [[ ]]. Many of the phrases or clauses placed within parentheses, ( ), represent double, or even triple translations — midrashic nature of the ancient commentary necessitating more than one rendition of the Biblical text. However, the lengthiest duplicate translations are labelled as Translation A, B, or C.

The line numbers in the left margin of the translations refer to the words following the slash marks (/) which divide the text. A slash is introduced the moment one must move ahead in translating to the next line of Hebrew text. However, I place between asterisks those words which belong to the preceding line.

William H. Brownlee
July 11, 1974

ACKNOWLEDGEMENTS

Recognition should be given to Professor Millar Burrows of Yale University and Professor Menahem Mansoor of the University of Wisconsin for my undertaking this project, which even upon the completion of the present tome does not mark the end of the project. For their part in this respect, see the following "Introduction."

It was in December, 1970, that Dr. Mansoor visited Claremont in connection with a lecture series, which was arranged for by Dr. Irving Allan Sparks of the Institute for Antiquity and Christianity at Claremont. This enabled us to discuss together the present manuscript in so far as it had by then emerged. In March, 1971, I had the privilege of conferring with Professor Mathias Delcor of the Catholic University of Toulouse, France, who was making a lecture tour of the United States. He too read and criticized my manuscript. Both men made helpful suggestions, sometimes as to the vocalization of the text, sometimes as to its interpretations, sometimes mentioning secondary works to be consulted.

Gratitude and credit are especially due to the Claremont Graduate School and to its arm, the Institute for Antiquity and Christianity, for they supported the project by raising money to pay for work-study assistants (Research Associates) and for typists. Students who have assisted me in this and other projects include Edgar W. Smith ('67-'68), Elmer A. Martens ('68-'69), Gerald W. Frens ('69-'72), and Charles Mabee ('72-'74). I am thankful for the critical attention given the manuscript by the editors of the Monograph Series of the Society of Biblical Literature, who have assisted in the final process of perfecting the manuscript.

Gratitude is due to scores of scholars around the world who have sent me copies of hundreds of articles, many of which I might never have seen apart from their generosity.

Alas, God only knows what debt I owe my wife and children for their patience and pride in my work in making possible my continued labors over many years.

Thanks are due Marvin Sweeney, Mark Kispert, and especially Myron D. Andes for their able assistance in proofreading.

William H. Brownlee
Claremont Graduate School
July 7, 1976

ABBREVIATIONS

Standard abbreviations which appear in all writings need not detain us here. The abbreviations for Biblical books and other ancient Jewish literature should be clear.

The sigla designating the various Dead Sea Scrolls are those set forth by Roland de Vaux in the *Revue Biblique*, LX, 1953, pp. 87f. The use of these sigla is well illustrated in the article published by P. Benoit and others in the same journal (*RB*, LXIII, 1956, pp. 49-67) and translated into English in the *Biblical Archaeologist*, XIX, 1956, pp. 75-96. A section on "Scroll Nomenclature and Abbreviations" appears also in my book *The Meaning of the Qumrân Scrolls for the Bible*, pp. xix-xxi. There I explained the system of numbered caves (as 1Q, 4Q, etc.) and of abbreviated literary designations. For the sake of a closer correlation between the sigla and English names, I proposed calling the formerly designated Dead Sea Manual of Discipline (DSD) the Society Manual to go with *Serekh Hay-yaḥad (1Q S)*, rather than the more literal Order (or, Rule) of the Community. Similarly, H goes better with Hymns (*Hôdāyôt*) than the more literal Thanksgiving Psalms. The War of the Sons of Light Against the Sons of Darkness may be appropriately called the Military Manual to agree with the siglum M (*Milḥāmāh*), etc.

The abbreviations set forth here are bibliographical–being intended to aid the understanding of the references in the Bibliography itself and in the rest of the book. For shortened citations of titles, one should see the annotated Bibliography.

AJSL = American Journal of Semitic Languages and Literature
ALBO = Analecta Lovaniensia Biblica et Orientalia
ASOR = American Schools of Oriental Research
ASV = American Standard Version of the Holy Bible
BA = Biblical Archaeologist
BASOR = Bulletin of the American Schools of Oriental Research
BDB = Brown-Driver-Briggs. See Francis Brown under Miscellaneous
    Works in the Bibliography.
BHT = Beiträge zur historischen Theologie
Bi Or = Bibliotheca Orientalis
BJRL = Bulletin of John Rylands Library
BThB = Biblical Theology Bulletin
BZAW = Beihefte zur *Zeitschrift für die alttestamentliche Wissenschaft*
CBQ = Catholic Biblical Quarterly

1

CDC = Cairo Fragments of the Damascus Covenant (the so-called Zadokite Work). The pages of these codices are designated by Roman numerals; but the chapter and verse numbers which appear in Charles, *Apocrypha and Pseudepigrapha*, Vol. II, pp. 799 ff. are given in Arabic numbers. Thus xx, 10 ff. = 9:36f.

CS = *Cahiers Sioniens*

DJD = Discoveries in the Judaean Desert [of Jordan]

DSS, I = *The Dead Sea Scrolls of St. Mark's Monastery*, Vol. I (edited by Burrows, Trever, Brownlee)

DSS + p. = Millar Burrows, *The Dead Sea Scrolls*

DSSE = Geza Vermes, *The Dead Sea Scrolls in English*

ET = *Expository Times*

ETL = *Ephemerides Theologicae Lovanienses*

Frg. = numbered scroll fragment

HThR = *Harvard Theological Review*

ICC = International Critical Commentary

IEJ = *Israel Exploration Journal*

JA = *Jewish Antiquities*, by Josephus

JW = *Jewish Wars*, by Josephus

JJS = *Journal of Jewish Studies*

JBL = *Journal of Biblical Literature*

JQR = *Jewish Quarterly Review*

JSS = *Journal of Semitic Studies*

JThS = *Journal of Theological Studies*

KJV = King James Version of the Holy Bible

KS = *Kirjath Sepher*

li. = line / lis. = lines

Meaning = W. H. Brownlee, *The Meaning of the Qumrân Scrolls for the Bible*

MT = Massoretic text of the Hebrew Bible

NAB = New American Bible

NC = *Nouvelle Clio*

NEB = New English Bible

NRTh = *Nouvelle Revue théologique*

NTS = *New Testament Studies*

NTT = *Norsk Teologisk Tidsskrift*

OS = *Oudtestamentische Studiën*

PEQ = *Palestine Exploration Quarterly*

RB = *Revue Biblique*

RHR = *Revue de l'histoire des religions* (with Dupont-Sommer and without citation of volume = Tome CXXXVII, 1950, pp. 129-71)

RQ = *Revue de Qumran*

RSR = *Recherches de science religieuse*

RSV = Revised Standard Version of the Holy Bible

SDB = *Supplement au Dictionnaire de la Bible*

SH = Scripta Hierosolymitana
STh = *Studia Theologica*
Text = W. H. Brownlee, *The Text of Habakkuk in the Ancient Commentary from Qumran*
ThS = *Theological Studies*
ThZ = *Theologische Zeitschrift*
ThLZ = *Theologische Literaturzeitung*
VT = *Vetus Testamentum*
ZAW = *Zeitschrift für die alttestamentliche Wissenschaft*
ZKTh = *Zeitschrift für katholische Theologie*
ZNW = *Zeitschrift für die neutestamentliche Wissenschaft*
ZRG = *Zeitschrift für Religions- und Geistesgeschichte*
ZThK = *Zeitschrift für Theologie und Kirche*

CIRCLETS OVER LETTERS

Not all Hebrew letters are equally preserved in the manuscript. Where a letter has suffered major damage, a circlet (°) appears above it. On the other hand, a distinction is made between degrees of preservation, so that those letters least well-preserved are generally inside the brackets, whereas those better preserved are outside the brackets. Yet there are borderline cases, consequently, one should always consult the photographic reproductions.

BIBLIOGRAPHY AND METHODS OF CITATION

Below are the works cited directly and, in the case of certain texts, indirectly. Many other worthwhile articles and books will be cited in the subsequent volume. Naturally, works which are primarily concerned with interpreting the historical allusions will receive more attention, when later on I turn to historical interpretations.

A strenuous effort has been made to make the references clear and yet simple. A few works frequently cited are listed by author only. In the case of A. Dupont-Sommer's first and basic translation of 1Q p Hab, I have cited it regularly as "Dupont-Sommer, *RHR*, p.," without specifying the volume number. In the case of Karl Elliger's book, *Studien zum Habakuk-Kommentar vom Toten Meer*, mention of the author alone has been deemed sufficient whenever citing the translation and accompanying notes on pp. 166-225; but references to views expressed by him elsewhere in the book are specified as to page.

Footnotes have been avoided, bibliographical references being inserted into the text of the exposition. Whenever citations interrupt grammatical connections, the bibliographical reference is placed within parentheses. Out of regard for simplicity I have avoided the use of such reference devices as *op. cit., ibid.,* and *loc. cit.* When, within the same pericope, after a previous reference to an author (and/or author and work) + page, there is further reference to the same author, this refers to the same work and to the same page. Whenever one has moved on to a later page, this is indicated. In case one takes up another work by the same author, this is also specified; but this necessitates a renewed mention of the earlier work, if one wishes to cite it again within the same pericope. Mathias Delcor's basic book *Essai sur le Midrash d'Habacuc* is generally cited by author and page, without indication of title; but following any citation of another work by the same author, it has been found necessary to mention the earlier work by title (*Midrash*) at the resumption of references to it.

Not only is there a table of abbreviations which we may consult in interpreting the bibliographical references; but also, after pertinent items in the bibliography, specific methods of citation are mentioned.

If this seems involved, at least it gives fuller information than the bare allusion to authors and their works by a single letter as in the apparatus of Elliger.

TEXTS AND PRIMARY SOURCES

Allegro, John. *Qumrân Cave 4, I (4Q 158 — 4Q 186)*, DJD, V. Oxford: Clarendon, 1968.

Baillet, M.; J. T. Milik; R. de Vaux. *Les 'Petites Grottes' de Qumrân; Exploration de la falaise, les grottes 2Q, 3Q, 5Q, 6Q, 7Q á 10Q, le rouleau de cuivre*, DJD, III. Oxford: Clarendon, 1962.

Barthélemy, D.; J. T. Milik. *Qumran Cave I*, DJD, I. Oxford: Clarendon, 1955.

Benoit, P.; J. T. Milik; R. de Vaux. *Les Grottes de Murabba^cât*, DJD, II. Oxford: Clarendon, 1961.

Black, Matthew. *Apocalypsis Henoch Graece*. Leiden: E. J. Brill, 1970.

Burrows, Millar; John C. Trever; William H. Brownlee. *The Dead Sea Scrolls of St. Mark's Monastery*, Vol. I. New Haven: ASOR, 1950 (also a second printing, with corrections, of no date). (Cited as *DSS*, I)

————. *The Dead Sea Scrolls of St. Mark's Monastery*, Vol. II, Fascicle 2. New Haven: ASOR, 1951.

Charles, R. H. *The Ethiopic Version of the Hebrew Book of Jubilees*. Oxford: Clarendon, 1899.

————. *The Apocrypha and Pseudepigrapha of the Old Testament*, 2 vols. Oxford: Clarendon Press, 1913.

Colson, F. H. *Philo with an English Translation*, IX, "Every Good Man is Free," Loeb Classical Library. Cambridge, Mass.: Harvard University Press. London: William Heinemann, 1932.

Colson, F. H.; G. H. Whitaker. *Philo with an English Translation*, IV, "The Migration of Abraham," Loeb Classical Library. Cambridge, Mass.: Harvard University Press. London: William Heinemann, 1941.

Epstein, I (ed.) *The Babylonian Talmud*. London: The Soncino Press, 1935.

Freedman, H. and Maurice Simon (editors). *Midrash Rabbah*, Genesis (translated by H. Freedman), Lamentations (translated by A. Cohen). London: Soncino Press, 1939.

Habermann, A. M. *^cEdah we-^cEduth: Three Scrolls from the Judean Desert, Edited with Vocalization, Introduction, Notes and Indices*. Jerusalem: Maḥbaroth le-Sifruth, 1952. (Cited as *^cEdah*)

————. *Megilloth Midbar Yehuda: The Scrolls from the Judean Desert, Edited with Vocalization, Introduction, Notes and Concordance*. Jerusalem: Maḥbaroth le-Sifruth, 1959. (Cited as *Megilloth*)

Jellinek, Adolph. *Bet ha-Midrasch, Sammlung kleiner Midraschim und vermischter Abhandlungen aus der ältern jüdischen Literatur*, III. Jerusalem: Bamberger Wahrmann, 2nd ed., 1938. (Published in Germany, 1856)

Kittel, Rudolf; P. Kahle (editors). *Biblia Hebraica*, 3rd ed., and 7th ed., newly edited by A. Alt and O. Eissfeldt. Stuttgart: Württembergische Bibelanstalt, 1971.

Levi, Israel. *The Hebrew Text of the Book of Ecclesiasticus, Edited with Brief Notes and a Selected Glossary*. Leiden: E. J. Brill, 1951.

Lohse, Eduard. *Die Texte aus Qumran, hebräisch und deutsch, mit masoretischer Punktation, Übersetzung, Einführung und Anmerkungen*. Darmstadt: Wissenschaftliche Buchgesellschaft, 1964. (Cited as Lohse)

Marcus, Ralph (translator). *Josephus, Jewish Antiquities*. Vols. VI-VIII (Vol. VIII with Allen Wikgren), Loeb Classical Library. Cambridge, Mass.: Harvard University Press. London: Heinemann, 1937, 1963.

Ploeg, J. van der; A. S. van der Woude with B. Jongeling. *Le Targum de Job de la Grotte XI de Qumrân*. Koninklijke Nederlandse Akademie van Wetenschappen. Leiden: E. J. Brill, 1971.

Rabin, Chaim. *The Zadokite Documents: I. The Admonition; II. The Laws, Edited with a Translation and Notes*. Oxford at Clarendon, 1954.

Rahlfs, Alfred. *Septuaginta, id est Vetus Testamentum Graece iuxta LXX Interpretes*. Stuttgart: Württembergische Bibelanstalt, 3rd ed., 1949.

Schechter, Solomon. *Fragments of a Zadokite Work, Documents of Jewish Sectaries*, Vol. I. Cambridge University Press, 1910.

Smend, R. *Die Weisheit des Jesus Sirach*. Berlin: G. Reimer, 1906.

Starcky, J. "Psaumes apocryphes de la grotte 4 de Qumrân (4Q Ps′ vii-x)," *RB*, LXXIII, 1966, pp. 353-371.

Sukenik, E. L. מדבר יהודה. מגילות גנוזות מתוך גניזה קדומה שנמצאה במדבר יהודה. Survey I, 1948; Survey II, 1950. Jerusalem: Bialik Institute. (Cited as *Megillot Genuzot*, I and II)

_____. אוצר המגילות הגנוזות שבידי האוניברסיטה העברית (edited by Nahman Avigad). Jerusalem: Bialik Institute, Hebrew University, 1954.

Thackeray, H. St. J. *Josephus, the Jewish War*. Loeb Classical Library. Cambridge, Mass.: Harvard University Press. London: William Heinemann, 1927, 1928.

Trever, John C. *Scrolls from Qumran Cave 1: the Great Isaiah Scroll, the Order of the Community, the Pesher to Habakkuk from Photographs by John C. Trever* (edited by F. M. Cross, D. N. Freedman, J. A. Sanders). Jerusalem: The Albright Institute of Archaeological Research and the Shrine of the Book, 1972.

Vaux, R. de. "Quelques textes hébreux de Murabbaᶜat," *RB*, LX, 1953, pp. 268-75.

Williams, W. Glynn. *Cicero, the Letters to His Friends, with an English Translation*, Loeb Classical Library. Cambridge, Mass.: Harvard University Press; London: William Heinemann, 1927, 1952.

Winstedt, E. O. *Cicero, Letters to Atticus, with an English Translation*. Loeb Classical Library. London: William Heinemann. New York: G. P. Putnam's Sons, 1912, 1939.

WORKS ON THE QUMRAN LITERATURE

Allegro, John. *The Treasure of the Copper Scroll*. Garden City, N. Y.: Doubleday, 1960.

_____. *The Dead Sea Scrolls, a Reappraisal*. Baltimore: Penguin Books, 2nd ed., 1964.

Atkinson, K. M. T. "The Historical Setting of the Habakkuk Commentary," *JSS*, IV, 1959, pp. 238-63.

Baer, Yitzhak. " 'Pesher Habakkuk' and its Period" (Hebrew), *Zion*, XXXIV, 1969, pp. 1-42.

Bartke, Hans. *Die Handschriftenfunde am Toten Meer*. Berlin: Evangelische Haupt-Bibelgesellschaft, 1953.

Barthélemy, D. "Le grand rouleau d'Isaie trouvé près de la Mer Morte," *RB*, LVII, 1950, pp. 530-49.

_____. "Notes en marge de publications récentes sur les manuscrits de Qumran," *RB*, LIX, 1952, pp. 187-218.

Benoit, P., et al. "Le Travail d'édition des fragments manuscrits de Qumran," *RB*, LXIII, 1956, pp. 49-67. (English translation in *BA*, XIX, 1956, pp. 75-96).

Bergmeier, Roland. "Glaube als Werk? Die 'Werke Gottes' in Damaskusschrift II, 14-15 und Johannes 6,28-29," *RQ*, VI, No. 22, 1967, pp. 253-60.

Betz, Otto. *Offenbarung und Schriftforschung in der Qumransekte*, Wissenschaftliche Untersuchungen zum Neuen Testament (ed. by J. Jeremias and Dr. O. Michel). Tübingen: J. C. B. Mohr, 1960.

Black, Matthew. *The Scrolls and Christian Origins*. New York: Charles Scribner's Sons, 1961.

_____. "The Account of the Essenes in Hippolytus and Josephus," *The Background of the New Testament and Its Eschatology* (W. D. Davies and D. Daube, editors). Cambridge University Press, 1956, pp. 172-75.

Bonsirven, Joseph. "Révolution dans l'histoire des origines Chrétiennes?" *Études*, CCLXVIII, 1951, pp. 213-18.

Brown, Raymond E. "The Qumrân Scrolls and the Johannine Gospel and Epistles," *CBQ*, XVII, 1955, pp. 403-19, 559-74.

Brownlee, William H. "The Jerusalem Habakkuk Scroll," *BASOR*, No. 112, Dec., 1948, pp. 8-18.

_____. "Further Light on Habakkuk," *BASOR*, No. 114, April, 1949, pp. 9f.

_____. "Further Corrections of the Translation of the Habakkuk Scroll," *BASOR*, No. 116, Dec., 1949, pp. 14-16.

_____. "The Original Height of the Dead Sea Habakkuk Scroll," *BASOR*, No. 118, April, 1950, pp. 7-9.

_____. "Excerpts from the Translation of the Dead Sea Manual of Discipline," *BASOR*, No. 121, Feb., 1951, pp. 8-13.

_____. *The Dead Sea Manual of Discipline*, BASOR, Supplementary Studies, Nos. 10-12, New Haven, Conn.: ASOR, 1951. (Cited by title + page)

_____. "Biblical Interpretation among the Sectaries of the Dead Sea Scrolls," *BA*, XIV, 1951, pp. 54-76.

_____. "The Historical Allusions of the Dead Sea Habakkuk Midrash," *BASOR*, No. 126, April, 1952, pp. 10-20.

_____. "The Servant of the Lord in the Qumran Scrolls," *BASOR*, No. 132, Dec., 1953, pp. 8-15; No. 135, Oct., 1954, pp. 33-38.

_____. *The Dead Sea Habakkuk Midrash and the Targum of Jonathan*, a mimeographed paper issued by the author, Feb. 2, 1953.

_____. "The Habakkuk Midrash and the Targum of Jonathan," *JJS*, VII, 1956, pp. 169-86.

_____. "Messianic Motifs of Qumran and the New Testament," *NTS*, III, 1956-57, pp. 12-30, 195-210.

_____. Review of *The Dead Sea Scriptures in English Translation* by Theodor Gaster. *JBL*, LXXVII, 1958, pp. 383-86.

_____. *The Text of Habakkuk in the Ancient Commentary from Qumran*, JBL Monograph, XI. Philadelphia, 1959. (Cited as *Text*)

_____. *The Meaning of the Qumrân Scrolls for the Bible*. New York: Oxford University Press, 1964. (Cited as *Meaning*)

_____. "The Significance of 'David's Compositions,'" *RQ*, V, No. 20, 1966, pp. 569-74.

_____. "Jesus and Qumran," *Jesus and the Historian* (edited by F. Thomas Trotter). Philadelphia: Westminster Press, 1968.

_____. "Anthropology and Soteriology in the Dead Sea Scrolls and in the New Testament," *The Use of the Old Testament in the New and Other Essays, Studies in Honor of William Franklin Stinespring* (edited by James M. Efird). Durham, N.C.: Duke University Press, 1972. (Cited as "Anthropology and Soteriology")

_____. "Whence the Gospel according to John," *John and Qumran* (edited by James H. Charlesworth). London: Geoffrey Chapman, 1972. (Cited as "Whence John")

_____. "The Background of Biblical Interpretation at Qumrân," *Qumrân, sa piéte, sa théologie et son milieu* (edited by M. Delcor), Paris: Duculot, 1978, pp. 183-93.

Bruce, F. F. *Biblical Exegesis in the Qumran Texts*. Grand Rapids, Mich.: Eerdmans, 1959.

Buchanan, George W. "The Priestly Teacher of Righteousness," *RQ*, VI, No. 24, 1969, pp. 553-58.

Burrows, Millar. *The Dead Sea Scrolls*. New York: Viking Press, 1955.

_____. *More Light on the Dead Sea Scrolls, New Scrolls and New Interpretations, with Translations of Important Recent Discoveries*. New York: Viking Press, 1958. (Cited as *More Light*)

Carmignac, Jean. "Interprétations de Prophetes et de Psaumes," *Les Textes de Qumran* (edited by J. Carmignac, E. Cothenet and H. Lignée). Paris: Letouzey et Ané, 1961. (Cited as *Textes*)

_____. "Notes sur les Peshârîm," *RQ*, III, No. 12, 1961-62, pp. 505-38.

_____. *Christ and the Teacher of Righteousness* (translated by Katherine G. Pedley). Baltimore and Dublin: Helicon Press, 1962. (Cited as *Christ and the Teacher*)

Chamberlain, John V. *An Ancient Sectarian Interpretation of the Old Testament Prophets: A Study in the Qumran Scrolls and the Damascus Fragments*. Duke University Ph.D. Dissertation, 1955.

Chemouilli, Henri. Review of *Text and Language in Bible and Qumran* by M. H. Goshen-Gottstein. *RQ*, No. 10, 1961, pp. 297-98.

Cross, Frank Moore, Jr. "The Essenes and Their Master," *CC*, LXXII, Aug. 17, 1955, pp. 944f.

_____. *The Ancient Library of Qumran and Modern Biblical Studies*. Garden City, N.Y.: Doubleday, 1958. (Cited as *Ancient Library*)

Dagut, M. B. "The Habakkuk Scroll and Pompey's Capture of Jerusalem," *Biblica*, XXXII, 1951, pp. 542-48.

Davies, W. D. "'Knowledge' in the Dead Sea Scrolls and Matthew 11:25-30," *HThR*, XLVI, 1953, pp. 113-39.

Delcor, Mathias. *Essai sur le Midrash d'Habacuc*. Paris: Éditions du Cerf, 1951. (Cited by author, except after another work by the same author, then as *Midrash*)

_____. "Le Midrash d'Habacuc," *RB*, LVIII, 1951, pp. 521-48.

_____. "L'eschatologie du Documents de Khirbet Qumran," *RSR*, XCIV, 1952, pp. 363-86.

_____. "L'immortalité de l'âme dans le livre de la Sagesse et dans les documents de Qumrân," *NRTh*, LXXVII, 1955, pp. 614-30.

_____. *Les Hymnes de Qumran (Hodayot): Texte hébreu, introduction, traduction, commentaire*. Paris: Letouzey et Ane, 1962. (Cited as *Hymnes*)

_____. "L'Hymne à Sion du rouleau des Psaumes de la grotte XI de Qumrân," *RQ*, VI, No. 21, 1967, pp. 71-88.

Del Medico, H. E. *Deux Manuscrits Hébreux de la Mer Morte: Essai de traduction du "Manuel de Discipline" et du "Commentaire d'Habakkuk" avec notes et commentaires*. Paris: Librairie Orientaliste, Paul Geuthner, 1951. (Cited as *Deux Manuscrits*)

_____. *L'Enigme des manuscrits de la Mer Morte*. Paris: Librairie Plon, 1957.

_____. *The Riddle of the Scrolls*. London: Burke, 1958. (Cited as *Riddle*)

Detaye, C. "Le cadre historique du Midrash d'Habacuc," *ETL*, XXX, 1954, pp. 323-43.

Driver, G. R. *The Hebrew Scrolls from the Neighbourhood of Jericho and the Dead Sea*. London: Oxford University Press, 1951. (Cited as *Hebrew Scrolls*)

_____. Review of *The Scriptures of the Dead Sea in English* by Theodor Gaster, *JThS*, IX, 1958, pp. 347-48.

_____. *The Judean Scrolls: The Problem and a Solution*. Oxford: Blackwell, 1965. (Cited as *Judean Scrolls*)

Dupont-Sommer, André. "Le 'Commentaire d'Habacuc' decouvert près de la Mer Morte," *RHR*, CXXXVII, 1950, pp. 129-71. (Cited as *RHR* + p.)

_____. Interview in *Figaro Littéraire*, Feb. 24, 1951.

_____. "Le Maître de Justice fut il mis à mort?" *VT*, II, 1952, pp. 276-78.

_____. "Quelques remarques sur le *Commentaire d'Habacuc*, à propos d'un livre récent," *VT*, V, 1955, pp. 115-29.

_____. *The Jewish Sect of Qumran and the Essenes* (translated by R. D. Barnett). London: Vallentine, Mitchell & Co., 1954.

_____. *The Essene Writings from Qumran*. Oxford: Blackwell, 1961.

Edelkoort, A. H. *De Handschriften van de Dode Zee*. Baarn: Bosch und Keunig, 1952.

Eissfeldt, Otto. "Der Anlass zur Entdeckung der Höhle und ihre ähnliche Vorgänge aus älterer Zeit," *ThLZ*, LXXIV, 1949, cols. 597-600.

Elliger, Karl. *Studien zum Habakkuk-Kommentar vom Toten Meer*. BHT, Vol. XV, Tübingen: J. C. B. Mohr, 1953.

Finkel, A. "The Pesher of Dreams and Scriptures," *RQ*, IV, No. 15, 1963, pp. 357-70.

Fitzmyer, Joseph A. *Essays on the Semitic Background of the New Testament*, Missoula, Mont.: Scholars Press, 1974. (Cited as *Essays*)

Freedman, David N. "The 'House of Absalom' in the Habakkuk Scroll," *BASOR*, No. 114, April, 1949, pp. 11f.

Gärtner, Bertil. *The Temple and the Community in Qumran and the New Testament*. Cambridge University Press, 1965.

Gaster, Theodor H. *The Dead Sea Scriptures in English Translation.* Garden City, N.Y.: Doubleday, 1st ed., 1956; 2nd ed., 1964. (1st ed. cited by author + p.)

Glanzmann, G. S. "Sectarian Psalms from the Dead Sea," *ThS,* XIII, 1952, pp. 487-524.

Goossens, Roger. "Les Kittim du Commentaire d'Habacuc," NC, IV, 1952, pp. 138-70.

Gordon, R. P. "The Targum to the Minor Prophets and the Dead Sea Texts: Textual and Exegetical Notes," *RQ,* VIII, 31, 1974, pp. 425-29.

Goshen-Gottstein, M.H. "Studies in the Language of the Dead Sea Scrolls," *JJS,* IV, 1953, pp. 104-07.

_____. "Die Qumran-Rollen und die hebräische Sprach-wissenschaft, 1948-1958," *RQ,* I, 1, 1958, pp. 103-12.

_____. *The Qumran Scrolls and Their Linguistic Status* (Hebrew). Studies in Hebrew and Biblical Philology, I. Jerusalem/Tel Aviv & Schocken, 1959.

_____. *Text and Language in Bible and Qumran* (Hebrew). Jerusalem/Tel Aviv: Orient Pub. House, 1960.

_____. "Philologische Miszellen zu den Qumran-texten," *RQ,* II, 5, 1961, pp. 43-52.

_____. "Linguistic Structure and Tradition in the Qumran Documents," *SH,* IV, 1965, pp. 101-37.

Greenberg, Moshe. Review of *The Language and Linguistic Background of the Isaiah Scroll* by E. Y. Kutscher.

Greenfield, Jonas C. Review of *The Qumran Scrolls and Their Linguistic Status* by M. H. Goshen-Gottstein. *RQ,* III, No. 10, 1961, pp. 296-7.

Grintz, Y. M. "סין(א) איסיים-בית היחד'—אנשי," *Sinai,* XVI, 32, pp. 11-43.

Harris, John G. *The Qumran Commentary on Habakkuk.* London: Mowbray, 1966. (cited by author + p.)

Jeremias, Gert. *Der Lehrer der Gerichtigkeit.* Göttingen: Vandenhoeck und Ruprecht, 1963. (Cited as *Der Lehrer* + p.)

Johnson, Sherman E. "Paul and the Manual of Discipline," *HThR,* XLVIII, 1955, pp. 157-65.

Jongeling, B. "Les formes *QṬWL* dans l'hebreu des Manuscrits de Qumran," *RQ,* I, No. 4, 1959, pp. 483-94.

Kaddari, M. Z. "The Root *TKN* in Qumran Texts," *RQ,* V, No. 18, 1965, pp. 219-24.

Keck, Leander E. "The Poor among the Saints in Jewish Christianity and Qumran," *ZNW,* LVII, 1966, pp. 54-78.

Kosmala, Hans. *Hebräer - Essener - Christen.* Leiden: E. J. Brill, 1959.

Kuhn, Karl Georg. "Die in Palästina gefunden hebräischen Texte und das Neue Testament," *ZThK,* XLVII, 1950, pp. 192-211.

Kutscher, Eduard Yeḥezkel. "Concerning the Language of the Dead Sea Scrolls" (Hebrew), *Lešonenu,* XXII, 1958, pp. 89-106.

_____, *The Language and Linguistic Background of the Isaiah Scroll,* Leiden: E. J. Brill, 1974.

Lambert, Gustave. "Le Maître de Justice et la Communauté de l' Alliance," *NRTh,* LXXIV, 1952, pp. 259-83. (Cited as Lambert + p.)

_____. "Traduction de quelques 'Psaumes' de Quamrân et du 'pêsher' d'Habacuc," *NRTh,* LXXIV, 1952, pp. 284-97. (Cited as Lambert + p.)

Lambert, G. and G. Vermès. "Les Manuscrits du Désert de Juda: Les 'Aperçus' de M. Dupont-Sommer," *NRTh,* LXXIII, 1951, pp. 385-98.

Land, F. A. W. van't; A. S. van der Woude. *De Habakkuk-rol van ᶜAin Fašha, Tekst en Vertaling, met een Woord voorauf van Prof. Dr. Th. C. Vriezen.* Assen: van Gorcum, 1954. (Cited as van't Land)

LaSor, William S. *The Dead Sea Scrolls and the New Testament.* Grand Rapids, Mich.: Eerdmans, 1972.

Laurin, R. B. "The Question of Immortality in the Qumran *Hodayot,*" *JSS,* III, 1958, pp. 344-55.

Lehmann, O. H. "Materials Concerning the Dating of the Dead Sea Scrolls, I - Habakkuk," *PEQ,* LXXXIII, 1951, pp. 32-54.

Liebermann, Saul. "Light on the Cave Scrolls from Rabbinic Sources," *Proceedings of the American Academy for Jewish Research,* XX, 1951, pp. 395-404.

Mansoor, Menahem. *The Thanksgiving Hymns.* Studies on the Texts of the Desert of Judah (edited by J. van der Ploeg). Leiden: E. J. Brill. Grand Rapids, Mich.: Eerdmans, 1961.

Maier, Johann. *Die Texte vom Toten Meer.* Munich / Basel: Ernst Reinhardt, 1960.

Marcus, Ralph. "Pharisees, Essenes, and Gnostics," *JBL,* LXXIII, 1954, pp. 157-61.

Martin, Malachi. *The Scribal Character of the Dead Sea Scrolls.* Louvain: Publications Universitaires, Vols. I and II, 1958. (Vol. II, pp. 661-70, cited by section number)

Michaud, Henri. "Un Passage conteste d'un des Rouleaux de la Mer Morte," *VT,* II, 1952, pp. 83-85.

_____. "A Propos d'un passage des Hymnes (1Q *Hôdayôt* II, 7-14)," *RQ,* I, No. 3, 1959, pp. 413-16.

Michel, A. *Le Maître de Justice d'après les Documents de la Mer Morte, la littérature apocryphe et rabbinique.* Abignon: Maison Aubanel Père, 1954.

Milik, J. T. "Fragments d' un Midrash de Michée dans Manuscrits de Qumran," *RB,* LXIX, 1952, pp. 412-18.

_____. "Le Testament de Lévi en Araméen, fragment de la Grotte 4 de Qumran," *RB,* LXII, 1955, pp. 398-406.

_____. *Ten Years of Discovery in the Wilderness of Judea* (Translated by J. Strugnell). Naperville, Ill.: Alec R. Allenson, 1959.

Molin, Georg. (His first translation of 1Q p Hab, presented by K. Schubert as the conclusion of his own article,) *ZKTh,* LXXIV, 1952, pp. 57-62.

_____. "Der Habakkukkommentar von ͨEn Fešḥa in der alttestamentlichen Wissenschaft," *ThZ,* VIII, 1952, pp. 340-57.

_____. *Die Söhne des Lichtes: Zeit und Stellung der Handschriften vom Toten Meer.* Vienna / Munich: Herold, 1954. (Cited by author only, except for clarity)

North, Robert. "The Damascus of Qumran Geography," *PEQ,* LXXXVI, 1955, pp. 1-14.

Nötscher, Friedrich. *Zur theologischen Terminologie der Qumran-Texte.* Bonner biblische Beiträge, X. Bonn: Peter Hanstein, 1956.

Oswald, Eva. "Zur Hermeneutik der Habakkuk-Kommentar," *ZAW,* LVIII, 1956, pp. 243-56.

Philonenko, Marc. "Sur l'expression 'corps de chair' dans le Commentaire d'Habacuc," *Semitica,* V, 1955, pp. 39-40.

Ploeg, J. van der. "Les Rouleaux de la Mer Morte," *Bi Or,* VIII, 1951, pp. 1-13.

_____. "L'immortalité de l' homme d'après les textes de la Mer Morte," *VT,* II, 1952, pp. 171-75.

_____. "L'usage du parfait et de l'imparfait comme moyen de datation dans le Commentaire d'Habacuc," *Les Manuscrits de la Mer Morte.* Colloque de Strasbourg 25-27 mai 1955. Paris: Presses Universitaires de France, 1957, pp. 25-35.

_____. *The Excavations at Qumran, a Survey of the Brotherhood and Its Ideas.* London / New York / Toronto: Longman's, Green and Co., 1958.

_____. "The Belief in Immortality in the Writings of Qumran," *Bi Or,* XVII, 1961, pp. 118-24.

Rabin, Chaim. "Notes on the Habakkuk Scroll and the Zadokite Documents," *VT,* V, 1955, pp. 148-62.

_____. *Qumran Studies.* London: Oxford University Press, 1957.

Rabinowitz, Isaac. "The Second and Third Columns of the Habakkuk Interpretation-Scroll," *JBL,* LXIX, 1950, pp. 31-49.

_____. "Sequence and Dates of the Extra-Biblical Dead Sea Scroll Texts and 'Damascus Fragments,'" *VT,* III, 1953, pp. 175-85.

_____. "The Guides of Righteousness," *VT,* VIII, 1958, pp. 391-404.

_____. "*Pêsher / Pittârôn.* Its Biblical Meaning and Its Significance in the Qumran Literature," *RQ,* VIII, No. 30, 1973, pp. 219-32.

Ratzaby, Yehuda. "Remarks concerning the Distinction between *Waw and Yodh* in the Habakkuk Scroll," *JQR*, XLI, 1950, pp. 155-57.

Reicke, Bo. *Handskrifterna från Qumran*. Symbolse Biblical Upsalienses, Supplementhöften till Svensk Exegetisk Årsbok. Uppsala: Wretmans Boktryckeri, 1952. (Cited as *Handskrifterna*)

Ringgren, Helmer. *The Faith of Qumran: Theology of the Dead Sea Scrolls* (translated by Emilie T. Sander). Philadelphia: Fortress Press, 1963.

Roberts, B. J. "Some observations on the Damascus Document and the Dead Sea Scrolls," *BJRL*, XXXIV, 1951-52, pp. 366-87.

Roth, Cecil. *The Historical Background of the Dead Sea Scrolls*. New York: Philosophical Library, 1959.

Rowley, H. H. "The Internal Dating of the Dead Sea Scrolls," *ETL*, XXVIII, 1952, pp. 257-76. (also in *ALBO*, II, pp. 30 ff.)

_____. *The Zadokite Fragments and the Dead Sea Scrolls*. New York: MacMillan, 1952.

_____. "The Historical Background of the Dead Sea Scrolls," *ET , LXIII, 1952, pp. 378-84.*

Samuel, A. Y. *Treasure of Qumran: My Story of the Dead Sea Scrolls*. Philadelphia: Westminster Press, 1966.

Schoeps, Hans-Joachim. "Handelt es sich wirklich um ebionitische Dokumente?" *ZRG*, III, 1951, pp. 322-36.

Schubert, K. "Die Jüdischen und judenchristlichen Sekten im Lichte des Handschriftenfunde von En Fešcha," *ZKTh*, LXXIV, 1952, pp. 1-62.

Segal, M. H. "The Habakkuk 'Commentary' and the Damascus Fragments," *JBL*, LXX, 1951, pp. 131-47.

Segert, Stanislav. "Zur Habakkuk-Rolle aus dem Funde vom Totem Meer," I-VI, *Archiv Orientální*, XXI, 1953, pp. 218-39; XXII, 1954, pp. 99-113; pp. 444-59; XXIII, 1955, pp. 178-83, 364-73, 575-619. (Cited by section numbers).

Silberman, L. H. "Unriddling the Riddle, a Study in the Structure and Language of the Habakkuk Pesher," *RQ*, III, No. 11, 1961, pp. 323-64. (Cited as "Riddle")

Sjöberg, Erik. "The Restoration of Column II of the Habakkuk Commentary of the Dead Sea Scrolls," *STh*, IV, 1952, pp. 120-28.

Slomovic, Elieser, "Toward an Understanding of the Exegesis in the Dead Sea Scrolls," *RQ*, VII, No. 25, 1969, pp. 3-15.

Stauffer, Ethelbert. "Zur Frühdatierung des Habakukmidrasch," *ThLZ*, LXXVI, 1951, cols. 667-74.

Stenzel, M. "Habakkuk II 15-16," *VT*, III, 1953, pp. 97-99.

Stern, S. M. "Notes on the New Manuscript Find," *JBL*, LXIX, 1950, pp. 19-30.

Sutcliffe, F. *The Monks of Qumran as Depicted in the Dead Sea Scrolls*. Westminster, Md.: Newman Press, 1960. (Cited as *Monks*)

Szyszman, S. "A propos du Karaïsme et des Textes de la Mer Morte," *VT*, II, 1952, pp. 343-48.

_____. "Sur la Geniza du Caire," *VT*, III, 1953, pp. 411-13.

_____. Review of *Karaite Anthology* by Leon Nemoy, *VT*, V, 1955, pp. 328-35.

_____. Review of *The Judean Scrolls and Karaism* by Naphtali Wieder, *RHR*, CLXVIII, 1965, pp. 62-74.

Talmon, Shemaryahu. "Notes on the Habakkuk Scroll," *VT*, I, 1951, pp. 33-37.

_____. "*Yom Hakkippurim* in the Habakkuk Scroll," *Biblica*, XXXII, 1951, pp. 549-63.

_____ "The Calendar Reckoning of the Sect from the Judaean Desert," *Aspects of the Dead Sea Scrolls, Scripta Hierosolymitana*, IV, 1965, pp. 162-99.

Tamisier, R. "A Prototype of Christ?" *Scripture*, V, 1952, pp. 35-39.

Teicher, J. L. "The Dead Sea Scrolls-Documents of the Jewish-Christian Sect of Ebionites," *JJS*, II, 1951, pp. 67-99.

_____. "The Teaching of the Pre-Pauline Church in the Dead Sea Scrolls," *JJS*, III, 1952, pp. 139-50; IV, 1953, pp. 1-13.

_____. "The Habakkuk Scroll," *JJS*, V, 1954, pp. 47-59.

Trever, John C. *The Untold Story of Qumran.* Westwood, N. J.: Fleming H. Revell, 1965.

Vaux, R. de. Review of *Observations sur le Commentaire d'Habacuc découvert près de la Mer Morte* and *Aperçus préliminaires sur les Manuscrits de la Mer Morte* by A. Dupont-Sommer, *RB*, LVIII, 1951, pp. 437-43.

_____. "Fouille au Khirbet Qumrân." *RB*, LX, 1953, pp. 83-106.

_____. *Archaeology and the Dead Sea Scrolls.* London: Oxford University Press, 1973.

Vermèes, Géza. "A propos des 'Aperçus préliminaires sur les Manuscrits de la Mer Morte' de M. A. Dupont-Sommer," *CS*, V, 1951, pp. 58-69.

_____. "Les Manuscrits du Désert de Juda," *NRTh*, LXXIII, 1951, pp. 385-98.

_____. "La Communauté de la Nouvelle Alliance d'après ses écrits récemment découverts," *ETL*, XXVII, 1951, pp. 70-80.

_____. "Quelques traditions de la Communauté de Qumran," *CS*, IX, 1955, pp. 25-58.

_____. *Discovery in the Judean Desert.* New York: Desclée, 1956. (Cited as *Discovery*)

_____. "The Symbolical Interpretation of Lebanon in the Targums: The Origin and Development of an Exegetical Tradition," *JThS*, IX, 1958, pp. 1-12.

_____. *The Dead Sea Scrolls in English.* Gloucester, Mass.: Peter Smith, 1963. (Cited as *DSSE*)

Wallenstein, M. "A Hymn from the Scrolls," *VT*, V, 1955, pp. 277-83.

Weis, P. R. "The Date of the Habakkuk Scroll," *JQR*, XLI, 1950, pp. 125-54.

Wernberg-Møller, P. *The Manual of Discipline: Translated and Annotated with an Introduction.* Studies on the Texts of the Desert of Judah (edited by J. van der Ploeg). Leiden: E. J. Brill, 1957.

Wieder, Naphtali. "The Habakkuk Scroll and the Targum," *JJS*, IV, 1953, pp. 14-18.

_____. "The term קץ in the Dead Sea Scrolls and in Hebrew Liturgical Poetry," *JJS*, V, 1954, pp. 22-31.

_____. *The Judean Scrolls and Karaism.* East and West Library. London: Horovitz Publishing Co., 1962.

Winter, Paul. "Two Non-allegorical Expressions in the Dead Sea Scrolls," *PEQ*, XCI, 1959, pp. 38-46.

Worrell, John. "עצה: 'Counsel' or 'Council' at Qumrân?" *VT*, XX, 1970, pp. 65-74.

Woude, A. S. van der. *Die messianischen Vorstellungen der Gemeinde von Qumrân.* Assen: Van Gorcum, 1957. (Cited as *Die messianische Vorstellungen*)

_____. *Bijbelcommentaren en Bijbelse verhalen; vertaald door A. S. van der Woude, met een voorwoord van J. van der Ploeg.* Amsterdam: Proost en Brandt, 1958. (Cited as Bijbelcommentaren)

Yadin, Yigael. *The Scroll of the War of the Sons of Light against the Sons of Darkness* (translated by Batya and Chaim Rabin). London: Oxford University Press, 1962.

_____. "The Temple Scroll," *New Directions in Biblical Archaeology* (edited by David Noel Freedman and Jonas C. Greenfield). Garden City, N. Y.: Doubleday, 1969, pp. 139-148, and Fig. 56, facing p. 121.

Yalon, Chanokh (Enoch). Review of *Megillot Genuzot II* by E. L. Sukenik, *KS*, XXVI, 1950, pp. 239-48.

_____. Review of *The Dead Sea Scrolls of St. Mark's Monastery*, edited by Millar Burrows, *et al.*, *KS*, XXVII, 1951, pp. 163-76.

Zeitlin, Solomon. " 'A Commentary on the Book of Habakkuk': Important Discovery or Hoax?" *JQR*, XXXIX, 1949, pp. 237-47.

_____. "Scholarship and the Hoax of the Recent Discoveries," *JQR*. XXXIX, 1949, pp. 337-63.

_____. "The Hebrew Scrolls: Once More and Finally," *JQR*, XLI, 1950-51, pp. 1-58.

_____. "The Hebron Pogrom and the Hebrew Scrolls," *JQR*, XLIII, 1952-53, pp. 140-52.

MISCELLANEOUS WORKS

Albright, William F. *From the Stone Age to Christianity.* 2nd ed. Baltimore: Johns Hopkins Press, 1964.

Bentzen, Aage. *Introduction to the Old Testament.* Copenhagen: G. E. C. Gad, 2nd ed., 1952.

Bergmeier, Roland. "Zum Ausdruck in Ps. 1.1, Hi. 10.3, 21.16 und 22.18," *ZAW*, LXXIX, 1967, pp. 229-32.

Black, Matthew. "The Account of the Essenes in Hippolytus and Josephus," *The Background of the New Testament and Its Eschatology* (edited by W. D. Davies and D. Daube). Cambridge University Press, 1956, pp. 172-5.

Bloch, Renée. "Ézéchiel XVI: exemple parfait du procéde midrashique dans la Bible," *CS*, IX, 1955, pp. 193-223.

_____. "Midrash," *Supplement au Dictionnaire de la Bible*, V, 1957, cols. 1263-81.

Boström, Gustav. *Paronomasi den äldre hebreiska maschalliteraturen*, Lund: Gleerup, 1928.

Brekelmans, C. H. W. "The Saints of the Most High and Their Kingdom," *Oudtestamentische Studiën*, XIV, 1965, pp. 305-29.

Bronner, Leah. *Sects and Separatism during the Second Jewish Commonwealth.* New York: Bloch, 1967.

Brown, Francis, S. R. Driver, C. A. Briggs. *A Hebrew and English Lexicon of the Old Testament* (Based on the lexicon of William Gesenius, as translated by E. Robinson). Oxford: Clarendon Press, 1959.

Brownlee, William H. "Books of Maccabees," *IDB* (edited by George Buttrick). New York / Nashville: Abingdon Press, 1962, pp. 201-15.

_____. "Habakkuk," *Hasting's Dictionary of the Bible* (edited by F. C. Grant and H. H. Rowley). New York: Charles Scribner's Sons, 1963.

_____. "The Placarded Revelation of Habakkuk," *JBL*, LXXXII, 1963, pp. 319-25.

_____. "The Composition of Habakkuk" *Hommages à André Dupont-Sommer* (edited by A. Caquot and M. Philonenko). Paris: Adrien-Maisonneuve, 1971, pp. 255-75. (Cited as "The Composition of Habakkuk")

_____. "Psalms 1—2 as a Coronation Liturgy," *Biblica*, LII, 1971, pp. 321-36.

_____. "The Book of Ezekiel," *The Interpreter's One-Volume Commentary on the Bible* (edited by Charles M. Laymon). Nashville / New York: Abingdon Press, 1971, pp. 411-35.

Cody, Aelred. "When is the Chosen People Called a Gôy?" *VT*, XIV, 1964, pp. 1-6.

Dahood, Mitchell. "Some Northwest Semitic Words in Job," *Biblica*, XXXVIII, 1957, pp. 306-20.

_____. *Psalms. 2 Vols.* The Anchor Bible. Garden City, N. Y.: Doubleday, 1968.

Daube, David. *The Sudden in the Scriptures.* Leiden: E. J. Brill, 1964.

Delcor, Mathias. "Les sources du Deutéro-Zacherie et ses Procédés d'emprunt," *RB*, LIX, 1952, pp. 385-411.

_____. *Le Livre de Daniel*, Sources Bibliques, Librairie Lecoffre. Paris: J. Gabalda et Cⁱᵉ Éditeurs, 1971.

Driver, G. R. "Hebrew Notes," *ZAW*, LII, 1934, pp. 51-6.

_____. "On Hēmāh 'Hot Anger, Fury' and also 'Fiery Wine,' " *ThZ*, XIV, 1958, pp. 133-35.

Driver, S. R. *Notes on the Hebrew Text of the Books of Samuel.* Oxford: Clarendon Press, 1890.

Fohrer, Georg. *Introduction to the Old Testament* (a revision and rewriting of Ernst Sellin, translated by David Green). Nashville / New York: Abingdon Press, 1968.

Frost, S. B. "Apocalyptic and History," *The Bible and Modern Scholarship* (edited by J. P. Hyatt). Nashville / New York: Abingdon Press, 1965, pp. 78-113.

Gaster, Moses. *The Samaritans*. London: Oxford University Press, 1925.

Gesenius, Friedrich Heinrich Wilhelm. *A Hebrew and English Lexicon of the Old Testament, Including Biblical Chaldee* (from the Latin of William Gesenius by Edward Robinson, with corrections and large additions, partly furnished by the author in manuscript, and partly condensed from his larger Thesaurus, as completed by Roediger). Boston: Crocker and Roedinger, 1871 (Cited as Gesenius)

Ginsberg, H. L. *Studies in Daniel*. New York: Jewish Theological Seminary of America, 1948.

_____. "The Oldest Interpretation of the Suffering Servant," *VT*, III, 1953, pp. 400-04.

Godbey, Allen Howard. "The Hebrew *Mašal*," *AJSL*, XXXIX, 1922-23, pp. 89-108.

Gottwald, Norman K. *Studies in the Book of Lamentations*. Chicago: A. R. Allenson, 1954.

Harkavy, Alexander. *Hebrew and Chaldee Dictionary to the Old Testament*. New York: Hebrew Publishing Co., 1914.

Henry, Matthew. *An Exposition of the Old and New Testament*, Vol. IV. New York / Chicago / Toronto: Fleming H. Revell (date unknown, but "original preface," 1712).

Hempel, Johannes. *Die althebräische Literatur und ihr hellenistisch-jüdisches Nachleben*. Wildpark-Potsdam: Akademische Verlagsgesellschaft Athenaion, 1930.

Holt, J. M. "So He May Run Who Reads It," *JBL*, LXXXIII, 1964, pp. 298-302.

Hölscher, G. *Hesekiel—der Dichter und das Buch: Eine literarkritische Untersuchung*. BZAW, XXXIX, 1924.

Humbert, Paul. *Problèmes du Livre d'Habacuc*. Neuchatel: Secretariat de l'Universite, 1944.

Jastrow, Marcus. *A Dictionary of the Targumim, the Talmud Babli and Yerushalmi, and the Midrashic Literature*. New York: Pardes Publishing House, 1950. (Cited as *Dictionary*)

Kennicott, B. *Vetus Testamentum Hebraicum cum variis lectionibus*, Oxford, 2 vols., 1776, 1780. (Cited as Kennicott)

Kaufmann, Yehezkel. *The Religion of Israel*. Chicago: University of Chicago Press, 1963.

Köhler, L. and Walter Baumgartner. *Lexicon Veteris Testamenti Libros*. Leiden: E. J. Brill, 1953. (Cited as Köhler-Baumgartner)

Kraus, Hans-Joachim. *Psalmen*, II. Biblischer Kommentar, XV. Neukirchen: Neukirchener Verlag, 1960.

Lambert, Gustave, "Que signifie le nom divin *YHWH*?" *NRTh*, LXXIV, 1952, pp. 897-917.

Le Déaut, Roger. "Apropos a Definition of Midrash." *Interpretation*, XXV, 1971, pp. 259-82.

_____. "The Current State of Targumic Studies." *BThB*, IV, 1974, pp. 3-32.

Marcus, Ralph. "Pharisees, Essenes, and Gnostics," *JBL*, LXXIII, 1954, pp. 157-61.

Meyer, Rudolf. "Zur Geschichte des hebräischen Verbums," *VT*, III, pp. 225-35.

Montgomery, James A. *A Critical and Exegetical Commentary on the Book of Daniel*. ICC. Edinburgh: T & T Clark, 1927.

Noth, Martin. "Die Heiligen des Höchsten," *NTT*, LVI, 1955, pp. 146-61 (also in *Gesammelte Studin*. Munich: Kaiser, 1957, pp. 274-90)

Pope, Marvin. *Job*. The Anchor Bible. Garden City, N. Y.: Doubleday, 1965.

Rad, Gerhard von. *Genesis* (translated by John H. Marks). The Old Testament Library. Philadelphia: Westminster, 1961.

_____. *Old Testament Theology*. II. (translated by D. M. G. Stalker). New York: Harper and Row, 1965.

Radin, Max. *The Jews among the Greeks and Romans*. Philadelphia: Jewish Publication Society of America, 1915.

Sawyer, J. F. A. "Hebrew Words for the Resurrection of the Dead," *VT*, XXIII, 1973, pp. 218-34.

Scott, R. B. Y. *Proverbs. Ecclesiastes*. The Anchor Bible. Garden City, N. Y.: Doubleday, 1965.

Segal, M. H. *A Grammar of Mishnaic Hebrew*. Oxford: Clarendon Press, 1927.

Stendahl, Krister. *The School of St. Matthew*. Acta Seminarii Neotestamentici Upsaliensis. Lund: C. W. K. Gleerup, 1954.

Thomas, D. Winton. "A Consideration of Some Unusual Ways of Expressing the Superlative in Hebrew," *VT*, III, 1953, pp. 209-24.

Torrey, C. C. *The Second Isaiah*. Edinburgh: T & T Clark, 1928.

Vaux, Roland de. *Ancient Israel: Its Life and Institutions* (translated by John McHugh). New York / Toronto / London: McGraw-Hill, 1961.

Vermès, Géza. "The Symbolical Interpretation of Lebanon in the Targums: the Origin and Development of an Exegetical Tradition," *JThS*, IX, 1958, pp. 1-12.

_____. *Scripture and Tradition in Judaism*. Studia Post-Biblica, IV. Leiden: E. J. Brill, 1961.

Webster, Noah (the following dictionaries in his tradition): *Webster's New Collegiate Dictionary*. Springfield, Mass.: G. & C. Merriam Co., 1961. *Webster's Third New International Dictionary of the English Language, Unabridged* (Philip Babcock, editor). Springfield, Mass.: G. & C. Merriam Co., 1968.

Weiser, Artur. *The Old Testament: Its Formation and Development* (translated by Dorothea Barton). New York: Association Press, 1961.

Widengren, G. *Tradition and Literature in Early Judaism and the Early Church*. Leiden: E. J. Brill, 1963.

Wright, Addison G. "The Literary Genre Midrash," *CBQ*, XXVIII, 1966, pp. 105-38, 417-57 (subsequently published as a book with the same title, at Staten Island: Alba House, 1967).

Yadin, Yigael. "Expedition D—the Cave of the Letters," *IEJ*, XII, 1962, pp. 227-257.

_____. *Masada: Herod's Fortress and the Zealots' Last Stand*. New York: Random House, 1966.

_____. *Bar-Kokhba, The Rediscovery of the Legendary Hero of the Second Jewish Revolt against Rome*. New York: Random House, 1971.

TRANSLITERATIONS AND VOCALIZATIONS

Pointed Hebrew texts are presented in connection with the translation of each pericope, which contains a Biblical quotation and its interpretation (or, *pēšer*). Elsewhere, one generally finds the Hebrew and Aramaic words cited in transliteration; but whenever it is advantageous to quote a nonvocalized form, I have presented it either in Hebrew characters or in a strictly consonantal transliteration. In a few cases a Hebrew word may be spelled in Anglicized form, as the word "midrash" when one is discussing ancient Jewish interpretation; but when discussing this as a Hebrew term, it is written "*midrāš*." As for *pēšer*, this newcomer into exegetical discussion is usually given in transliterated Hebrew; but in titles and a few other places, the Anglicized form "Pesher" appears. (For the significance of the term, see the Introduction.)

The consonants are transliterated here in the standard manner, except that I have made concessions to modern Hebrew pronunciation, which recognizes only three aspirated letters (*b/v, k/kh, p/f*). Consonantal *Wāw*, however, is presented in the classical manner as *W/w*, in order to distinguish it from the aspirated Bêt (*v*). Vocal *Šĕwâ*s (schwas) are transliterated as *ĕ*, which leaves the raised *e* (*ᵉ*) for the *Ḥātēf Sĕgôl*, the other *Ḥātēf*s also being raised letters. A dot over an *h* indicates that it is sounded after a vowel, as when pointed with *mappîq*.

The transcriptional method is the same as in my book *Meaning*, pp. xv-xviii, except for the marking of long vowels. There I marked all the long vowels with a caret (ˆ), avoiding the macron (¯), which in popular English denotes other sounds than those intended. However, in the present work, I have distinguished between long vowels which are represented by consonants (or written *plene*) and those which are not so indicated (written *defectiva*). The former are marked with a caret and the latter by the macron.

However, *plene* short vowels are not so indicated in the transliteration; for to use the caret in these cases would be misleading. Thus *QYṢY* (vii, 13) is *qiṣṣē*, not *qîṣṣē*, for, despite the use of the *Yôd* as a vowel letter, the vowel here is short. Similarly, *lĕ'ummîm* (spelled *L'WMYM*) at x,8 must surely employ a *Wāw* for the short *u*, as vocalized by Habermann, and not the long *û* of Lohse's pointing.

It is the vocalic use of *Wāw*, indeed, which has been perplexing to scholars. In nouns, Lohse and Habermann (with one exception just mentioned) interpret this as indicating a long vowel, by vocalizing regularly with a *Ḥōlem* or a *Šûreq*, even when the traditional vocalizations of the MT indicate a

16

pronunciation with *Qāmeṣ Ḥāṭûf* and *Qibbûṣ*, respectively. It is possible that Qumrân pronunciation differed in these cases; but it is more likely that the vowel letters represent various vowel sounds, the short as well as the long. The important thing indicated by a *Wāw* is that we have an *O*-class vowel. Whether it is long or short is not indicated, except as one may infer this from tradition and the rules concerning open and closed syllables. The manuscripts from Qumrân give an important indication that *Qāmeṣ Ḥāṭûf* was still pronounced as a short *o*, and not as *ā* (English *ä*) after the manner of the ordinary *Qāmeṣ*. One may well doubt that a *Ḥāṭēf* vowel would ever be designated by a vowel letter, and hence he may posit a full vowel in such cases; but the same skepticism need not extend to the short vowels themselves. The vowel letter probably stands for a full vowel, but not necessarily for a long vowel.

In the case of verbs in the *puʿal*, Habermann recognizes that *Wāw* does stand for *Qibbûṣ* and so he vocalizes accordingly; but Lohse points with a *Šûreq*. Particularly in cases of the inflection of the infinitive both Habermann and Lohse are in error by vocalizing with a *Ḥōlem*, rather than with a *Qāmeṣ Ḥāṭûf*. Thus they have pointed בְּשׁוֹמְעָם at ii,7, rather than בְּשָׁמְעָם; and עוֹמְדוֹ at viii,9, rather than עֻמְדוֹ. In fact, their pointings suggest that they are erroneously reading participles rather than infinitives! However, it is only the infinitive which may receive a suffix as the *nomen actionis*.

Although one wishes to make the vocalizations correspond as fully as possible with Qumrân pronunciation, the vowel letters do not seem sufficiently precise for absolute certaintly. In most cases of *scriptio plena*, one finds the same class of vowel indicated as in the MT. Of course there are exceptions, as in the vocalization of proper nouns. (See *Meaning*, pp. 165-68). There are also some variations in the accentuation of verbs. The long *ô* of the *qal* imperfect singular (*yiqtôl*) is regularly retained in the plural (*yiqtôlû*), a type of spelling attested in the MT, in pausal positions. These are not artificial lengthenings, but the retention by the MT of older, uncontracted forms which preserve the tradition of a penultimate accentuation of the verb before the plural ending. (See Yalon in *KS*, xxvi, 1950, pp. 241 f.; Rudolf Meyer, *VT*, III, pp. 225-35; Wernberg-Møller, *The Manual of Discipline*, p. 9.)

Unless there is a scribal error involved, in *YŠWPṬNW* at xii,5, we have a *yĕqotel* or *yĕquṭel* form in the place of a *yiqtôl*. Habermann and Lohse recognize this, by their pointing, but they vocalize this with a long vowel as יְשׁוֹפְטֶנּוּ; whereas I would point this with a short *o*, as יִשָׁפְטֶנּוּ (*yĕšofṭennu*), after the analogy of the Massoretic forms פָּעֲבְדֵם (Exod. 20:5), וַעֲבָדְם (Deut. 13:3) and תֹּאכֲלֵהוּ (Job 20:6). It is noteworthy that in each occurrence the pronominal suffix is present. Such formations elsewhere, without the pronominal suffix, would probably receive long vowels.

Commonly, 1Q p Hab has *hifʿil* infinitives in which the *Hē* is elided after the prefixed preposition *Lāmed*; but these and other orthographic features are mentioned at the appropriate places under the exposition.

One peculiar spelling of *BBYT* ("in the house of") is at xi,6, אבית, which (as explained under ¶31) indicates a pronunciation *abbēt*, growing out of the desire to keep the initial letter of בית hard, despite the general practice at that time of softening the letter *b* to *v* after a vowel. This explanation of the odd spelling requires that one vocalize the traditional orthography at viii,1 as בְּבֵית. From the contraction הריץ at xiii,1, one might have pointed all other occurrences of this word as הָאָרֶץ; but, as Malachi Martin has shown, we have the hand of more than one scribe in 1QpHab; so that not all occurrences of this word have been made by the same hand. Perhaps, therefore, these different scribes varied in their pronunciation. Surely קצוות at ix,14 indicates a different pronunciation from קצות of the MT; yet this is what Lohse insists upon. Habermann's קַצְוּוֹת is better; but on the basis of spellings in 1Q Isaᵃ I have adopted the pointing קְצָוּוֹת. (See the discussion under ¶28) Admittedly, we are only on the threshold of understanding the pronunciations of Hebrew at Qumrân; and as more and more texts are published, new advances will be made. See the works of M. H. Goshen-Gottstein, cited in the bibliography. For a full discussion of the orthographic peculiarities of this scroll see Karl Elliger, pp. 59ff.; Stanislav Segert, *Archiv Orientálni*, XIII, 1953-55 (*passim*) and Malachi Martin, *The Scribal Character of the Dead Sea Scrolls*, Vol. I, 1958. In *The Text of Habakkuk in the Ancient Commentary from Qumran* (prepared in 1954), I have analyzed the orthographic variants of the Habakkuk citations and have given an analytic summary on pp. 96-108.

On the linguistic sideof the Qumrân literature, see also: M. H. Goshen-Gottstein, "Philologische Miszellen zu den Qumrantexten," *RQ*, No. 5, pp. 43-51; *The Qumran Scrolls and Their Linguistic Status* (reviewed by Jonas C. Greenfield in *RQ*, No. 10, 1961, pp. 296f.); *Text and Language in Bible and Qumran* (reviewed by Henri Chemouilli in *RQ*, No. 10, 1961); "Linguistic Structure and Tradition in the Qumran Documents," *SH*, IV, 1965, pp. 101 ff.; E. Y. Kutscher, "Concerning the Language of the Dead Sea Scrolls," *Lešonenu*, xxii, 1958, pp. 89-106; *the Language and Linguistic Background of the Isaiah Scroll* (reviewed by Moshe Greenberg in *JBL*, LXXIX, 1960, pp. 278-80).

INTRODUCTION

The Qumrân Manuscripts

My firsthand acquaintance with the Dead Sea Scrolls of the first Qumrân Cave reaches back to 1948, when Dr. John C. Trever and I were Fellows of the American School of Oriental Research in Jerusalem, and Professor Millar Burrows was the Director. On February 21, 1948, four ancient manuscripts came to the School for photography, being brought there by the Metropolitan A. Y. Samuel and Mar Butros Sowmy of the St. Mark's Monastery of the Old City of Jerusalem. One of the manuscripts had already been identified by Trever as the entire book of Isaiah; but the rest were unknown.

That first day was taken up with their photography. Hence we had to await the photographic prints before we could begin studying the texts. John Trever was the expert photographer; but I assisted him both in the photographing and in the developing. The first prints were very small; but, with the aid of a magnifying glass, we began their study as fast as we could develop the prints. On two later occasions, we photographed the manuscripts anew— first in black and white and later in color. The black and white photographs were published by the American Schools of Oriental Research (referred to hereafter as the ASOR) under the title *The Dead Sea Scrolls of St. Mark's Monastery*, Vol. I, 1950; Vol. II, 1951 (to be cited as *DSS* I or II). Trever's colored photographs were not published until 1972: *Scrolls from Qumrân Cave I, the Great Isaiah Scroll, the Order of the Community, the Pesher to Habakkuk*.

In the first volume of texts by the ASOR (*DSS* I), there are physical descriptions of the Isaiah and Habakkuk manuscripts. I wrote all the introductory material on the Habakkuk Commentary. The transcriptions were made by Millar Burrows, John C. Trever and me; but wherever we differed, Dr. Burrows made the final decisions.

When the Dead Sea Scrolls were first discovered, we called them the Jerusalem Scrolls, although we were told that they had been found by bedouins in a cave of the Judean Wilderness, somewhere near the Dead Sea. Archbishop Samuel even knew of Khirbet Qumrân, for he had visited the area in his youth, and he relates this experience in his book *The Treasure of Qumran*. In March, 1948, he told us about the area, mentioning also the cemetery, and he expressed the hypothesis that perhaps this was the site of an ancient Essene monastery. We had hoped to be able to visit the region, to find the cave and to excavate it. Trever obtained a permit from the Antiquities Department for us to excavate the cave, and arrangements were made for bedouins to guide us; but, near the end of March, he was informed by Samuel that the Haganah was conducting military maneuvers in the Judean Wilderness, so that it would be unsafe for us to go there. Hence, we all returned from the American School to the United States without attempting to explore the area.

Bedouins and scholars have conducted extensive and persistent explorations since then. Eleven manuscript-producing caves have been found in the Qumrân region alone; and, since many manuscripts have also been found in other areas of that desert, we need to distinguish different kinds of Dead Sea Scrolls from one another, so that the manuscripts first published as Dead Sea Scrolls are now more precisely called Qumrân Scrolls, and DSH (the Dead Sea Habakkuk Commentary) has become known as 1Q p Hab (the *pēšer* to Habakkuk from Cave One of Qumrân). Among the finds of the Qumrân Caves are other important *pěšārîm*; but 1Q p Hab is by far the most complete. (On the meaning of *pēšer* as a designation of this new kind of interpretative document, see the discussion below. On the manuscript discoveries, see John C. Trever, *The Untold Story of Qumran*; Frank M. Cross, Jr., *The Ancient Library of Qumran*).

Translating the Habakkuk Pesher

My first translation of this scroll was a hasty, tentative production, which was issued very quickly in order to satisfy the scholarly world which was clamoring for these texts. A rough translation was prepared in Jerusalem, March, 1948. For personal reasons, I was unable to proceed further until the fall of the year, when without an opportunity to correct this early draft sufficiently, I was persuaded to permit its publication in the *BASOR* of December, 1948. My later articles were constantly correcting, either explicitly or implicitly, my first translation. Yet eighteen years later, when in 1964 I began preparation of the present translation, I discovered that there were many passages which had not yet been fully understood. The new insights came mainly by ascertaining more exactly how the Biblical text was construed by the ancient author of the pesher (*pēšer*). Since then, until now, I have been actively working at the preparation of the present volume—though many other responsibilities have often meant that the progress was slow.

This fresh translation and exposition of 1Q p Hab was planned already in 1950, when after the publication of *DSS* I, Millar Burrows wrote me of his desire to publish a second volume which would include technical studies, as well as the Hebrew text of the Manual of Discipline. My extensive reading and note taking on this midrashic work began at that time, with the purpose of preparing both a critical commentary of the document as a whole and a study of the Biblical text which it contains. However, I was unable to prepare any of the material for publication until my semester leave from teaching, the fall of 1954, at which time I prepared *The Text of Habakkuk in the Ancient Commentary from Qumran*, (hereafter cited as *Text*). Meanwhile, already in 1951, we had published the text of the Manual of Discipline as Vol. II, Fascicle 2—with the intention that Fascicle 1 would ultimately be published and would contain technical studies based on the scrolls. When after several years, it appeared there were no funds for publishing Fascicle 1, Dr. Burrows released for publication elsewhere my *Text*; and so it appeared as Vol. XI of the Monograph Series of the *Journal of Biblical Literature*, in 1959.

The Relation of This to Other Studies

At long last, the present work dealing with the interpretative material of 1Q p Hab is presented as a companion of *Text*. Built into the earlier work were cross-references to the present volume, which at various points would vindicate inferences as to the meanings of the textual variants for the ancient interpreter. These cross-references have now become meaningful; for they anticipated the sections (or pericopes) as numbered here—numbers assigned by A. Dupont-Sommer in his translation and notes(*RHR*, CXXXVII, 1950, pp. 129-171—cited hereafter as *RHR*).

Despite the many, recent, new insights as to how the text of Habakkuk stands related to the appended interpretations, most of the inferences drawn in 1954 are strongly supported here—an exception being the variant § 123 (*Text*, p. 79). Neither that nor the present work is concerned with higher critical or form critical study of the Book of Habakkuk; but "The Composition of Habakkuk" in *Hommages à André Dupont-Sommer*, pp. 255-275, is concerned with that need.

The present volume is not only a companion and complement to *Text*, but it is an introduction to all the Qumrân Biblical commentaries as a whole. In 1963, through the suggestion of Dr. Menahem Mansoor I agreed to attempt a volume on all these *pĕšārîm*. This launched me upon a much larger project —one calling for two volumes instead of one. Hence the present work is devoted solely to the Habakkuk *pēšer*, with the expectation that a forthcoming volume will include all the others. Yet there may be ancillary aspects which may call for even a third volume.

In this first volume, I examine critically the readings, restorations, translations, and interpretations that have hitherto been advanced. I present my own pointed Hebrew text, including restorations, and give a translation, section by section—each being followed by an "exposition" which discusses the readings, restorations, translations, and the interpretative methodology of the ancient commentator.

The greatest interest in the Biblical commentaries of Qumrân for many scholars lies in the historical allusions; and hence they devote more space to discussing the history than to anything else. However, the present tome devotes relatively little attention to historical interpretation, insisting that this great task should be the last to be undertaken, after all of the texts have been carefully studied and interpreted. Before making the historical allusions concrete, one must determine the nature of the events mentioned; and these should generally not be identified one by one, but collectively, in the context of all the allusions. Thus, though I believe that the world conquerors who are called Kittim (Kittî'îm) by the scroll are the Romans, I give little attention to this here; for this should be treated systematically on the basis of the total evidence. As for the Righteous Teacher's most frequent opponent, the Wicked Priest, seldom do I suggest his identity. Where historical parallels are cited, this is done mostly in order to illustrate the kind of person or event to which the commentary alludes, not to prove that this is the actual history to which allusions are made. Hence, sometimes rival suggestions are mentioned without arguments for or against any one of them.

As early as 1952 (in BASOR, No. 126), I presented a tentative scheme of historical interpretation; and that was later broadened so as to include the data of other scrolls—as in NTS, Vol. III, 1956, pp. 12-15, and The Meaning of the Qumrân Scrolls for the Bible (cited hereafter as Meaning), pp. 101-104, 130-137. Nothing in more recent researches has altered substantially my previous theories as to the historical background of the Qumrân literature. Thus, I still believe that the tenses in 1Q p Hab indicate that the Righteous Teacher and his chief opponents belong to the past and that the Kittim belong either to the present or the imminent future. This view has been well supported by J. van der Ploeg, "L'usage du parfait et de l'imparfait comme moyen de datation dans le Commentaire d'Habacuc," Les Manuscrits de la Mer Morte, pp. 29-35.

Although I am reticent as to the identity of the Wicked Priest (or, Priests), I have been compelled by the exegesis of ¶33 (at xii, 4f.) to suggest the identity of the Man of Lies in an excursus appended to ¶17; for, if the former speaks of the Righteous Teacher as "Judah the Law Doer," then this tentatively recalls the story of a certain Judas (or Eleazar) who rebuked John Hyrcanus (or Jannaeus), an event to which allusion may be made in ¶17. Just as a scholar cannot at first be certain of all historical allusions, so also the readers of the present tome must await future work to know what I may finally decide as to the identity of persons and events alluded to in this and all the other Scrolls.

The initial publication of "The Jerusalem Habakkuk Scroll" (BASOR, No. 112, Dec., 1948) provoked an immediate challenge to its authenticity by Solomon Zeitlin, in his article "A Commentary on the Book of Habakkuk—Important Discovery or Hoax?" JQR, XXXIX, 1949, pp. 235-247. Despite his continued polemics, it is certain that palaeographic, archaeological, and linguistic studies have cumulatively placed the antiquity of the manuscripts of Qumrân beyond all reasonable doubt. (See esp., R. de Vaux, Archaeology and the Dead Sea Scrolls, 1973 and F. M. Cross, Jr., "The Development of the Jewish Scripts," The Bible and the Ancient Near East,

1961, pp. 133-202.) A palaeographic dating of 1 QpHab to the second half of the first century B.C. seems probable. This is not an autograph copy; for, as Malachi Martin has shown, this document was copied by two principal scribes and it required correction by other hands as well. Thus the actual date of the composition would be still earlier. Hence, if its numerous references to the Kittim refer to the Romans, then it would seem natural to date the writing of this *pēšer* to a time after 63 B.C., when Pompey took Jerusalem. Since, however, all the references to the Kittim employ verbs in the Hebrew imperfect, some scholars have interpreted them as predictions of the Roman conquest of Palestine. The references to the Romans are sufficiently general to allow for this possibility, there being no allusions to Pompey's capture of particular places, not even of Jerusalem.

When study of the other *pĕšārîm* has been completed, new light should be shed upon the meaning of 1Q p Hab as well. Hence, already, cross references are built into the present work which anticipate some important parallels in the other commentaries.

What is a Pesher?

There has been a terminological debate as to whether this scroll and others like it should be classified as a commentary, a midrash, or a pesher (*pēšer*). In my opinion, it is all three, "commentary" being the most general term, and the other terms successively narrowing the classification. Thus "commentary" may be defined as by *Webster's Third New International Dictionary* as "a systematic series of explanations or interpretations of the text of a writing." Surely no one denies that in the *pĕšārîm* we have a "series of explanations" of the Biblical text, or that the presentation is "systematic." In this latter respect, most of them are formally more systematic than the Rabbinic midrashim; for they quote the text in regular blocks and introduce the interpretations with regular formulae, which contain the word *pēšer*, such as: *pēšer had-dāvār ᶜal* ("the prophetic meaning of the passage concerns"), *pišrô ᶜal*("its prophetic meaning concerns"), and *pišrô ᶜašer* ("its prophetic meaning is that"). When there is a need to interpret a particular portion of text, one may find an equational statement like " 'Lebanon' is the Council of the Community"; or, a whole clause may be repeated, introduced by the words *wa-ᵓašer ᵓāmar* ("and as for that which He said") and followed by a formula containing *pēšer*. Some of the *pĕšārîm*, however, are less systematic, meandering through the Scriptures in a selective way (as 4Q Florilegium and 11Q p Melchizedek). In their direct quotations of other Scriptures in interpreting a given passage, they resemble more closely the Rabbinic midrash.

"Midrash" is defined by *Webster's New Twentieth Century Dictionary, Unabridged*, 2nd ed., as "any of the Jewish commentaries and explanatory notes on the Scriptures, written between the beginning of the Exile and c. 1200 A.D." The nature of "Jewish commentaries" is not explained. Therefore, *Webster's Third New International Dictionary* helps when it defines "midrash" as "an ancient Jewish exposition of a passage of the Scriptures that may be either halakic or haggadic in type." The two types concern mainly legal exposition and interpretative narrative, respectively. If the midrash be restricted to only these two categories, then the *pěšārîm* are not midrashic, for they are neither legal nor anecdotal. Accordingly, it has been plausibly argued that one has in the Qumrân Scrolls neither commentary nor midrash, but something new, the pesher. Yet haggada may be used for any non-halakic interpretation.

A famous article on "midrash" is that of Renée Bloch, in *SDB*, V, Cols. 1263-81. She began her discussion with a rather broad definition:

> Il désigne un genre édifiant et explicatif étroitement rattaché à l'Ecriture, dans lequel la part de l'amplification est réelle mais secondaire et reste toujours subordonnée à la fin religiouse essentielle, qui est de mettre en valeur plus pleinement l'oevre de Dieu, la Parole de Dieu.

She sharpens this definition by her list of characteristics (cols. 1265 f.): (1) It finds its point of departure in Scripture. (2) It has a homiletical quality. (3) It is attentive to the text. (4) Through reinterpretation, it adapts the text to present needs. (5) There are two main types, aggadah (=haggadah) and halakah. She turns to the Biblical origins of midrash, tracing the development of Jewish interpretation from the Hebrew Scriptures into the intertestamental and New Testament literature. She describes much of the post-Exilic Jewish writing as midrashic (i.e., exemplifying some of the traits of midrash) and midrash in fact. She infers that 1Q p Hab is some sort of midrash by characterizing it as "une paraphrase actualisante des deux premiers chapitres d'Habacuc, met en oeuvre tous les procédés midrashiques connus" (Col. 1277).

Addison G. Wright has criticized Mlle. Bloch for defining midrash too broadly, first of all in a lengthy article ("The Literary Genre Midrash," *CBQ*, XXVIII, 1966). Yet he too, despite his more restricted use of the term midrash, concludes that the Qumrân *pěšārîm* are to be considered midrashim. He deals summarily with the various views on pp. 418-22; but he concludes that "The *pěšārîm* then are haggadic midrash." This position seems to subsume the *pěšārîm* completely within the Rabbinic realm; and since they are not halakah, it categorizes them under haggadah. Wright suggests that the terms "Qumrân" or "Essene" could express the secondary differences." However, I believe that unlike Qumrân halakic interpretation, which is more nearly Rabbinic, the *pěšārîm* are sufficiently different from their closest Rabbinic counterparts that they warrant a distinct classification of their own. It is important to indicate both affinity and distinction in any nomenclature adopted. (For a response to both Bloch and Wright, see Roger Le Déaut, "Apropos a Definition of Midrash," *Interpretation*, XXV, 1971, pp. 259-82.)

I first explored the strong affinities between *pēšer* and midrash in the *BA*, Sept., 1951. In a mimeographed paper in 1953, I argued that a new class of midrash, the midrash pesher, was needed:

The present author had previously pointed out the basic differences as to literary form, approach, and interest between DSH and the other midrashim, but on the nature of the principles of exegesis employed he preferred the term Midrash to that of Commentary. As long as all these factors are recognized, however one classifies DSH is simply a matter of definition and terminology. Rather than invent an entirely new genus called *Pēšer* which relates DSH to nothing previously known, it seems more logical to the present writer to recognize a new species of Midrash, calling DSH (and the fragments of other works of the same kind found in the Scroll Cave of Qumrân) an example of *Midrash Pēsher*, a classification which is at once related to the midrashim and at the same time distinguished from the previously known classes thereof, *Midrash Halakah* and *Midrash Haggadah.*
(The Dead Sea Habakkuk Midrash and the Targum of Jonathan, p. 12)

The proposed terminology, midrash pesher, was adopted by Krister Stendahl in his book *The School of St. Matthew,* in 1954, p. 184.

It is not solely a matter of arbitrary preference, for the people of Qumrân themselves made use of the word midrash (*midrāš*) in various ways. Thus the Rule of the Community (or Society Manual, 1Q S), at viii, 15, employed this noun for the study of the Scriptures. The cognate verb *dāraš* ("to study, or expound") is not lacking either. Thus 1Q S vi, 6f. requires that at all times there be a minimal group of ten men, of whom there must "be a man who expounds the Torah day and night continually as they take turns with one another." The expected Anointed One of Aaron is in certain of the texts called the *dôrēš hat-tōrāh* (the Expounder of the Torah). Even more specifically in Florilegium (4Q 174, i, 14), an interpretation of Psalms 1–2 is headed: "A midrash of 'Blessed is the man who walks not in the counsel of the wicked.' " This quotation from Ps. 1:1 serves both as a heading of the unitary Psalm (=our Pss. 1–2); and it is at one and the same time the first portion of the text selected for interpretation. Hence it is followed immediately by the phrase *pēšer had-dāvār* ("the prophetic meaning of the passage"). This suggests that the Qumrân word for a commentary may have been *midrāš*, whereas their term for the interpretation of individual portions of the text was *pēšer*. (See my article, "Psalms 1–2 as a Coronation Liturgy," *Biblica,* LII, 1971, p. 321, n. 2). Unfortunately, we have no title pages preserved of any of the *pěšārîm.* According to this usage, 1Q p Hab is indeed a midrash; and if one wishes to characterize it further, he may qualify it appropriately as midrash pesher. Hence, I have given the present volume its title, *The Midrash Pesher of Habakkuk.* I also sometimes refer to the manuscript as a commentary, for I also believe that 1Q p Hab is that as well—though of course a peculiar kind of commentary.

One still needs to ask what is meant by the word *PŠR*, whether as noun, or as verb. From the Qumrân exegesis, one notes its preoccupation with explaining the fulfillment of Old Testament prophecy in the recent past of the commentator or in the imminent consummation of history. Except for Eccles. 8:1, it is not found in Biblical Hebrew; but it does occur several times in the Aramaic text of Daniel, both as a verb (5:12, 16) and as a noun (2:4-7; 4:3, 15f.;

5:12, 15f., 26; 7:16). Like its Hebrew cognate *PTR*, it was especially used of interpreting dreams (as in Gen. 40:5-22; 41:8-18). It is this use which has suggested to some scholars that the basic meaning of the word is an untying of knots or a solution of enigmas. If this were so, one might wonder why the verb *PTR/PŠR* is never used of riddles, but that rather one used the verb *higgîd* (Jud. 14:14, 15, 17, 19), or as in the Targum of Jonathan to the same passages, *ḥ*ᵃ*wāh*—both verbs having the simple meaning "declare, divulge." To be sure Dan. 5:12 attributes to Daniel "an excellent spirit, knowledge, and understanding to interpret dreams, explain riddles, and loosen knots." These varied expressions may all refer to Daniel's ability to declare and interpret the dreams of Nebuchadnezzar. Yet, semantically, each verb for solving the inexplicable is linked with its own special noun, without interchangeability. Hence there is no semantic equation of *PŠR* with the loosening of knots. The nearest thing to this concept is *šivrô* ("its breaking open"), which is employed of the Midianite's dream in Jud. 7:15—a passage in which the Targum of Jonathan uses the word *pišrēh* ("its prophetic meaning").

Isaac Rabinowitz has made a strong case for understanding *pēšer* as "presage," a rare English word employed both as verb and as noun (in *RQ*, Tome 8, pp. 219-232). The Hebrew cognate noun *pitrôn*, according to him, refers not only to the act of presaging a dream, but also to its realization in history. Hence his translation of Gen. 40:5 (p. 222) is very persuasive and illuminating: "now the two of them dreamed significantly, each his own dream on the same night, each *according to the reality presaged by his dream.*" One may contrast with this the enigmatic rendering of the King James Version: "And they dreamed a dream both of them, each man his dream in one night, *each man according to the interpretation of his dream.*" Likewise, Rabinowitz has shed a new light upon Gen. 41:13: "Then exactly that which he presaged for us came to pass: me *it* restored to my position, and him *it* hanged." The King James Version attributed the restoration and the hanging to Joseph himself! Modern versions of the Bible have avoided difficulties of this kind, not through any new semantic insights, but by boldly translating what one sensed should be the meaning. After carrying his investigation into the Book of Daniel, as well, he concluded (pp. 225f.): "The term *pēsher*, in fine, never denotes just an explanation or exposition, but always a presaged reality, either envisaged or emergent or else observed as already actualized."

Then moving into the Qumrân literature, Rabinowitz takes up 1Q p Hab xii,2 f., giving on p. 227 a rather impressive translation: "The word's presage is upon (*PŠR HDBR ᶜ L*) the wicked priest in order to pay him his requital with the very treatment he accorded poor people." My translation (at ¶33) makes the same point: "The prophetic fulfillment of the passage concerns the Wicked Priest, by heaping upon him the same recompense which he heaped upon the poor." This is one clear example of *pēšer* still having the meaning of "the reality presaged" (a phrase of Rabinowitz), or as I have rendered it "the prophetic fulfillment." However, in many statements "prophetic meaning" is more suitable, especially in equational statements, such as xii,7: "Its prophetic meaning is: The 'city' is Jerusalem." In context, it is always apparent that a fulfillment of "the prophetic meaning" has either been realized or is imminent, so that ordinarily one does not need to employ the actual word "fulfillment." 1Q p Hab xii,2 is an exception, since the presage is conceived of as itself bringing the punishment of which Habakkuk spoke.

In the same passage, Isaac Rabinowitz rendered ^{c}*al* after *pēšer* as "is upon," rather than "concerns." In context this seems to fit; but when this suggestion is examined against the background of all the formulaic usages of the *pĕšārîm*, this nuance for ^{c}*al* appears doubtful. That ^{c}*al* does not regularly mean "upon" in the formulae *pišrô* ^{c}*al* and *pēšer had-dāvār* ^{c}*al* may be argued from some rare deviations from the idiom. In 4Q p Isa^b ii,1 one reads: "The prophetic meaning of the passage for the last days *pertains to* the punishment of the land (הארץ לחובת) by sword and famine." Here the preposition *lĕ* has replaced ^{c}*al*. The same enlarged formula of interpretation appears with variation at 4Q p Isa^c 22, ii,10: "The prophetic meaning of the passage for the last days *concerns* [^{c}*al*] the congregation of the expounders of smooth things." Another illustration is 4Q Catena 10-11, line 9: "The prophetic meaning of the passage *pertains to the victory* (לנצח) of the heart of men of [truth (?) over their fears (?)]." These parallels make it clear that *lĕ* and ^{c}*al* in these formulae are synonyms, with no appreciable difference in meaning.

A related matter is the meaning of $^{\,2a}$*šer*. The suggestion of Rabinowitz is that in some of the passages where it has been translated "who" it means "that" (either as a simple conjunction or as purposive). Whenever this word follows directly *pišrô* or *pēšer had-dāvār*, the conjunctive use is clear: "Its prophetic meaning is *that* such and such did, or will, happen." However, whenever it comes after *pišrô* ^{c}*al* + a noun, it is surely the relative pronoun modifying the noun—e.g., "Its prophetic meaning concerns the Wicked Priest *who* did such and such." Rabinowitz suggests that even in these cases $^{\,2a}$*šer* may sometimes have the conjunctive sense (pp. 227 f.): "Its presage is *upon* the Wicked Priest: *that* [= so that] he did such and such." There are instances where this sense is definitely to be excluded, as when $^{\,2a}$*šer* is complemented with a pronominal suffix appended to a following verb or noun, as in 1Q p Hab vii,4, 11; viii,2; ix,9f.; xi,12; xii,13. Sentences in which $^{\,2a}$*šer* may be the subject of the verb naturally lack this kind of grammatical confirmation; but nothing requires a departure from the norm that in such cases we should read the relative pronoun.

Rabinowitz, of course, would recognize that sometimes $^{\,2a}$*šer* after the noun is the relative pronoun; but that it ever means anything else remains to be proved. The proposed conjunctive meaning is simply a logical corollary to his interpretation of *pišrô* ^{c}*al* as meaning "Its presage is *upon*," which (as we have seen) appears doubtful. Hence, I conclude that the conjunctive use of $^{\,2a}$*šer* in the interpretative formulae occurs only immediately after *pišrô* or *pēšer had-dāvār*, and that ^{c}*al* in the same position also serves simply to introduce the interpretation. The comparable use of $^{\jmath a}\check{s}er$ and $^c al$ (despite the different constructions) gives further support for the view that $^c al$ in such cases does not have the pregnant (or even menacing) sense of "upon," but that it simply introduces the subject *concerning which* the Biblical passage speaks.

It does not follow from Rabinowitz' wholly correct understanding of *pēšer* as used in the Bible, that the word "in the Qumran Scrolls may not correctly be held to mean 'meaning, interpretation' in any exegetical or expository sense" (p. 230). Nor may one assert: "Neither in method nor in form is a Pesher any kind of *midrash*" (p.231)—for even Qumrân used the word *midrāš* to head its interpretation of Pss. 1–2. Moreover, what concerns us in the Scrolls is not purely symbolical interpretation as in dreams or omens, but a presaging based upon texts. It is, therefore, by no means astonishing that 4Q Florilegium regards such *pēšer* as *midrāš* and that the verb *dāraš* and the noun *pēšer* are used in close proximity in 4Q Ordinances, frag. 5, lis. 5f. It seems that the kind of meaning which *pēšer* indicates here is not a "prophetic meaning," but a halakic meaning! If so, this is extraordinary. Yet a further development is found in 4Q 180, lis. 1 and 7, where it means a discourse on a given subject.

The Place of Pēšer in Interpretative Tradition

It is important to see how the Qumrân *pĕšārîm* grew out of the late prophetic and apocalyptic thought of the Old Testament. In "Biblical Interpretation in the Dead Sea Scrolls" (*BA*, Sept., 1951), I did not deal with this side of the subject, concentrating rather upon the hermeneutic principles, reserving this aspect of the subject till later. Meanwhile, other scholars have not neglected altogether this subject, especially as regards the relationship of *pēšer* interpretation to the Book of Daniel. (See Karl Elliger, *Studien zum Habakuk-Kommentar von Totan Meer*, Chap. VI, pp. 118-164 and F. F. Bruce, *Biblical Exegesis in the Qumran Texts*.)

It is particularly important to see how Qumrân interpretation was prepared for by apocalyptic thought of post-Exilic Judaism. The eschatological orientation of late Hebrew prophecy would seem to be connected in some way with the desirable "day of Yahweh" of which the contemporaries of Amos spoke (at 5:18). The canonical prophets who followed the lead of Amos turned this into a day of doom for all, including Israel. After the doom had befallen Jerusalem, rather definitively in 587 or 586 B.C., Judah became the victim of looters from Edom (Jer. 49:7-22; Obadiah) and the object of scorn by all. In the wake of such a bitter experience the plea of Lamentations 1:21c arose: "Bring Thou the day Thou hast announced, and let them be as I am." Here is a call for a new Day of Yahweh, in which the nations will be punished, that Israel may be set free. (Cf. Ezek. 28:24-26; 30:2f.). Thus the hopes associated with the oldest conception of the Day of Yahweh came to the fore again, and it is probable that they never did die out in pre-Exilic times, being kept alive by the "false prophets" and to a limited extent even by the canonical prophets. Frank Moore Cross (*Canaanite Myth*,

pp. 343 ff.) rightly traces apocalyptic conceptions to ancient mythology.
In any case, Lam. 1:21 indicates that the accomplishment of doom upon Judah did not seem to be an adequate fulfillment of the Day of Yahweh. A new day must come to bring judgment on Israel's foes and deliverance to the Jews. (See Norman K. Gottwald, *Studies in the Book of Lamentations*, pp. 87 f.). This expectation is clear in all the post-Exilic prophets. M. Delcor's study of Deutero-Zechariah shows how earlier prophecies were being reapplied to later expectations in the early Hellenistic period (*RB*, LIX, 1952, pp. 385-411.). A roughly contemporary prophecy is Ezek. 38–39, which declares specifically that Gog will fulfill events predicted by earlier prophets:

> Are you he of whom I spoke in former days by my servants the prophets of Israel, who in those days prophesied for years that I would bring you against them? (38:17)
>
> Behold, it is coming and it will be brought about, says the Lord GOD. That is the day of which I have spoken. (39:80

If one demands to know which prophets had foretold this eschatological foe, the only clues to the answer are to be found in the literary borrowings, which constantly (as G. Hölscher has shown) reapply phraseology which was first used of Assyria and Chaldea to the coming of Gog of the land of Magog. Foremost among these earlier prophets, as these borrowings show, were Isaiah, Jeremiah and the genuine Ezekiel. (See G. Hölscher, *Hesekiel—der Dichter und das Buch*, pp. 177-189.)

Similarly, Dan. 9 reinterprets Jeremiah's seventy years (Jer. 25:11; 29:10) as seventy weeks of years. When II Chron. 36:21 explained the seventy years as atoning for the previous non-observance of the Sabbatical year, the reference was to 490 years prior to the Exile; but since the glowing hopes of restoration envisaged by Deutero-Isaiah and other prophets had not been fully achieved, the author of Daniel extended the 490 years from the Exile downward, only the Sabbatical years being counted in calculating the seventy years. This interpretation was not developed from meditating upon the Book of Jeremiah alone; for as Daniel states, "I, Daniel, perceived in the books." These books probably also included Leviticus (cf. 26:24, 34). Such reapplication of the Scriptures appears in many another passage of Daniel, as H. L. Ginsberg has shown (*Studies in Daniel*; and "The Oldest Interpretation of the Suffering Servant," *VT*, III, 1953, 400-404). Thus Chaps. 8–12 constantly reapply the language of earlier prophecies to the reign of Antiochus Epiphanes.

Against such a background, the reapplication of the ancient prophecies to the historical times of the Qumrân covenanters is merely carrying on the traditions of late Hebrew prophecy and early Jewish apocalyptic. Even in the Book of Habakkuk, as shown in *Hommages à André Dupont Sommer*, p. 275, and in *The Meaning of the Qumrân Scrolls for the Bible*, pp. 67f., post-Exilic additions give an eschatological reinterpretation to the prophet's message. The editorial heading to the book describes the whole as "The oracle of God which Habakkuk the prophet *saw* (*ḥāzāh*)." In other words, it was conceived of as a "vision" (*ḥāzôn*), the very word employed metaphorically by Habakkuk himself at 2:2f. (Similarly, cf. Isa. 1:1; Ob. 1.) The understanding of the prophecy of Habakkuk as a vision of the endtime was therefore no new conception on the part of the author of 1Q p Hab. What was new in the scroll was a systematic and detailed dicussion, showing how each prophetic word had already been fulfilled, or soon would be fulfilled.

Visions, according to Daniel, must each receive their *pēšer* (*pĕšar* in Aramaic). What is required, however, is not merely a gifted expositor, but an inspired interpreter (Dan. 2:27-30) to whom God reveals the mystery (2:19), and to whom God has imparted His wisdom and Spirit (5:11f., 14). Curiously, Daniel was not given the power to interpret his own dreams or visions, but he was dependent upon an angel to interpret these (Cf. 7:15 ff.; 8:15 ff.; 9:20 ff.). Similarly, 1Q p Hab declares that the prophet Habakkuk did not understand the full import of his own inspired words, and so it was necessary to await the coming of a charismatic exegete "to whom God made known all the mysteries of the words of His servants the prophets" (1Q p Hab vii,4f., discussed in ¶20). It is even said that the Righteous Teacher spoke "from the mouth of God" (ii,2f., in ¶7). This strongly suggests that by the time the Qumrân *pĕšārîm* were written, their Teacher had been identified with the coming Prophet who is mentioned in 1Q S ix,11 and who figures in the opening selections of 4Q Testimonia.

Whether or not this speculation is correct, the Righteous Teacher in his role as interpreter functioned like the Prophet Daniel, and hence the verb לפשור is employed of him at ii,8. In Daniel, the root *PŠR* is restricted to visions, except in the case of the handwriting on the wall, whose inscription may be considered an objective text, since its words were interpreted with a certain amount of midrashic verbal play, as I pointed out in *Meaning*, p. 41.

If Dan. 1–6 is a compilation of older legends, then it is possible that Daniel's use of *PŠR* antedates Eccles. 8:1, the only Hebrew passage where the term is used in the Old Testament. Its text may be instructively compared with that of the Targum:

Massoretic Text

מי כהחכם ומי יודע פשר דבר

Who is like the wise man? And who knows the prophetic meaning of anything (or, of a single word)?

Targum

מן הוא חכימא דיכול למקם כל קבל חכמא דיְיָ
ולמדע פשר מליא כנבייא

Who is that wise man who is able to determine anything according to the wisdom of YHWH, and to know the prophetic meaning of things (or, of words), as the prophets do?

Now *pēšer dāvār* of Ecclesiastes may be compared with *pěšar millětā⁾* of Dan. 5:26; and *pěšar millayyā⁾* of the Targum occurs exactly as in Dan. 7:16. In the Qumrân Scrolls we frequently find *pēšer* joined with *had-dāvār*; but never is *dāvār* left undetermined (as in Eccles. 8:1) or given in the plural (as in the Targum to the same passage). Isaac Rabinowitz has suggested that Ecclesiastes means: "And who has knowledge of a (prophetic) word's presage?" Yet, it is noteworthy that the Targum does not read: "And to know the presage of the words of the prophets." Rather it is "to know the presage of things, as the prophets do." Since the Prophets in general were not interpreters of words, but of events, *millayyā⁾* probably refers to the latter. In Dan. 7:16, likewise, it does not refer to words, but to details of the vision. Therefore, Ecclesiastes probably means: "And who knows the presage of anything?" Nevertheless, it is instructive that this late targum interprets the knowledge of *pēšer* as a prophetic type of knowledge.

If one infers rightly that 1Q p Hab and the other *pěšārîm* of Qumrân were not actually composed by the Righteous Teacher but were written some decades after his death, one will then need to explain why all this presaging of the meaning of the prophetic words should be attributed solely to him. This attribution is probably due not alone to the fact that he was the great exponent of this kind of Biblical interpretation, but also to the fact that many of the interpretative features actually do go back to him, having been handed down by his disciples orally within the Qumrân society. In this process of transmission, his interpretations were modified and supplemented before being committed to writing. As we have seen, Biblical exposition was one of the continuous activities of the Community. It was expected that in its study sessions, new understanding (or revelations) would take place. (Cf. 1Q S i, 9; v,9; vi,6-8; viii,1 f., 15; ix, 13, 19.) Each member was expected to share his insights with the rest, as 1 Q S viii,11 f. states: "And every matter which was hidden from Israel and is found by a man who studies (*had-dôrēš*), let him not hide it from these [others] out of fear of a backsliding spirit." Wernberg-Møller has well stated, that "the idea of a constant stream of revelations, gained by the study of the Torah, appears to be something fundamentally characteristic of the spiritual activity of the society." (See his volume, *The Manual of Discipline*, p. 47, n. 21). Although the contexts of these passages in 1Q S would favor understanding the revelations as legal regulations, the new disclosures probably included the *pēšer* interpretations as well. Thus the Teacher's own interpretations would be constantly extended, as they were applied to new texts or to new situations.

One should not view midrashic exegesis and eschatological interpretation as mutually exclusive categories; for both elements are clearly present in the *pěšārîm*. In the translations, I sometimes need to give more than one interpretation of a selection of Scripture, in order to disclose the ascription of different meanings to the same prophetic words. Where it is simply a matter of a word or phrase, a secondary meaning is presented within parentheses; but where a whole verse is construed in more than one way, these are separated as Translation A, B, etc. My own exposition of the individual pericopes constantly calls attention to the midrashic techniques of the ancient interpreter. The validity of the interpretations for the Qumrân covenanters, however, did not rest simply upon the techniques employed, but especially upon the charismatic gift of the interpreter.

A history of Biblical interpretation at Qumrân would not be complete without some indication of its relationship to the practice of targuming the Scriptures in the synagogues. Targums too reveal free interpretations based upon midrashic methods and a concern for fulfilled prophecy. An outstanding example is the interpretation of Hannah's prayer (I Sam. 2:1-10) in the Targum of Jonathan:

(1) Hannah prayed in the spirit of prophecy and said: "Already Samuel, my son, is destined to be a prophet over Israel. In his days they will be delivered from the power of the Philistines; and by his hands signs and mighty deeds will be wrought for them. Therefore, my heart is confident through the destiny which Yahweh has apportioned me. And as for Heman the son of Joel, the son of my son Samuel, it is destined that he and fourteen of his sons should sing songs to the lyre and the lute, with their brethren the Levites, offering up praise in the sanctuary. Therefore, my horn is exalted in the portion that Yahweh has assigned me."

And also concerning a miraculous punishment that is destined to befall the Philistines, [she prophesied] that they were destined to bring the ark back in a new wagon, and with it the sacrifice of guilt offering. Therefore, sang the congregation of Israel: "I shall open my mouth to utter boasts against my scorners, for I rejoice in Thy redemption."

(2) Concerning Sennacherib the king of Assyria she prophesied and said: "He and all his troops are destined to come up against Jerusalem and a great miracle will be wrought upon him. There the corpses of his army will fall. Therefore, all peoples, nations and tongues will acknowledge Him, singing: 'None is holy, but Yahweh, for none is more pure than Thou.' And Thy people will sing: 'None is mighty, but our God.' "

(3) Concerning Nebuchadnezzar the king of Babylon she prophesied and said: "Ye Chaldeans and all peoples who are destined to rule over Israel. Do not vaunt yourself to boast and boast. Let no revilement come from your mouth, for Yahweh is the God who knows everything, and His Judgment is aimed at all His creatures. And also it is destined that you will be recompensed with punishment for your sins."

(4) Concerning the kingdom of Greece she prophesied and said: "The bows of the Greek warriors will be broken, whereas those of the house of the Hasmonean who had been weak, will have mighty deeds wrought for them."

(5) Concerning Haman's sons she prophesied and said: "Those who were satisfied with bread, proud of their wealth, and affluent in riches will be impoverished. In reversal, they will hire themselves out for bread, for the food of their mouth. Mordecai and Esther who were destitute became rich and forgot their poverty. In reversal, they became freedmen. Thus Jerusalem that has become like a barren woman is destined to be filled with her exiled people; whereas Rome which was full of many peoples will have her armies come to an end. She will take captive, but will herself become desolate.

(6) "All these are the mighty deeds of Yahweh Who is sovereign over the world: He puts to death, but commands that life be renewed. He brings down to Sheol, but He is

also ready to bring up into eternal life. (7) Yahweh makes poor and makes rich. He abases, also exalts. (8) Out of the dust He raises up the poor. From the dunghill He raises up the destitute, that they should be seated with the righteous, the great ones of the world; and He makes them inherit seats of honor, for human works lie exposed before Yahweh. In the netherworld, He established Gehinnom for the wicked; but for the righteous who do His will He has provided the earth. (9) He will keep the bodies of his righteous servants from Gehinnom; but the wicked will be damned in Gehinnom, in darkness—that it may be known that it is not the one endowed with might who is acquitted on the Day of Judgment. (10) Yahweh will shatter the scorners who rise up to reproach His people. Against them, from heaven, He will thunder with majestic voice. Yahweh will exact His recompense of judgment from Gog and from the camp of robber peoples who are coming with him from the ends of the earth; but He will give His own King the power and will make the kingdom of His messiah."

By interpreting the Lord's "anointed" as the Messiah, the targumists were led to infer that Hannah had predicted the whole history of her people from her own time to that of the future messianic kingdom. With its wealth of historical details presented in chronological fashion, the targumic version of Hannah's prayer is reminiscent of Dan. 11. One might also compare Hannah's words with the Sibylline Oracles. A striking contrast is the clarity and explicitness of Hannah's predictions as presented in the Targum; but back of these lie Hannah's own words which are as confusing as those of any Sibyl, if all this is what the inspiring Spirit meant!

One discerns the influence of other Scriptures upon the Targum, not simply by the historical data gleaned from the Biblical narratives (such as the psalm-singing descendants of Samuel, referred to in I Chron. 6:18), but also by interpretations influenced by prophetic predictions. Thus, in Vs. 4, the smashing of the bows of the *Greek* warriors may have been inferred from Zech. 9:10-13. That the "weak" (Hebrew, *nikhšālîm;* Aramaic, *ḥᵃlāšîn*) are "those of the house of the Hasmonean," i.e., the sons of Mattathias, could have been inferred from Dan. 11:33-35, where those who stumble (*nikhšělû*) in those times are promised "a little help" (Judas Maccabeus?). Similarly, in Vs. 5, the comparison of Jerusalem with a barren woman may derive from Isa. 54:1-3; and the contrastive destiny of Rome may stem from what is said of Babylon in Isa. 47. Two different meanings are given the "noble" (*nĕdîvîm*) of Vs. 8: they are both "the righteous" (as in Prov. 17:26) and "the great ones" (as in many other passages). So also, the interpretations in the *pĕšārîm* of Qumrân were often influenced by other Scriptures, usually without direct quotations to show this.

The words of the *pĕšārîm* are as farfetched as those of the Targum to Hannah's prayer. Like them, also, one is left to puzzle out for himself the relationships between the interpretation and the Biblical text. It is only through careful and ponderous comparison that one can see the relationships and discern how various words and phrases were interpreted. Likewise, in the *pĕšārîm* one must diligently compare the alleged prophetic meanings with the words of the prophet himself, if he is to know how to understand and to translate either the Biblical quotation or its interpretation. Often the words of Scripture are punned in ingenious ways. To grasp what the ancient midrashist made of the divine oracles, one must read orally, and not just visually; for to the ancient interpreter the words never lost their oral character. Also, one must not keep in separate categories all the various homonyms, as though they were different and unrelated words. It is not altogether clear that there was even the notion of such distinctions as may be listed in a modern lexicon, as roots I, II, or III. Rather, it could be that these were all thought of as different meanings of one and the same word. Not only was it legitimate to select any one of these meanings which suited the purpose of the interpreter, without regard to the original context; but it was also legitimate to employ more than one meaning in an exposition, for such things belonged to "the mysteries of the words of God's servants the prophets."

A number of concepts are shared by this Targum with Qumrân interpretation. First of all there is the common concept that psalmody is prophecy. (Cf. *Meaning*, pp. 69 f., 271 ff.; *RQ*, No. 20, 1966, pp. 571 f.). Thus there is the constant transferral of the words of Hannah's song to later times—though not so drastically as in the Qumrân texts, whose historical allusions relate mostly to the last two centuries B.C. There are also genuinely eschatological elements such as references to the Day of Judgment, the resurrection, and punishment in the netherworld (v. 9; cf. 1Q p Hab ¶¶23, 28, 29, 35). All this, as argued above, was prepared for in post-Exilic prophecy and in apocalyptic prediction, which reinterpreted earlier prophecy, but without presenting a continuous systematic restatement of earlier texts, as was done by targum and *pēšer*.

There is even a presentational similarity between targuming and the giving of *pēšer* interpretations. In the former case, a portion of Scripture was read first of all in Hebrew and was then followed by a restatement in Aramaic. In the *pēšārîm*, quotations are given sequentially, interlarded with their alleged prophetic meanings. Both the quotations and their interpretations are given in Hebrew, and we know them only from written texts. Still there is enough formal similarity between *pēšer* and targum, that one wonders whether the written style of the *pĕšārîm* arose from an oral practice of interlarding the reading of the Hebrew Scriptures with *pēšer*. Perhaps this was the method of the Righteous Teacher in instructing his adherents.

Many scholars have recognized a midrashic process underlying the targums. Renée Bloch (in "Midrash," cols. 1278 f.) discussed briefly the Palestinian Targum found in the Cairo Geniza, stating that "it is much more a midrash than a version." The so-called Genesis Apocryphon from the first Qumrân Cave clearly contains elements of both translation and midrash, so that some passages are more a version and others more a midrash. The 11Q Targum of Job is strictly a version, yet the interpretative element is more strongly present than has been perceived by many. The relationship of targum and midrash is discussed by Roger Le Déaut in his article, "The Current State of Targumic Studies," *BThB*, IV, 1974, pp. 3-32.

One may here take note of Renée Bloch's article "Ézéchiel XVI: exemple parfait du procédé midrashique dans la Bible," *CS*, IX, 1955, pp. 193-223. By meticulously comparing the vocabulary of Ezek. 16 with other Scriptures, she deduced that this allegory of the Lord's marriage with the foundling girl is an "account following with curious exactitude the events of sacred history, such as are recounted in the sequence of Genesis to Kings (vs. 3: the sojourn of the patriarchs in Palestine; vs. 6: the covenant with Abraham; vss. 7-8; the covenant with Moses, etc.)." (This summary is from "Midrash," col. 1272). Actually, her study constitutes a brilliant explication of the midrashic process behind the Targum of Jonathan, showing how its interpretation (which she adopted) was derived by comparing Scripture with Scripture. So impressive were the data that she uncovered, that she wrongly attributed this targumic understanding of the allegory to the prophet himself.

Her interpretation, however, is far from that of Ezekiel's intended meaning. Unlike Chap. 23, Chap. 16 does not begin its historical allusions prior to the Conquest. It treats the history of Jerusalem, beginning with the Canaanite town and ending with her as the capital city of Israel (later, of Judah). (See my treatment in *The Interpreter's One-Volume Commentary on the Bible*, pp. 420 f.).

The Purpose of Pesher

What purposes did *pēšer* exegesis serve? Drawing an analogy from the sage and prophet Daniel, the counsellor of kings, Isaac Rabinowitz (p. 232) has suggested: "So too, doubtless, the writers of these presage-texts intended them to be used in the deliberations of policy by the pietists' leadership." Yet, the real purpose of the Book of Daniel, despite Daniel's repeated presence in the royal court, was not for kings, but for the Jewish people as a whole, that through the predictions of Daniel they might understand their own day as a part of the divine plan for history which was fast approaching its consummation. So, likewise, the Righteous Teacher's function as a presager was not for the court of any ruler, nor solely for the deliberative guidance of the leadership among his own adherents, but for the benefit of all who would hear and believe and identify themselves with his Community. In so far as others transmitted, added to, or reapplied his prophetic interpretations, their expositions would serve the same purposes. These purposes may be listed as follows:

(1) To vindicate the Righteous Teacher against his enemies.

Scriptural proofs were adduced to show that the work and sufferings of the Teacher had been predicted of old, and that the evil and blasphemous works of the Wicked Priest and the Man of Lies had all been foretold. This showed that the character of each was, according to his title, righteous, wicked, or false.

(2) To vindicate the followers of the Teacher against their opponents.

Thus, "the men of truth, the doers of the Law" are led to see themselves as justified by past events and as about to be vindicated by future events. Proof that they are in the right is supported even by *pěšārîm* which do not mention the Righteous Teacher, the Wicked Priest, or the Man of Lies. Thus in 4Q p Nahum, Ephraim and Manasseh (the Pharisees and the Sadducees) are doomed, and the glory of Judah (that of the Teacher and his followers) will in the end be disclosed.

(3) To strengthen the faith and endurance of the Teacher's adherents.

Thus 1Q p Hab, ¶22, reassures the languid that the time of God's salvation is coming according to its divine schedule. And ¶24 comforts the doers of the Law with the assurance that they will be saved from damnation through their steadfast faith in their True Teacher.

(4) To warn the wavering of the dangers of apostasy.

That there would be traitors to the truth disclosed by the Teacher was foretold in the Scriptures (1Q p Hab, ¶7). Their doom was also predicted, both what would befall them in this life (¶25) and what will befall them in the future Judgment (¶28).

(5) Through learning and obedience to prepare the way of Yahweh in the Wilderness of Judea.

This is stated explicitly in 1Q S, viii, 14-16. Interestingly, 4Q S^e reads not "to prepare the way of Him" (i.e., Yahweh), but "the way of Truth"—since for the people of Qumrân Yahweh is the God of Truth, and progress in the Truth is preparation for His coming.

(6) To instruct the Community regarding the future.

Such hopes and expectations sustain the Community in their present hour of suffering and perplexity. Since the future prospect derives from the Scriptures and has been authoritatively interpreted by their own Teacher, it is important that they live every moment with the correct expectation in view. Thus the *pěšārîm* were an important source of indoctrination.

Postscript

Appearing too late for use here is the thesis of Daniel Patte, *Early Jewish Hermeneutic in Palestine*, Missoula, Mont.: Society of Biblical Literature, Dissertation Series, No. 22, 1975. Dr. Patte covers with considerable breadth and depth of knowledge the whole area of the present introduction and more. His dissertation, like that of Dr. John V. Chamberlain, follows closely my presentation of the Hermeneutic principles of 1Q p Hab as given in the *BA*, Sept., 1951. At the same time he makes original suggestions of his own. His philosophical distinctions between exegesis and hermeneutic and between Rabbinic hermeneutic and Qumrân hermeneutic are helpful.

THE MIDRASH PESHER OF HABAKKUK

¶ 1 (i, 1-5)

1 [שֻׂוּעְתִּי וְלֹוא] הַמַּשָּׂא אֲשֶׁר חָזָה חֲבַקּוּק הַנָּבִיא עַד אָנָה יהוה [שֻׂוַּעְתִּי וְלֹוא

2 [חֵלֶת דֹּור] תֹו עַל פִּשְׁרֹו תֹושִׁיעַ וְלֹוא חָמָס אֵלֶיךָ אֶזְעַק תִּשְׁמָע

3 הַבָּא[וֹת עֲלֵיהֶם

4 יִצְ[עֲקוּ עַל

1 (1:1)   [THE ORACLE WHICH THE PROPHET HABAKKUK
        RECEIVED BY REVELATION.

   (1:2)   How long, O LORD], do I implore,

2   and [Thou] not /[hear?
         Crying out to Thee, "Violence!"
             and Thou not save?

             Its prophetic meaning concerns the ex]pectation of the generation

3-4   of /[. . . . that are com]ing upon them /[. . . . . . They make] outcry

5   against /. . .

¶1 *Exposition*

It is probable that this is the first column of the scroll; for it is not likely that a whole column of introduction to this *pēšer* should have preceded. The title verse of Isaiah (Isa. 1:1) together with the commentary upon it occupied at least four lines in the Isaiah Commentary from the Third Qumrân Cave; but that is a verse containing much more historical substance than Hab. 1:1. The width of this column is determined by lis. 10-13. A. M. Habermann has reconstructed a much narrower column (in both his *ᶜEdah*, p. 43, and his *Megilloth*, p. 43) which did not allow him room to include 1:1 in the first line. In fact he has boldly restored the entire text of this column. Many of his restorations have been followed by Yitzhak Baer, " 'Pesher Habakkuk' and Its Period" (Hebrew), *Zion,* XXXIV, 1969, pp. 1-42, with reference here to pp. 13f.

i, 2. *Tôḥelet,* "expectation" or "hope." This is the restoration of Dupont-Sommer (*Essene Writings,* p. 259), van der Woude (*Bijbelcommentaren,* p. 29); Carmignac (*Textes,* p. 93); and Lohse (pp. 258f.). Alternative restorations are *maḥᵃlat,* "sickness" (Habermann, followed by Baer), *naḥᵃlat,* "inheritance," *tĕḥillat,* "beginning" (Vermès, *DSSE,* p. 235).

i,3. The first word is restored as *ʾaḥᵃrôn* by Habermann (*Megilloth*), Vermès (*DSSE,* p. 235) and Baer, and is suggested by Carmignac–so as to obtain the phrase "last generation" ("*la génération future*") as in ii,7 and vii,1 (in which lines the article appears with both words). The absence of the article here favors taking *dôr* as a construct.

For the restoration *hab-bāʾôt,* "the things that are coming," see, after S. M. Stern (*JBL,* LXXIX, 1950, p. 25), ii,7 and vii,1. In the former the Righteous Teacher foretold the coming things; but in vii,1 it was Habakkuk. The present context follows so closely the reference to the prophet in 1:1 that a reference to Habakkuk is probable here.

i,4. Elliger's restoration *yizᶜᵃqû* rests upon the Hab. text *ʾezᶜaq,* and is read by Elliger *et al.* However, the perfect *zāᶜᵃqû* (Baer, p. 14) is equally possible, as also the perfect or imperfect *ṢᶜQ.* Michel restores *ṣāᶜᵃqû* (*çaᶜaqou,* p. 18, n. 1), which has the stylistic support of the Commentary by interpreting the Biblical word with a synonym. Habermann's restoration of [*niz*]ᶜᵃqû ᶜ*al* [*he-ḥāmās*] ("They are called together unto violence") like almost anything else is possible in this fragmentary text; but it departs from Habakkuk in not taking *ḥāmās* as the anguished outcry of the oppressed. See G. von Rad, *Genesis,* p. 206.

THE MIDRASH PESHER OF HABAKKUK

¶2 (i, 5-6)

לָמָּה תַרְאֵנִי אָוֶן וְעָ[מָל תַּבִּ]יט   [5
הַבִּיט] אֶל בְּעֹשֶׁק וּמָעַל   [פִּשְׁרוֹ אֲשֶׁר   6

5 (1:3a)   [Why dost Thou make me see trouble
                    and lo]ok upon [tra]vail? /
6   Its prophetic meaning . . . God [looked]
       upon oppression and treachery.

¶2 *Exposition*

i,5f. Dupont-Sommer (*RHR*, p. 131) first restored here vs. 3*a-b* (in which he was followed by Molin, p. 11, and Habermann, ᶜ*Edah*, p. 43; *Megilloth*, p. 43); but in *Essene Writings*, p. 258, he reserves vs. 3*b* + *c* for li. 7. Vermès (*DSSE*, p. 235) places the whole of vs. 3 in lis. 5f.; but this would overcrowd li. 6.

Concerning li. 6, Theodor H. Gaster wrote me, Jan. 11, 1949: "I strongly suspect that the prefix ב in בעשק was governed by the verb ראה (or הביט), the sense having been something like יביט or יראה אל בעשק ומעל, 'God looks upon oppression and treachery.'" Either verb, perfect or imperfect, is suitable here. In the commentary, עשק = און and מעל = עמל. Note the verbal play in the second equation. F. A. W. van't Land and A. S. van der Woude wished to read מעל in the Biblical text as well. Concerning this, see my refutation in *Text*, §1a. Mathias Delcor (in personal communication) notes that in the Targum both verbs are first person (shifting the action from God to the prophet). Similarly, in the Syriac the second verb is first person. The preserved subject ᵓēl in the commentary supports the second person restorations in harmony with the MT.

THE MIDRASH PESHER OF HABAKKUK

¶3 a-b (i, 7-10)

[וְשׁוֹד וְחָמָס לְנֶגְדִּי] 7
[יִגְז[ֹ]ל[ֹ]וּ ה[ֹ]וֹן וַיְהִ]י רִיב [פִּ]שְׁרוֹ 8
מ[רִ]יבָה וְחָ[שְׁב]וּ הוֹאָה פֵשֶׁר [וּמָדוֹן יִשָּׂא 9
] 10

3a

7 (1:3bα)   [Destruction and pillage are before me]. /
8   [Its prophetic meaning . . . . . .] They r[o]b
    w[ealth] / . . . .

3b

(1:3bβ)   Strife [occurs /
9   and contention arises.
          Its prophetic meaning] . . . .
      [s]trife; and they p[lot] ruin. /
10   . . .

¶3 a-b *Exposition*

The extant part of li. 7 is blank. This indicates a paragraphing in the manuscript after the previous Habakkuk quotation, with the interpretation being reserved for the next line (cf. ii,11; vi,9; x,1; xi,11; but contrast xii,5). The question is how much text could be contained on the non-extant part of li. 7. Since there was no need to crowd, it appears doubtful that more than Hab. 1:3*bα* appeared on it. Carmignac (*Textes*, p. 93), Dupont-Sommer (*Essene Writings*, p. 258), Elliger and van der Woude (*Bijbelcommentaren*, p. 29) place all of vs. 3*b* here; but Carmignac notes: "The dimensions of the lacuna lead one to suppose that the author cited this text, perhaps, in an abridged form." One may avoid this by reserving 3*b* for i,8f., where it may be partially preserved on li. 8. This corresponds in part with the reading of Habermann (*ʿEdah*, p. 43; *Megilloth*, p. 43), who confusedly telescopes lis. 7-8. The following display shows my restoration:

ביוֹאוּ וַיַּשּׁעֲ חוּאַה

צַרִיבֹ וֹחַושּׁעָן חוֹאַ֯ת

This is a scissors-and-paste job made from the photographs, with retouching.

i,8. For "rob wealth," see viii,11 and xii,10. For *ḥāmās* = "pillage," cf. xi,17; xii,9f. (¶33).

i,9. *Mĕrîvāh* interprets *rîv* of i,8. Habermann restores וֹח[מאה]. But the letters supplied are too large to fit the lacuna. Since what Habermann takes as the left side of the *Hē* may be a *Wāw*, it is easier to restore after Elliger וֹח[שבוֹ]. The word *HWʾH* (*hûʾâh*) may be read as the longer form of the pronoun *HWʾ* (*hûʾ*), a spelling which is well attested in 1Q Isaᵃ, 1Q S, and elsewhere. However, as Elliger and Glanzmann observe, 1Q p Hab in all other instances uses the shorter form. Therefore, read this either as *hōwâh* (with *ʾĀlef* interpreted as a vowel letter) or as *hôʾāh* (with *ʾĀlef* replacing consonantal *Wāw*).

THE MIDRASH PESHER OF HABAKKUK

¶4 (i, 10-11)

עַל כֵּן תָּפוּג תּוֹרָה 10

11 [פִּשְׁרוֹ עַל מַטִּיף הַכָּזָב וְאַנְשֵׁי עֲדָתוֹ] אֲשֶׁר מָאֲסוּ בְתוֹרַת אֵל

10 (1:4aα)   Therefore, the Law is relaxed. /
11   [[Its prophetic meaning concerns the Prophet of Lies and the men
of his congregation]] who rejected the Law of God. /

¶4 *Exposition*

i,11. This brief form of the introductory formula seems likely in view of the brevity of the space for interpretation. There is no certainty with regard to this restoration; but if ᵃ*ašer* follows the designation of the party concerned, we have a relatively long designation. Cf. "the house of Absalom and the men of their council who" (v,10), "the adherents of the truth, the doers of the Law who" (vii,11 f.). Note that the "*Man* of Lies" (ᵓ*îš hak-kāzāv*) is said to have "rejected the Law in the midst of their whole c[ongregatio]n" at v,11 f. The "*prophet* of Lies" at x,8 f. is said to have "misled many into . . . establishing through falsehood a congregation." Either designation could have occurred here. Both titles are apparently identical in meaning. ᵓ*îš hak-kāzāv* parodies ᵓ*îš hā-*ᵓᵉ*lôhîm* ("the man of God" = "prophet of God"). *Maṭṭîf hak-kāzāv* means "he who drips (or prophesies) lies." See also 1Q p Micah, ¶2 (li. 11). For the "man of lies," see ii,1 f. (¶7), also 4Q p Psalms i,26 (¶7), also the restored text of 1Q p Hab ¶30. From ¶29 it seems clear that the "prophet of lies" was a chief priest, since he is said to have built a city. His abrogation of the Law in the present pericope and in ¶17 may be compared with the same charge made against the Wicked Priest in ¶25 (viii,9 f.) and ¶26 (viii,16 f.). On the role of the Prophet of Lies, see Otto Betz, pp. 92-98.

Noteworthy is the misspelling of מאסו as מאשו; but more important is the derivation of this idea from Habakkuk. Lou H. Silberman ("Riddle," *RQ*, III, 1961, p.335) has suggested that the idea of rejection comes from *pûq* = Aramaic *nĕfaq*, which in the *haf*ᶜ*ēl* means "drive away, expel." Though this is possible, the commentary is close to the idea of a slackened or benumbed Law.

THE MIDRASH PESHER OF HABAKKUK

¶5 (i, 12-14)

[וְלוֹא יֵצֵא לָנֶצַח מִשְׁפָּט כִּיא רָשָׁע מַכְתִּי]רْ אֶת הַצַּדִּיק   12
[פִּשְׁרוֹ הָרָשָׁע הוּא הַפּוֹהֵן הָרָשָׁע וְהַצַּדִּיק] הוּא מוֹרֵה הַצֶּדֶק   13
[   ] [אֲשֶׁר   14

12 (1:4aβ)   [Justice emerges not victorious;
    (1:4bα)   but the wicked he]ms in the righteous. /
13   [Its prophetic meaning is that the "wicked" is the Wicked
14   Priest, and the "righteous"] is the Righteous Teacher / [whom . . .]

45

¶ 5 *Exposition*

i, 12. *Lā-neṣaḥ* is here rendered "victorious" ("in victory"). In so far as Aquila is preserved, his Greek recension translates the expression εἰ νῖκος, as also do Paul (I Cor. 15:54), Aquila, and Theodotion at Isa. 25:8. Aquila's text of Hab 1:4 is not preserved, however. The LXX translation both here and usually elsewhere is εἰς τέλος. However, εἰς ν[ε]ῖκος occurs at II Sam. 2:26; Amos 1:11; 8:7; Jer. 3:5; and Lam. 5:20. Interestingly the LXX also translates the last clause of Hab. 3:1 (*la-měnaṣṣēaḥ bingînōtāi*) as τοῦ νικῆσαι ἐν τῇ ᾠδῇ αὐτου ("to conquer through his song"). Glanzmann (*ThS*, IV, 1952, p. 499), finds this meaning at 1Q H iv, 13, 25, and points out that in Phoenician the root *NṢḤ* means "to prevail over." Despite the usual translation "forever" in the Scriptures, according to Glanzmann, "there are places where the sense is vastly improved by understanding *NṢḤ* as 'victory'–including Hab. 1:4." If we adopt this meaning, the sense is the same as Isa. 42:3c ("He will truly [*le-ʾemet*] bring forth justice."). Note the citation at Matth. 12:20 which translates *leʾemet* with εἰς νῖκος. Cf. 1Q S iv, 19, "At that time, the truth on earth will emerge victorious." Cf. also Job 23:7 in Pope, *Job,* The Anchor Bible, p. 156.

The restoration of i, 13, first introduced with פשר אשר (*BASOR*, No. 112, 1948, p. 9), is one word too long; however, Habermann's restoration which omits also the first word is too brief and ignores the expectancy of always finding *pēšer* immediately after a primary citation of Scripture.

The fortunate preservation of "He is the Righteous Teacher" as an interpretation of "the righteous" in 1:4b indicates that this must have been preceded by an interpretation of the "wicked" as "the Wicked Priest." Perhaps, this was the first introduction of these characters in the *pēšer*, and certainly at a logical point, where the text itself indicates a persecuted righteous one who is the object of injustice on the part of the wicked man.

The first word of the title *môrēh haṣ-ṣedeq* is in the construct, and so it does not receive the article as would be necessary if one were to obtain the unambiguous reading "the one teaching righteousness." The second word is either a subjective or an objective genitive. Most of the time in the Qumrân Scrolls it is probably the former, giving us "the Righteous Teacher" in opposition to his opponent "the Wicked Priest." On the other hand, when the antithetical figure is "the Prophet of Lies," we should think of the objective genitive, "the Teacher of *ṣedeq*." "Righteousness," in such cases is not a suitable translation of *ṣedeq*, for we need a term which connotes truth as well as goodness. For this reason, in the following translations, I sometimes translate the phrase as "the Teacher of Right" – having in mind both rightness of doctrine and right behavior. *Ṣedeq* could also be taken to refer to the Teacher's legitimacy, "the Rightful Teacher." This last would be a suitable rendering, provided *hak-kôhēn hā-rāšāᶜ* could mean "the Unlawful Priest." However, the Scrolls never refer unambiguously to the illegitimacy of this priest, but only to his wicked deeds. On the Righteous Teacher, see O. Betz, pp. 75f.

G. W. Buchanan (*RQ*, No. 24, 1969, pp. 553-558) believes that he has found a parallel to this teacher's title in *Midrash Těhillîm,* Ps. 102:18, which he has translated as follows:

> Another interpretation of *He will turn to the prayer of the destitute* [is this]: Rabbi Isaac said, "With reference to the generations, they said that they had no prophet, no priestly teacher of righteousness, and no temple which would atone for them."

The key phrase is *wě-lôʾ kôhēn môrēh ṣedeq,* which Buchanan explains as an allusion to II Chron. 15:3, which in his translation reads as follows: "Many days for Israel there will be no true God, no priestly teacher (ולא כהן מורה) and no Torah." On the basis of this passage, he has deduced that *môrēh haṣ-ṣedeq* designated an office which might be held by many different persons. The man at Damascus (mentioned repeatedly in CDC) who bore this title would be a different person from the man who held this office at Qumrân.

Theodor H. Gaster (p. 5) also argues that one should think of a succession of teachers, "a kind of 'apostolic succession.' " He regularly translates this phrase as "the teacher who expounds the Law aright." However, emphasis is placed upon his interpretation of "the mysteries of the words of God's servants the prophets" (vii, 4f. [¶ 20]), so that it is not primarily the Law which he interprets. Gaster has also argued that the reading *MWRY* in 1Q p Mic indicates the plural, "those who expound the Law correctly." Actually, one has here simply a phonetic spelling, the *Yôd* standing for *Ṣērê*. This passage will be discussed below in connection with xii, 4 (¶ 33). (See also my review of Gaster's book in *JBL,* LXXVII, 1958, pp. 383 ff.) Moreover, the fact that an era can be calculated after the Teacher's death in CDC xix, 35f. (=9:29) and xx, 13ff. (=9:39) shows that it was not considered a continuing office in the Community at Damascus.

The word *môreh* as used at Qumran can mean "guide," as in CDC i,11 (=1:7): "And He raised up for them a Guide of Righteousness to lead them in the way of His heart." (See here Isaac Rabinowitz, "The Guides of Righteousness," *VT,* VIII, 1958, pp. 391-404). However, no one meaning is exhaustive, for when the *môrēh haṣ-ṣedeq* stands opposed to the *maṭṭîf hak-kāzāv,* the connotation is that of one "who showers truth" in antithesis to him "who drips lies." Actually the title was probably borrowed from Joel 2:23 which was interpreted to mean:

> Be glad, O sons of Zion,
>   and rejoice in the LORD, your God;
> for He has given you *the one who showers* [or, *teaches*] *righteousness,*
>   He has poured out to you abundant rain,
>   the early and the latter rain, first.

With this one may compare also the last clause of Hos. 10:12, which may have been construed to mean: "that he may come and teach [or, shower] righteousness to you." In agreement with Joel's phrase *ham-môreh liṣdāqāh*, one reads in 1Q p Hab ii, 2 *môrēh haṣ-ṣĕdāqāh*. In accordance with Hosea's phrase *yōreh ṣedeq*, we should probably recognize the title *yôrēh hay-yaḥad* in CDC xx, 14 (=9:39) — the spelling of the second word being there corrupted as *HYḤYD*. This last designation probably means "the Founder of the Community" (as argued in *NTS*, III, 1956, p. 13). However, according to CDC i,9f. (=1:6), this "founder" did not appear on the scene until after twenty years of groping by a slowly emerging movement. Though the connotations of *môreh* at Qumrân were many, the denotation of the word is in every place that of "teacher."

In opposition to Buchanan, one argues that the phrase *môrēh ṣedeq* in *Midrash Tĕhillôt* does not have the broad range of meaning that *môrēh haṣ-ṣedeq* has at Qumrân, that it means simply any "legitimate [or, authoritative] teacher." In this regard it may be compared with *mĕšîaḥ haṣ-ṣedeq* in 4Q Patriarchal Blessings (1i.3), "the legitimate [or, true] messiah"—this latter being restricted to one individual by the use of the article, just as *môrēh haṣ-ṣedeq* regularly has the article at Qumrân. The whole phrase *wĕ-lô᾿ kôhēn môrēh ṣedeq* as found in *Midrash Tĕhillôt* may be translated either as "and no priest as authoritative teacher," or (taking a clue from Gaster) as "and no priest who teaches the Law aright." Since for the Pharisees it was unimportant that an authoritative teacher be a priest, this parallel is indeed interesting. Is this reference to the priestly teacher due solely to the literary influence of II Chron. 15:3, or did Rabbi Isaac have his own peculiar priestly interest? Nothing in the context of the midrash serves to identify this rabbi as to date and provenance. In any case, he belonged to a different milieu from that of the Qumrân manuscripts, so that his meaning of the phrase *môrēh ṣedeq* does not need to have any connection with the Qumrân usage.

Of greater similarity to Qumrân is the Karaite interpretation of Joel and Hosea. Daniel al Kumisi's commentary (dating from the end of the ninth century) interpreted *ham-môreh liṣdāqāh* of Joel 2:23 as follows:

According to my view it is the *môrēh ṣedeq*, Elijah, who will be sent to Israel to teach them the laws, as it says [Hos. 10:12], "Till he come and teach righteousness to you"; and it also says [Mal. 3:24] "And he shall turn the heart of the fathers to the children," and this will be before (the coming of) Gog as it says [Mal. 3:23], "Before the coming of the great and dreadful day of the LORD."

This important passage was first cited by P. R. Weis, *JQR*, XLI, 1950, p. 135. As indicated above, also the Qumrân title was partly derived from Hos. 10:12, but not simply as a description of an office, but as the designation of an eschatological teacher who holds that office. This similarity, however, does not prove dependence of the Qumrân Scrolls upon Karaite literature; for any such suggestion is refuted by the solid archaeological and palaeographic evidence for the much greater antiquity of the Scrolls. This correspondence is due rather to coincidence in interpreting the prophets, or even to ultimate Karaite dependence upon Qumrân interpretation.

In a series of articles, S. Szyszman has argued that Karaism is derived from the Essenes in historical continuity. (See the bibliography.) N. Wieder (*The Judean Scrolls and Karaism,* pp. 253-255) has concluded similarly that various remnants of ancient Judean sects were drawn together in the formation of Karaism, and that vestiges of living tradition which derived ultimately from Qumrân contributed to *pēšer*-like exegesis among the Karaites.

Another possibility is that some earlier Dead-Sea-Scroll discovery may account for the presence of some affinities between the Karaites and Qumrân. Saul Liebermann (*Proceedings of the American Academy for Jewish Research,* XX, 1951, pp. 395-404) has called attention to a statement by Rabbi Moses Taku concerning Anan, the supposed eighth century founder of Karaism:

> And we have heard from our teachers that the heretic Anan and his friends used to write down heresies and lies and hide them in the ground. Then they would take them out and say: "This is what we found in ancient books."

Indeed, the Syrian Patriarch of Seleucia wrote about a discovery of scrolls in a cave near Jerico, which happened some time around A.D. 800—as noted by Otto Eissfeldt, *ThLZ,* LXXIV, 1949, cols. 596-600. Such a discovery may account for the presence of the Zadokite Work (or the Damascus Covenant) among the works discovered by Solomon Schechter in the geniza of a Karaite synagogue in Cairo. It could also explain the presence of the Hebrew text of the Wisdom of Sirach in that geniza. Manuscript finds at Qumrân and Masada prove that these medieval manuscripts must derive ultimately from ancient exemplars.

The title *hak-kôhēn hā-rāšāᶜ* is no doubt a deliberate caricature of the highpriestly title *hak-kôhēn hā-rōᵓš,* as suggested by Elliger (p. 266); but, if so, this implies that in many a passage where reference is made to "the Wicked Priest who did such and such," the identity of this chief priest must be inferred from the specific historical allusions, and that from passage to passage we may be dealing with different persons. This need not be thought strange, since Daniel 11 in its frequent references to "the king of the North" and "the king of the South" leaves the identity of the king in each case to be inferred from the historical allusions.

Nevertheless, in the present passage, the Wicked Priest and the Righteous Teacher are spoken of in such an absolute way, that this text may support the view that there is only one Wicked Priest, as well as one Righteous Teacher. Yet, one may argue that regardless of whether these titles designate one or more persons the intention of the present pericope is to present these men as exercising two contrastive offices, in a programmatic introduction to the *dramatis personae.*

i, 14. The sense of the missing half-line should be: "whom he [the Wicked Priest] oppressed in such and such a way." The missing statement would interpret the clause "Justice emerges not victorious"; and, perhaps, at the same time it would disclose an interpretation of the participle *makhtîr* ("hems in"). The Targum of Jonathan translates: "The wicked swallow (*měsal^cᵃmîn*) the righteous." One will recall here the use of the verb *BL^c* ("swallow") in Hab. 1:13, which is interpreted implicitly in ¶17 as the action of the Man of Lies. The word itself is used in the commentary at xi, 5 (¶31) to define the aim of the Wicked Priest in attacking the Teacher, but with the meaning "to make reel." An unexplained *ᶜāwôn* was committed by the Wicked Priest against the Teacher, according to ix, 9 (¶27). More specific is the charge of 4Q p Pss*ᵃ* iv, 8f. (¶23), which interprets Ps. 37:22 as referring to "the Wicked [Pries]t who kept w[atch over] the Right[eous Teach]er [in order tỏ sl]ay him [and to do violence to the Coven]ant and the Law which he sent him." This last passage may be particularly important for comparison here, since it indicates a violation of the Law in close agreement with Hab. 1:4. With such a violation one might compare also the Wicked Priest's attack upon the Righteous Teacher at the Day of Atonement (discussed in ¶31). None of these passages does more than illustrate the possibilities. Hence, no restoration has been attempted.

THE MIDRASH PESHER OF HABAKKUK

¶6 (i, 14-16)

|עַ[ל בֵּן יֵצֵא הַמִּשְׁפָּט   14
[מְעֻקָּל   פשר . . . .[וְלֹוא לְ]יֹ[ישֶׁר   15
[. . . . .]   16

14-15 (1:4bβ) [The]refore justice goes forth / [perverted.
16   Its prophetic meaning] . . . but not in [rectitude]/ . . . .

¶6 *Exposition*

What a pity the interpretation of this pericope has not survived, for if the Righteous Teacher had been subject to legal injustice (as suggested also by the preceding pericope) something would surely have been said about it here. The last surviving letter of line 15 is probably a *Bêt*, but it could be a *Mêm* or *Tāw*. This was followed by no more than three or four letters. This excludes the longer restoration of Habermann. The present restoration suggests that the missing word is the antithesis of *měʿuqqāl*.

THE MIDRASH PESHER OF HABAKKUK

¶7 (i, 16-ii, 10)

16   [רְאוּ בוֹגְדִים וְהַבִּיטוּ]

17   [וְהִתַּמְּהוּ תְּמָהוּ כִּיא פֹעַל פּוֹעֵל בִּימֵיכֶם לוֹא תַאֲמִינוּ כִּיא]

ii,1   יְסֻפָּר   [פֶּשֶׁר הַדָּבָר עַל]הַבּוֹגְדִים עִם אִישׁ

2   הַכָּזָב כִּי לוֹא]הֶאֱמִינוּ בְדִבְרֵי] מוֹרֵה הַצֶּדֶקֿה מִפִּיא

3   אֵל וְעַל הַבּוֹגְ]דִים בַּבְּרִית [הַחֲדָשָׁה כְּ]י[א לוֹא

4   הֶאֱמִינוּ בִּבְרִית אֵל[וַיְחַלְּלוּ] אֶת שֵׁ[ם קָ]וְדְשׁוֹ

5   וְכֵן   פֶּשֶׁר הַדָּבָר] עַל הַבּוֹ]גְדִים לְאַחֲרִית א

6   הַיָּמִים הֵמָּה עָרִיצֵ]ים בַּבְּר]ית אֲשֶׁר לוֹא יַאֲמִינוּא

7   בְּשׁוֹמְעָם אֶת כָּול הַבָּ]אוֹת עַל]הַדּוֹר הָאַחֲרוֹן מִפִּי

8   הַכּוֹהֵן אֲשֶׁר נָתַן אֵל בְּל]בּוֹ בִינָ]ה לִפְשׁוֹר אֶת כָּול

9   דִּבְרֵי עֲבָדָיו הַנְּבִיאִים [אֲשֶׁר בְּ]יָדָם סִפֵּר אֵל אֶת

10   כָּול הַבָּאוֹת עַל עַמּוֹ וַ[עֲדָתוֹ]

i.16   (1:5)[Look, O traitors, and see;/

17   wonder and be astonished!

       For He is working a work in your days

ii,1   ye will not believe, though] / it be foretold.

       The prophetic meaning of the passage concerns those who were

2   traitors along with the Man of / Lies, for they [did] not [believe the

3   words of] the Teacher of Right (which came) from the mouth of/ God.

       It also concerns those who were trait[ors to the] New [Covenant], f[or

4   they were not / faithful to the covenant of God, [but profaned] His

5   [h]oly na[me]. / And thus the prophetic meaning of the passage

6   [concerns] also [the trai]tors of the last / days. They are vio[lators of the

7   coven]ant who will not believe / when they hear all that is com[ing

8   upon] the last generation from the mouth of / the priest in [whose heart]

9   God has put [understandi]ng to give the prophetic meaning of all / the

10   words of His servants the prophets, [through] whom God foretold / all

       that is coming upon His people and [His] c[ongregation].

¶7 Exposition

i, 16f. The scroll had at least 17 lines (see *BASOR*, 118, 1950, pp. 7-9). Therefore, the citation of Hab. 1:5 may have begun at i,16. Of course, it is possible that some columns had as many as 18 lines. In that case, Elliger could be right in numbering the first two lines of this pericope as 17 and 18.

i, 16. The textual variant *bôgĕdîm* ("traitors") for M.T. *bag-gôyîm* ("among [or, upon] the nations") is implied both by the constant reference to "traitors" in the commentary and by the absence to any reference to the "nations." See *Text*, §3, citing the LXX; yet some follow the MT (Burrows, p. 265; Maier, I, p. 150; Vermès, *DSSE*, p. 236; Michel, p. 8); and Silberman ("Riddle," pp. 335f.) has suggested that this is unnecessary since the commentator might have arbitrarily altered the consonants (mentally) in order to achieve his interpretation. Yet the reading *bôgĕdîm* is probable and has been adopted by Elliger; van der Woude, *Bijbelcommentaren,* p. 30; Maier; Molin, p. 11; Carmignac, *Textes,* p. 94; Gaster, pp. 249, 265.

i, 17. "*He* is working a work." This has usually been translated as "*I* am working a work." The absence of the personal pronoun, however, is more congruent with the word *pôˁēl* being interpreted as third person. (See Brownlee, "The Composition of Habakkuk.") The same translation is given by van der Woude.

ii, 1. The verb *yĕsuppar* is interpreted here as meaning "foretold," after ii, 6f. For this meaning see 1Q H i, 23 and Isa. 52:15, and my paraphrase of the latter in *Meaning,* p. 295.

The reading הבוגדים replaces my original reading of ובוגדים. The hook of the upper left of the letter, which alone survives, resembles more closely the loop of a *Hē* than the point of a *Wāw*. Nevertheless, some have followed this reading and coupled it with a preceding synonym. Thus Michel, n. 1, p. 19, suggests רשעים ("impies"), read by Habermann in ˓*Edah*; and Baer, p. 14, would enlarge the reading by supplying the article before each word. In *Megilloth,* p. 43, Habermann restores האנשים. Such restorations, however, are too large, as the measure of li. 11, below, shows.

There appear to be three classes of *bôgĕdîm* in the interpretation, as Dupont-Sommer (*RHR,* p. 53, §7) first indicated. (See also Gert Jeremias, *Der Lehrer der Gerechtigkeit,* pp. 80ff.) The first class were "traitors along with the Man of Lies," who are mentioned in v, 8-12 (¶ 17) and CDC i, 11-ii, 1 (=1:9-17). This does not mean that they ever followed the Righteous Teacher. Rather, they never had "believed in the words of Teacher of Right"; but such unbelief constituted defection from the true Israel. Cf. Rom. 11:20. Cf. 1Q H ii, 9f.: "Thou hast made me a scorn and derision to the faithless [*bôgĕdîm*]." One stands or falls before God, according to his attitude toward the Teacher, who is probably the speaker in 1Q H vii, 12: "For all who contend against me shall be condemned in judgment, [to] make a distinction through me between the righteous and the wicked."

"The Teacher of Right" translates *môrēh haṣ-ṣĕdāqāh*, which occurs here instead of the usual *môrēh haṣ-ṣedeq*. The variation must have been made for emphasis. The revered Teacher in contrast with the Man of Lies taught what is right and true.

ii,2f. The restoration of Isaac Rabinowitz in *JBL*, LXIX, 1950, pp. 33, 39, is שמעו לדברי, which is based upon II Chron. 35:22: "He did not hearken to the words of Necho form the mouth of God." It is reinforced by CDC xx, 28, 32 (9:51, 53): "They hearkened (וישמעו) to the voice of the Teacher. . . . They gave ear (האזינו) to the voice of the Righteous Teacher." This restoration would appear probable, if it were not for the context. Therefore, continue to restore *heʾemînû* along with Habermann, Silberman, Burrows, Edelkoort (p. 53), Maier, Molin, Sutcliffe (*Monks*, p. 173), Carmignac, Gaster, Michel. However, *heʾezînû* might have occurred as a pun on Habakkuk's *taʾamînû*. Elliger and Lohse have followed Rabinowitz, with a slight change in the preposition, only *ʾel* for *lĕ*.

Since the Teacher was no Necho, II Chron. 36:12 is more significant than 35:22 for understanding his role; for Jeremiah was declared to be "the prophet from the mouth of Yahweh." Cf. Jer. 23:16; Ezek. 3:17. Gert Jeremias (*Der Lehrer*, pp. 81, 140-46) emphasizes the Teacher's prophetic role.

Those betraying "the New Covenant" would appear to be those who joined the sect and fell away. *Heʾemînû*, at ii, 4, in contrast with 1i. 2 and 1i. 6, does not mean simply "did not believe" (Brownlee, *BASOR*, 112; and others), but "were not faithful." However, a middle meaning, "They did not maintain their faith in the New Covenant," is also possible. Through this lapse of faith and loyalty "[they profaned] his [ho]ly Na[me]." One is not to think of profanity in the use of God's name. A close parallel with this defection is found in CDC xx, 10 f. (=9:36 f.):

> With a judgment like that of their fellows who turned away with the men of scoffing shall they be judged; for they uttered error against the statutes of righteousness and despised the covenant and the pledge of faith which they had affirmed in the land of Damascus; and this is the New Covenant.

ii, 4. Dupont-Sommer first restored "new" to obtain "the *new* covenant of God" (*RHR*, pp. 132, 140); but he later omitted this (*Essene Writings*, p. 259).

ii, 5 ff. This third class of *bôgĕdîm* consists neither of those who early in the history of the sect rejected the Righteous Teacher (ii, 1 f.), nor of those who after joining the sect have turned away (ii, 3 f.), for they have not yet heard the predictions of the Righteous Teacher. They belong to the "last days" and are a subsequent generation (probably that of the commentator), who live in the last days. Cf. Michel's rendering "génération suivante." This distinction as to time is indicated by the differences of tense: the perfect *heʾemînû* occurs at ii, 4: but the imperfect *yaʾamînû*, in ii, 6. Silberman (p. 336) has acknowledged:

> These [references to *bōgĕdîm*] point to three different groups of 'betrayers,' perhaps in chronological sequence. The first group belongs to the days of the *Moreh ha-Zedek;* the

second, to the period after the new covenant was entered into; the third, to the *future traitors*.

The expression "future traitors" is Gaster's translation at lis. 5f. In harmony with such an understanding of the third group is the translation of *had-dôr hā-ʾaḥᵃrôn* (li. 7) as "la generation future" (Carmignac, *Textes,* p. 94). The imperfect mood of the verb in li. 6 may be appealed to; but more probably "the traitors of the last days" are the author's own contemporaries, removed in time by at least one generation from the lifetime of the Teacher. The Kittim are also always referred to in the imperfect; but they probably belong to the present and not simply to the near future. Yet here and elsewhere one is led to consider the possibility that the midrash sometimes preserves traditions of interpretation, including predictions, that go back to the Teacher himself. Essenes reputed to have mantic ability are mentioned by Josephus, *JA,* XIII, xi,2 (§§ 311-313); XV, x,5 (§§ 373-379); XVII, xiii,3 (§§ 345-348); *JW,* I, ii,5 (§§ 78-80).

ii, 5. The *ʾĀlef* at the end of this line is according to Yigael Yadin preemptive, intended to prevent any interpolation in an incomplete line. This usage he has found in the Bar Kokhba manuscripts. See *IEJ,* Vol. 12, p. 256 and plate 48 C. See illustrations of this in his book, *Bar-Kokhba,* 1971, pp. 177, 179. However, the *Sitz im Leben* of this practice was in legal documents (deeds, contracts, etc.), so its exceptional occurrence here must be regarded as a scribal slip.

ii,6. "The viola[tors of the coven]ant," which was proposed by Sjöberg, "The Restoration of Column II of the Habakkuk Commentary of the Dead Sea Scrolls," *Studia Theologica,* IV, 1952, pp. 121ff. (here p. 123) is a more likely restoration than "the ruth[less of the nati]ons," ערי[צי האומ]ת, despite Rabinowitz' appeal (p. 41) to עריצי גוים in Ezek. 28:7; 30:11; 31:12; 32:12; for as Sjöberg (p. 127) points out, there is nothing to indicate that this third class of faithless ones is not also Jewish. Note also the *ᶜārîṣîm* of 4Q p Pssᵃ iii,12 (¶ 20) who are defined as "the ruthless of the [people, the wi]cked of Israel." Habermann (*Megilloth,* p. 43) restores ערי[צים מפירי הברי]ת, "the ruthless, the breakers of the covenant;" and Baer (p. 14) suggests ערי[צי דורשי חלקו]ת, "the ruthless, the seekers of smooth things." Carmignac has proposed ערול[י'לב וכלי]ות, "the uncircumcised of heart and kidneys;" but the letter *Lāmed* seems to be excluded by a faint trace of the lower bend of the letter *Ṣādê,* at the tattered edge of the manuscript. This seems clear in the original black and white photograph. However, Trever's colored photograph in *Scrolls from Qumrân Cave I* shows this less distinctly, since meanwhile the margin had crumbled slightly. The latter also makes it appear improbable that there ever was any ink above the hook (or presumed loop) as the reading *Lāmed* must presuppose. Moreover, the angle of the preserved hook is more agreeable to the right arm of an *ᶜAyin* or *Ṣādê.* Although the Old Testament sometimes associates the "heart" with the "kidneys" (or, "reins"), there is no example of either circumcision or uncircumcision being spoken of in connection with the kidneys.

ii, 7f. The "priest" whose predictions of things to come are spoken of is undoubtedly the Righteous Teacher whose interpretations of the "words of His servants the prophets" are mentioned also in vii, 4f. Cf. 4Q p Pss^a iii, 15 (¶ 21) and 4Q p Pss^a iv, 5 f. (¶ 26). "Its meaning concerns the priest, the [Righteous] Teacher." This passage of 1Q p Hab. does not imply, as Elliger (p. 171) supposes, that the Teacher may be still alive. Note that after the "gathering in" (or death) of the Teacher of the Community (CDC xx, 14 f. = 9:39), it was still possible to "listen to the voice of the Teacher" (CDC xx, 28, 32 = 9.50, 53). The teacher is dead, but is still to be heard. Cf. Heb. 11:4; John 10:16; Eph. 2:17f.

ii,8. "In whose [heart] God has put [insight] to interpret." The restoration was approximated by Rabinowitz (p. 33), who citing Ex. 36:2 and I Kings 10:24 / II Chron. 9:23 for the entire expression, supplied ḥokmāh (wisdom) rather than bînāh (insight), in which he has been followed by Burrows, Molin, Habermann (^cEdah, p. 44). However, IQ H xiv, 8 favors bînāh: הנותן בלב עבדו בינה ("who puts in the heart of His servant insight"). Cf. also 1Q H ii,10. Hence this restoration of Habermann (Megilloth, p. 43) and Vermès is to be preferred. Other restorations appear less likely: "in the mysteries of wisdom" (Molin), "in the house of Judah" (Dupont-Sommer, Lambert [p. 291], Bardtke [p. 125], Michel), "at that time" (Sjöberg), "in those days" (Gaster), "in the midst of the congregation" (Elliger, Maier, Lohse, van der Woude).

"Insight to interpret." The infinitive is cognate with the noun pēšer, which appears constantly in the Scroll in the sense of the "secret prophetic meaning" which only an inspired interpreter may expound. The noun itself is employed in the Aramaic text of Daniel. As an inspired interpreter, Daniel is declared to have "had insight [hēvîn] in all visions and dreams," according to Dan. 1:17. Cf. also Dan. 2:21, 23 and 5:11-12 for the ascription of ḥokmāh to Daniel. For the importance of this background for Qumrân interpretation, see Elliger (pp. 163f.), F. F. Bruce, Biblical Exegesis in the Qumran Texts, Grand Rapids, Mich.: Eerdmans, 1959, pp. 7f.; Silberman, ("Riddle," pp. 323-35).

ii, 9. On the verb sippēr ("foretold"), cf. above at ii, 1.

ii, 10. "Upon His people and [His] c[ongregation]," restores according to Elliger and Sutcliffe. Rabinowitz (followed by Dupont-Sommer; Lambert; Delcor, p. 22) restored [ועל הגואים] ("and upon the nations"). In BASOR, 112, pp. 9f., I supplied ב[ני ישראל למור[ה ("whom He has given unto the Ch[ildren of Israel for a teach]er." This overly long restoration was shortened only slightly by Edelkoort to "aande Is[raëlieten als leraar]." J. van der Ploeg (Bi Or VIII, p. 5), Barthélemy (RB, 1952, p. 209), Reicke (Handskrifterna, p. 29), van der Woude, and Carmignac (p. 96) have all supplied ישראל ("upon His people Israel")–a phrase very close to 1Q M x, 9. Habermann (^cEdah, p. 44),

Vermès (*Discovery*, p. 124; *DSSE*), Maier, and Lohse have restored ו[על ארצו], or more briefly ו[ארצו] ("and [upon] His land"). Unfortunately, the upper right hand tip of the fragmentary letter could be ש, א, or ע; and the preceding letter is ambiguously *Wāw* or *Yôd* in the penmanship of this Scroll. The reading "Israel" fits well and is possible paleographically. However, Elliger's reading, with its linking of synonyms accords well with the style of the commentary. Habermann (*Megilloth*) would restore ו[אשר אמר] ("and as for that which He said") and take this as the introduction to the next Biblical quotation; but that is entirely unsuitable, since this phrase is used elsewhere only for requotations of a portion of text previously quoted at greater length (vi, 1; vii, 3; ix, 1f.; x, 1f.).

The historical transposition of Hab. 1:5 to the "last days" and to the problem of disbelief in the Righteous Teacher finds an interesting parallel in Acts 13: 38-41 in the rejection of Jesus as preached by Paul at Antioch of Pisidia. In both cases the application is to an eschatological figure; but in Paul's application it is not merely disbelief in the teachings of Jesus but in God's work of salvation accomplished through him.

Otto Betz, pp. 88-99, develops the prophetic side of the Teacher's role at Qumrân in contrast with the Prophet of Lies. The literary allusions point clearly to affinities with the Old Testament prophets, and his opponent is a false prophet; and yet, according to Betz, Qumrân distinguished him as rather an interpreter of the prophets who stood on the threshold of the Messianic age.

THE MIDRASH PESHER OF HABAKKUK

¶8 (ii, 10-16)

כֹּ[יא הִנְנִי מֵקִים אֶת   10
הַכַּשְׂדָּאִים הַגּוֹי הַמַּ[ר וְהַנִּמְ]הָר   11
פִּשְׁרוּ עַל הַכִּתִּיאִים אֲ[שֶׁר הֵמָּ]ה קַלִּים וְגִבּוֹרִים   12
בַּמִּלְחָמָה לְאַבֵּד רַבִּים[וַעֲנוּגִים] בְּמֶמְשֶׁלֶת   13
הַכִּתִּיאִים יַרְשִׁ[יעוּ מִדִּבְרֵי הַבְּרִי]ת וְלוֹא יַאֲמִינוּ   14
[   ]ֹ[א] לְ[חֻקֵּי   15
[   ]   16

10   (1:6a) Look! (O bitter and hasty nation!)
11   I am raising up / the Chaldeans,
           that fierce and speedy nation. /
12   Its prophetic meaning concerns the Kittim, w[ho ar]e swift and
13   mighty / in war to destroy the s[of]t [and dainty]. Under the dominion
14   of / the Kittim, men will turn wick[edly away from the provisions of the
15   covenan]t and not be faithful / to the ordinances of [Go]d . . . /
16   . . . . .

59

¶8 Exposition

ii, 10. כ[כ] = כי. Here it simply introduces the quotation, as in Gen. 21:30; 29:12; Ex. 3:12; esp. Zech. 2:13 (=2:9). Cf. above concerning Hab. 1:5*b*.

ii, 11. For the spelling *kaśdā^ɔîm*, cf. *kaśdā^ɔîn* in the Aramaic of Dan. 3:8; 5:11. The Biblical text determines the width of the column and the size of the lacunae which appear in every line of this column from top to bottom.

ii,12. For the spelling *kittî^ɔîm*, cf. (after Barthélemy, *RB*, 1950, p. 544) *hā-^carĕvî^ɔîm* in II Chron. 17:11. In each case the usual O. T. spelling is *kittîm* and *hā-^carĕvîm*, respectively; but these are contractions of *kittîyîm* (Jer. 2:10) and *hā-arĕvîyîm* (II Chron. 26:7). The spellings with ^ɔ*Ālef* attest a quiescent *Yôd*. For the interpretation of *ham-mar* as *gibbôrîm*, see Silberman, "Riddle," pp. 336f.

ii, 13. The restoration suggested here is new: Cf. Isa. 47:1. Other restorations of the words which follow לאבד are: (1) [ועצומים] ר[ב]ים "great and mighty" (Sjöberg, *STh*, p. 127); (2) [כי ילחמו]ר[ב]ים "to destroy many should they war against" (Rabinowitz, *JBL*, 1950, pp. 33f.); (3) [והיתה הארץ]ר[ב]ים "many; and the earth [or land] will become (subject to)" (Dupont-Sommer, *RHR*, p. 140; Bardtke, p. 125; and Lohse); (4) [והיתה ארץ ישראל]ר[ב]ים "many and the land of Israel will become" (Michel, p. 19, n. 10); (5) רעים והבוגדים "to destroy the wicked; but 'the traitorous' " (Molin, p. 11); (6) רעים וחטאים "evil and sinners" (Habermann, both in ^c*Edah*, p. 45,; and *Megilloth*, p. 43); (7) רוזנים ולכניעם "to destroy rulers and subject them" (Burrows, p. 365; Elliger; the 2nd word in Driver, *Judaean Scrolls*, p. 127); (8) רוזנים ומלכים היורדים "rulers and kings who are brought down" (Baer, p. 5); (9) רבים ולהכניעם "to destroy many and subject them" (Maier, I, p. 150; II, p. 143; van der Woude, *Bijbelcommentaren*, p. 30; Gaster, p. 250). The reading of the first word as *rabbîm* or *ra^cîm* seems doubtful since the traces of the top of the second letter fit better the narrower space of a *Kaf*. *Rōzĕnîm* is excluded, since there is not room for both a *Zayin* and a *Nûn*. Cf. iv, 1. The second word of the restoration should perhaps provide the subject of the verbs of the next line. Concerning this, see other restorations below.

ii, 14. The following restorations have been proposed: (1) ר[ורש]עים "But the wi[cked. . . .]" (*BASOR*, 112; Delcor, p. 23; Habermann; Vermès [*DSSE*, p. 236]);) (2) ורש]עים הם לבטוח בשק[ר "And they are wick[ed so as to trust in false]hood" (Rabinowitz); (3) ורש]עים בה לראו[ת (Heb. uncertain) "And the wicked will see it" (Dupont-Sommer, *Essene Writings*, p. 259); (4) ירש]יעו על בני הברי[ת (by going back to preceding line) "[but the traitors] under the dominion of the Kittim *will act* [*wickedly against the men of the covenan*]*t* and will not believe in [Go]d's ordinances." (Molin, *ZKTh*, 1952, p. 58); (5) ירש]עו כי יעשה חטא[ת " will be guil[ty, for they will commit sin]s" (Molin, *Die Söhne des Lichtes*, p. 11); (6) ירש]ו ארצות רב[ות "will po[ssess many land]s" (Burrows, Elliger, Maier, Lohse); (7) ור]וצחים וגוזלים["namely, [or, As for] murderers and robbers" (Baer, p.5, his interpretation of the syntax being uncertain). Nos. 1 and 2 misread the traces of the last letter, which can only be a *Tāw*. No. 7 ignores the traces of letters partially preserved. Nos. 2 and 6 would in the immediate sequel charge the Kittim with disbelief in the ordinances of God, as also J. G. Harris interprets (p. 37). No. 4 is moving in the right direction; and its length (if inferred correctly from the German [*Die Abtrünnigen*] *aber werden unter der Herrschaft der Kittim* [*den Männern des Bundes Böses*] *tun*) is about right. Nos. 3, 4 and 5 seem to infer correctly that the theme of traitorous and unfaithful Jews has been carried forward from the previous pericope. Molin (both Nos. 4 and 5) restores *bôgĕdîm* in line 13, which has the advantage of providing a subject for the following verbs; but when this is followed by the preposition *bĕ*, this should mean rather "those who are traitors *to* the dominion of the Kittim"—a meaning unsuitable to the context. (Cf. viii, 10 f.) As subject, one might restore הרשעים as the second word of the lacuna of li. 13; but perhaps the subject of the verb was left indefinite.

On *yaršîᶜû min*, see 1Q *34* ii, 4; II Sam. 22:22 (= Ps. 18:22); but cf. *hiršîaᶜ ᶜal* at ix, 11 f., also *maršîᶜē bĕrît* of 1Q M i, 2 and Dan. 11:32. The choice of preposition and the addition of *divrê* are based upon space. For *divrê hab-bĕrît*, see 1Q S ii, 13.

ii, 15. Dupont-Sommer (*RHR*, p. 140) has suggested as alternatives for בחוקי [אל] either [בחוק[ם] or הברית] בחוקי; but the tip of the *Lāmed* is clear, as Elliger notes. The parallelism between "covenant" and "ordinance" (as restored at ii, 14 f.) is quite appropriate. The association of unbelief (or faithlessness) with violation of the covenant has occurred twice previously in this same column (lis. 3 f., 6).

The midrashic relationship between the interpretation and Hab. 1:6*a* depends upon one's restorations. Silberman ("Riddle," pp. 336 f.) has suggested that the idea of *gibbôrîm* ("strong") (li. 12) was inferred from Habakkuk's word *ham-mar*, derived from *mar* ("lord, master, *Herr, Besitzer*") or from *MRY* = *MRᵓ*, "be fat, strong." In this he may well be right. From the notion of fatness might be derived also the notion of "the soft and dainty" as I restore at li. 13; for this refers to the wealthy rulers who through self-indulgence are soft and effete, as in Deut. 28:54, 56; Isa. 47:1. In a sense, also, they are "mighty," but the commentator has deliberately twisted this into its opposite when applying the term to the genteel of his own nation. From the word *mar*, Silberman derives also the verb ירשו which (following Elliger and others) he restores at 1i, 14. However, at this point my restoration correlates with *MRH* as "be disobedient, rebellious"—as will appear from the following discussion.

The restoration of 1i.14 is not simply a matter of the continuing theme of infidelity and unbelief; but rather it seems that *hag-gôi ham-mar wĕ-han-nimhār* has been taken in two different ways. Firstly, it was construed correctly as in apposition to *hak-kaśdāᵓîm:*

Behold I am raising up the Chaldeans,

the bitter and hasty nation

(i.e., that fierce and speedy nation).

Secondly, it was contrued as listing another party also:

Behold, I am raising up the Chaldeans,

O bitter and hasty nation.

Thus the commentator was able to find a description of the Jewish nation in the second clause by reading a vocative. The Jews so described, according to him, are "under the dominion of the Kittim." It is not simply that the dominion of the Kittim is imposed upon such sinners as a punishment, but rather that those living under the Kittim become themselves like their overlords "bitter and hasty." The "bitter and hasty" of Israel are rebellious, like the malcontents of Saul's kingdom who joined David (I Sam. 22:2). According to Isa. 28:16: "He who believes does not hasten" from his place in the spiritual temple which God is building. Cf. IQ S viii,8. The forsaking of God is "evil and bitter" according to Jer. 2:19.

THE MIDRASH PESHER OF HABAKKUK

¶9 (ii, 16-iii, 2)

[הַהוֹלֵךְ לְמֶרְחֲבֵי אֶרֶץ לָרֶשֶׁת]   16

[מִשְׁכָּנוֹת לוֹא לוֹ פִּשְׁרוֹ עַל הַכִּתִּיאִים אֲשֶׁר בָּעֵמֶק]   17

וּבַמִּישׁוֹר יֵלְכוּ לַכּוֹת וְלָבוֹז אֶת עָרֵי הָאָרֶץ   iii,1

כִּיא הוּא אֲשֶׁר אָמַר לָרֶשֶׁת מִשְׁכָּנוֹת לוֹא לוֹ   2

ii,16 (1:6b) [Who march through broad places of the earth (or land)]

17   to seize /habitations not their own.

iii,1   Its prophetic meaning concerns the Kittim, who / will march, [*through vale*] and through plain to smite and to plunder the

2   cities of the land (or earth); / for that is what He said (1:6b) "to seize habitations not their own."

¶9 *Exposition*

ii, 16-17. The citation of Hab. 1:6*b* occurred at the bottom of Col. ii; but exactly how the words were divided between the last two lines is uncertain. Elliger and van der Woude (*Bijbelcommentaren*, p. 30) place the whole half-verse on 1i. 17 and start the interpretation at the beginning of a hypothetical eighteenth line. Habermann (*ᶜEdah,* p. 45; *Megilloth,* p. 44) puts the Biblical quotation on lines 15-16, ascribing only 16 lines to this column. Such variations from the norm of 17 lines, established by Col. xii, are possible. However, it is precarious to identify the *Lāmed* (traces of which appear at the beginning of ii, 16) with that of לרשת of the Biblical text, since to my eye (as also to that of Elliger) there appears also to be an infinitesimal fleck at the top of a *Wāw* just before the *Lāmed.* The *Lāmed* is usually flush with the margin when it stands at the beginning of a line. Only at x,1, does there appear an initial *Lāmed*, whose top is approximately as far to the left as is posited by Habermann for ii, 16.

iii,1. The verb *yēlēkhû* corresponds to the first word of the Biblical quotation; and *ū-vam-mîšôr* corresponds with the next two words. It, therefore, appears certain that very little interpretation is lost at the bottom of the preceding column. Habermann was on the right track when he placed at the end of the preceding line *baš-šĕfēlāh* ("through lowland"); for only this much would be necessitated by the "and" at the beginning of iii,1. However, if one insists that this "and" be preceded by an entire clause, then he will need to posit an eighteenth line for Col. ii. Habermann's resultant combination of words is attested by II Chron. 26:10; but it is not clear from that verse that "lowland" and "plain" are synonyms or designate different areas. The usual parallel to *mîšôr* is rather *ᶜēmeq* (Jer. 21:13; 48:8; I Kings 20:23, 28). The latter word is used in the Old Testament for such broad valleys as the Plain of the Jordan, and even for the coastal plain. The *mîšôr* is used as a geographical designation of the highlands of Transjordan (Delcor, p. 29); but it is probably used generically here. The "broad places of the Earth" are therefore interpreted as "broad valleys and plains" because these were required for the marching of large armies. The above excludes earlier alternatives for interpreting *bam-mîšôr.* "In uprightness" (BASOR, 112, p. 10) is unsuitable to context. More suitable would be "straight ahead" (Michel, p.9, "*endroite ligne*") and "unhindered" (van der Woude," "*ongehindered.*").

"To smite and to plunder the cities of the land," so van der Woude and Lohse. Both infinitives may be *qal* inf. const. of double ᶜ*Ayin* verbs. The root *KTT* (Michel, "*tailler en pièces*"), however, is used in the sense of crushing an enemy only in Zech. 11:6. It is not associated with the word *BZZ* ("to take plunder"); but as O. H. Lehmann (*PEQ*, 1951, p. 36) has pointed out, the verb *KTT* of Zech. 11:6 is so interpreted in the Targum. In that case one might wish to translate: "to *despoil* and to plunder the cities" (a linking of synonyms). Silberman ("Riddle," p. 337) apparently assumes derivation from *KTT* and interprets it as a midrash upon *lĕ-rešet* as though derived from *RŠŠ*, "beat down, shatter" (Jer. 5:17). Finkel (p. 368) suggests that the commentator knew the dual readings *LMRḤBY* and *LHḤRYB*, interpreting the latter to mean "to smite." Since no such reading is attested, however, it would seem preferable to find here a midrashic pun.

Reinforced by the above suggestions, the interpreter understood "to possess" to mean smiting and plundering. Even the holding and taxation of a city could be included under "plunder." It is best to point the first infinitive as a *hifᶜîl* of *NKH*, as Habermann and Elliger do, since in II Chron. 14:13 we find the sequential statements: ויכו את כל־הערים and ויבזו את כל־הערים. The omission of *Hē* in the *hifᶜîl* inf. is common in the scroll. The "habitations" of Hab. 1:6 are interpreted as "cities" also in the Targum. Perhaps we should render *haʾāreṣ* as "the earth," which is suitable if we think of the Kittim as a world-conquering power. However, an interesting requotation of 1:6b reinforces the equation of "habitations *not their own*" with "cities of the earth [or land]." "The land" seems better after all, for certainly the "land" of Palestine which had been given to the Israelites by God Himself cannot be said to belong rightfully to the Kittim.

iii, 2. The phrase which introduces that requotation has been variously translated, "for that is what *it* says" (most translators), "for it is He Who says" (*BASOR*, 114, p. 9); and "for that is what He said" (Michel, p. 9). 11Q p Melchizedek proves by the subjects supplied the verb אמר that this last is correct — only the subject can be either the prophet or God Himself. According to 1Q p Hab. ii, 9f., "God foretold through His servants the prophets all that is coming upon His people." To translate with a capital H ("*He*") ascribes the prophecy to God, but it includes the human agency. Since the Book of Habakkuk alternates between the prophet's own complaints and Yahweh's answers, it seems appropriate to employ "he" for the former and "He" for the latter.

THE MIDRASH PESHER OF HABAKKUK

¶10 (iii, 2-6)

אָיֹם   2

וְנוֹרָא הוּא מִמֶּנּוּ מִשְׁפָּטוֹ וּשְׂאֵתוֹ יֵצֵא   3

פִּשְׁרוֹ עַל הַכִּתִּיאִים אֲשֶׁר פַּחְדָּם [וְאֵי]מָ[תָ] ᴰ עַל־כָּוּל   4
הַגּוֹאִים

וּבְעֵצָה כָּול־מַחֲשַׁבְתָּם לְהָרַע וּבְגֹכֶל וּמִרְמָה   5

יֵלְכוּ עִם כָּול־הָעַמִּים   6

2-3	(1:7)	Dreadful / and fearsome are they;
		their judgment and their guile will go out from them. /
4		Its prophetic meaning concerns the Kittim whose terror [and]
4½-5		whose [dr]e[ad] will be upon all / the nations. / And in counsel,
		their whole purpose will be to do evil; and with cunning and
6		deceit / they will conduct themselves with all peoples.

¶10 *Exposition*

iii, 2 f. The only textual variant is the *plene* spelling of ᵓ*āyôm*. See *Text,* §§8, 8a. For the translation, see the commentary.

iii, 4. "Whose terror and whose dread." This interprets the words, "Dreadful and fearsome." The pronominal suffix of *wĕ-ᵓêmātām* was accidentally omitted, but was later inserted above the line. The *Mêm* resembles closely those of the main scribe, but not that of the corrector who supplied an omitted word above the first word of the next line.

iii, 4 1/2. *Hag-gôᵓîm*, which is thus supplied between the lines is not absolutely necessary to the sense. Yet in copying (or even in composing), omissions sometimes occur *between* the lines. The spelling with an ᵓ*Ālef* is to be explained by the fact that the *Yôd* of the original *gôyîm* (*kĕtîv* of Ps. 79:10b) has become quiescent. Yet this spelling appears only here in 1Q p Hab, in a correction addition. That the "terror and dread" of the *Kittîᵓîm* "will be upon all the nations" is inferred from the words *mimmennû. . . yēṣēᵓ.* The baneful influence of the Kittim "will go out *from them"* to *all the nations.* Contrast Isa. 42:3 f.

iii, 5f. "In counsel their whole purpose will be to do evil." This interprets *mišpāṭô* of the Biblical text — *mišpāṭ* being understood as a governmental decision reached through consultation. Dupont-Sommer (*RHR,* p. 132; *Essene Writings,* p. 260), Michel (p. 9), and van der Woude (*Bijbelcommentaren,* p. 31) render "with reflection," "deliberately;" but this is improbable. In 1QS vi, 22f., *mišpāṭ* and ᶜ*ēsāh* are linked together as synonyms. That the *mišpāṭîm* of the kittim are to be evil might have been inferred by taking Habakkuk in still another sense: "Their justice. . . will depart from them" — i.e., they will be unjust. Van der Woude interprets correctly: "op gericht kwaad te doen" ("to do evil in judgment").

"With cunning and deceit they will conduct themselves." Cf. the similar statement of 4Q p Nah ii, 2 (¶ 6). "Cunning and deceit" (which puzzles Silberman, "Riddle," pp. 337f.) interprets ושאתו. In the MT this is pointed *ū-śĕᵓêtô;* and one derives the word from the √ *nāśāᵓ* ("lift up"). In the scroll, however, we are apparently to read *ū-šĕᵓêtô* and to derive the word from the √ *nāšāᵓ* ("beguile, deceive"). In the LXX the word is interpreted as "income, tribute." In the Targum it is treated as a synonym of *mišpāṭ,* meaning "decree." Modern translations take the word here to mean "dignity." Cf. Michel, "grandeur;" Bardtke (p. 126), "Hoheit;" Carmignac (Textes, p. 96), "hégémonie," Contextually, the understanding of the Targum seems best. Gaster (p. 250) translated: "Out of itself proceed both its standard of justice and its (lust for) deception" — which interprets correctly.

THE MIDRASH PESHER OF HABAKKUK

¶11 (iii, 6-14)

וְקוֹל מִנְּמֵרִים סוּסָו וְחַדּוּ   6

מֵאָבֵי עֶרֶב   פָּשׁוּ וּפָרֻשׁוּ פָּרָשָׁו מֵרָחוֹק   7

יָעוּפוּ כְּנֶשֶׁר חָשׁ לֶאֱכוֹל כֻּלוֹ לְחָמָס יָבוֹא מְגַמֹּת   8

פְּנֵי הֶם קָדִים   [פִּשְׁרוֹ] עַל הַכִּתִּיאִים אֲשֶׁר   9

יָדוּשׁוּ אֶת הָאָרֶץ בְּסוּסֵ[יהֶם] וּבִבְהֶמְתָּם וּמִמֶּרְחָק   10

יָבוֹאוּ מֵאִיֵּי הַיָּם לֶאֱכוֹ[ל אֶת כָֹ]ל הָעַמִּים כְּנֶשֶׁר   11

וְאֵין שָׂבְעָה וּבְחֵמָה וָכַ[עַס וּבֵחֲרֹ]רֹן אַף וְזַעַף   12

אַפִּים יְדַבְּרוּ עִם[כָֹּו]ל הָעַמִּים כִּ[יא הוּא אֲשֶׁר   13

אָמַר מְ[גַמֹת פָּנָיו הֶם קָדִים]   14

6	(1:8)	Their horses will be swifter than leopards
7		and more agile / than evening wolves.
		Their steeds trample and scatter;
8		from afar / they will swoop as an eagle,
	(1:9a)	hastening to devour / all of it.
		Furiously will they come —
9	(1:9b)	the mutterings of / their face are the east wind.

10   Its prophetic meaning concerns the Kittim, who / will thresh the land with their horses and with their beasts; and from afar /

11 will they come, from (remote) shores of the sea, to dev[our a]ll the

12 peoples as an eagle, / but without being satisfied. With wrath and vex[ation, and with the hot breath of (their) nose and the angry

13 storm / of (their) face they will speak with [all the peoples; fo]r

14 that is what / He said, "The mu[tterings of their face are the east wind."]

68

¶11 *Exposition*

iii, 6-9. The Biblical text is here punctuated and translated in accordance with the interpretation which follows it. For the text-critical value of the variants, see *Text*, §§9-18. Finkel (p. 370) argues that the Qumrân interpreter "introduces word-splitting in the prophetic text and in its interpretation," citing the reading of iii,8 (as interpreted at iii,12f.) and the interpretation of Hab. 2:6 at viii,12f.

iii,6. In the above transcription, it is supposed that *qôl* (vs. 8) is the noun "lightness" (Jer. 3:9) used here attributively.

iii,7. One might read ᶜᵃ*rāv* ("wolves of the *steppe*") rather than ᶜ*erev*, ("wolves of the evening"); but cf. Zeph. 3:3. Wolves come out of hiding in the evening and prowl at night. *Pārāšāw* could be translated either as "their horsemen," or "their steeds"; but the commentary at iii, 10 derived from the verbs *pāšû u-fārĕśû* the notion that "they will thresh" (*yādûšû*). The root *pûš* apparently means, literally, "to spring or lunge," which suits "steeds" (horses) better; and the root *pāraś* means to "spread out." However, both verbs in the *nifᶜal* can mean "to be scattered" (Nah. 3:18; Ezek. 17:21; 34:12). Since "scattering" is part of the action of threshing, it is apparent that actions which are appropriate to threshing should be assigned to these verbs by the commentary.

iii,8. *Kĕ-nešer* could be rendered "as a vulture." But on this, cf. li. 11.

"To devour all of it." Proper scansion supports the Massoretic division of vss. 8-9, which places a period at the end of *le-ᵓekhôl* (as also all treatments of the Scroll text, except *BA*, Sept., 1951, pp. 62, 64 and Silberman, "Riddle," p. 338). However, the commentary at iii,11, "to devour *all* the peoples" indicates that *kullô* was construed with the preceding infinitive.

The word *lĕ-ḥāmās* does not appear to have been interpreted as "for violence," but "heatedly," or "furiously." Cf. iii,12.

iii,8 f. "The mutterings of their face are the east wind." (*mĕgammōt pānāw hēm qādîm*). The first word is here vocalized as a plural in agreement with *hēm*, which appears to be the pronoun used as a copulative verb. Yet it might be a singular noun interpreted as a collective and hence followed by *hēm* as is ᵓ*āmôn* in 1Q p Nahum iii,9 (¶12). The forced separation of *pĕnê* from *hēm* makes possible the reading *pĕnāw hēm*, in view of the ambiguity of *Wāw* and *Yôd* in this manuscript. The reading *qādîm* rather than *qādîmāh* allows for the "east wind" (as rendered by the Targum, Symmachus, Theodotion and the Vulgate). This sirocco is interpreted as angry speech. Cf. Job 8:12; 15:2; Hos. 12:2 (=12:1). The meaning of the M.T. *mĕgammat* is uncertain. The usual translation "with the *set* of their faces straight ahead" is only a guess. For the translation "mutterings," cf. Rabbinic *gimgēm* (*pilpēl* of *GMM*) "to stammer." The same word appears in Rabbinic Aramaic (*gamgēm*). Silberman ("Riddle," pp. 338 f.) interprets *mĕgammat pĕnêhem* after Ibn Ezra as meaning "before their faces, in front of them." He then would translate here, "In their presence [is] a scorching wind." However, Rashi (whom he also cites) interpreted in better accord with 1Q p Hab: "The *exhalation* of their face is like the East Wind, the strongest of winds."

iii,9f. Once more the Biblical text is applied to the Kittim. From the verb "thresh" and the noun "beasts" Ethelbert Stauffer ("Zur Frühdatierung des Habakukmidrasch," *ThLZ*, No. 11, cols. 667-74, and here col. 671) sought to find an allusion to Seleucid elephants which in the Greek version of I Maccabees are referred to as *thēria*, which might well translate the Hebrew *běhēmôt*. This word, however, should probably be vocalized as a collective singular (*běhemtām*), a term which here ambiguously covers both wild beasts (cf. "leopards" and "wolves" of the Biblical text) and domestic animals (livestock), which were used for threshing. If one thinks solely of "threshing," he will translate: "With their horses and (other) *livestock*." Since this is a figure for military exploit, however, he will interpret this to mean, "With their horses and (other) *beasts of burden*." In Hab. 3:12, the punishment of nations by Yahweh employs the verb *dûš*, as Baer (p. 7) observes. Note also that the idea of threshing was applied even to the Fourth Beast (or Kingdom) in Dan. 7:23: "and it will devour all the earth and thresh it and pulverize it." Manfred Lehman (*PEQ*, 1951, p. 36) has suggested that this verb "thresh" (*dûš*) was employed in the scroll by way of suggesting the destruction of kingdoms. He cites Isa. 41:15, where the Targum interprets the "mountains" and "hills" as "peoples" (*ᶜammĕmayyāᵓ*) and "kingdoms" (*malkĕwātāᵓ*). A sufficient analogy for this interpretation, however, is to be seen in Daniel. Though the root *dûš* occurs only in 7:23, a similar action is described in Dan. 7:7, 19; 8:7, 10 — where the Syriac employs in each case the root *dûš*. Cf. also 2:40. For the verbs "trample and scatter" (iii,7), cf. 7:23.

iii,11. "From the (remote) shores of the sea" (*mē-ᵓîyê hayyām*). This interprets the Biblical phrase "from afar." Such "shores" can be either islands or coastlands. The insertion of this phrase by way of identifying the conquering Kittim suits the Romans much better than the Seleucids — even though it may be argued that the coast of Syria would seem remote to ancient Palestinians.

"To devour all the peoples as an eagle." On the relation of this to the Biblical text, cf. above at iii,8. The bird is either an eagle or a vulture. The former feed primarily on live prey; and the latter, on dead prey. As a figure for ferociousness, the former is better. In Ezek. 17, both Babylonia and Egypt are portrayed as eagles. In I Enoch 90:2, the eagle represents the Greeks, or Macedonians; but in 1Q p Hab it is equally apt for the Romans. The ancient interpreter was doubtless aware of the description of Babylon in Deut. 28:49; but again he transferred the reference to the Kittim, for the language of Deut. 28:50 is similar to 1Q p Hab vi,10-12 (¶19). In IV Ezra 11, Rome is portrayed as an eagle flying up from the sea, as H. J. Schoeps has noted in *ZRG*, 1951, p. 325.

iii,12a. "Without being satisfied." A vulture has a more voracious appetite than an eagle; but this description was inspired by the nature of the Kittim.

iii,12*b*-13. Rabinowitz's restoration (*JBL*, 1950, p. 35) [יכ[עסו] ("will they be vexed") is equally satisfactory. The restorations of Dupont-Sommer (*RHR*, 1950, p. 141) [ובר[גז] and Habermann (*ᶜEdah*, p. 45; *Megilloth*, p. 44) [ובק[צף] ("and with rage") misread the second letter, which (though not fully preserved) can only be a *Kaf.* Silberman ("Riddle," p. 339) would restore [יכ[נסו] ("they gather together").

"With wrath and vex[ation and with the h]ot breath." The restoration followed here is that of S. M. Stern (*JBL*, 1950, p. 26) and was accepted by Burrows and Molin. Stylistically, this gives us two pairs of nouns for wrath, the first of each pair being introduced by the preposition *Bêt.* This series of words denoting anger was suggested by *lĕ-ḥāmās.* The root idea of this word, according to *BDB* is that of violence, but according to Jastrow (*Dictionary*, p. 478b) it means "to be heated, passionate." The latter suits well the interpretation of 1Q p Hab. Elliger restored *yakniᶜûm* (they will subdue them) rather than *wĕ-kha*[ᶜ*as.* This could conceivably interpret *lĕ-ḥāmās* as "for violence." However, one would expect much more to be made of the idea than mere subjection.

iii,12f. "With the hot breath of his nose (ᵓ*af*) and the fierce storm of their face (ᵓ*appayyim*)." For "nose" and "face" one may translate also "anger," but see Prov. 30:33. These are figurative terms, however; and the latter is used in Aramaic for "face." Both the Hebrew meaning "anger" and the Aramaic sense "face" are in the author's mind as is shown by the repetition of 1:9*a*: "For that is what it says, 'The mutterings of their *face* is the east wind." The meaning "face" for אפים is rarely attested even in Old Testament Hebrew, Gen. 48:12; II Sam. 14:4. The meaning "storm" for זעף has been suggested on the basis of Aramaic usage by Silberman. The connotations of both "storm" and "anger" are present — hence "angry storm" as an interpretation of the East Wind.

iii,13. Rabinowitz restores כול בני קדם ("all the orientals") rather than כול העמים ("all the peoples"). Though his restoration is longer, it is possible. This phrase for "orientals" is found in Isa. 11:14 and Jer. 49:28. However, *qādîm* as east wind is sufficiently accounted for in the commentary by the reference to angry speech. "All the peoples" is found in iii,11 and was restored here also by Dupont-Sommer and E. L. Sukenik (*Megillot Genuzot*, II, p. 89). For speech compared with "wind" (*rûaḥ*), cf. Job 6:26; 8:2. The east wind in the climate of Palestine is a hot, desert wind, blowing in from North Arabia. It was feared as damaging to crops. Cf. Gen. 41:6,23, 27; Ezek. 19:12. In the last passage (as also in Ezek. 27:26), the term is used allegorically for Chaldaea.

THE MIDRASH PESHER OF HABAKKUK

¶12 (iii, 14-17)

[וַיֶּאֱסוֹף כַּחוֹ]ל שֶׁבִי   14

[[פִּשְׁרוֹ עַל הַכִּתִּיאִים   15

                                                                    16

                                                                    17

14 (1:9c) [And they will gather] captives [like san]d. /
15   [Its prophetic meaning concerns the Kittim] . . ./
16-17   . . . . / . . . .

¶12 *Exposition*

This pericope has all but perished. All we have are the last vestiges of the Biblical quotation and slight traces of the upper tips of the third and fourth letters of the word *pišrô*. The context of the scroll suggests that this passage was applied to the Kittim. Nearly three lines of text are lost here. The gathering of captives "like sand" refers not only to their vast numbers, but it also may carry forward the figure of the east wind with its gathering sand storm.

THE MIDRASH PESHER OF HABAKKUK

¶13 (iii, 17-iv, 2)

[וְהוּא בַּמְּלָכִים] 17
iv,1 יְקַלֵּס וְרֹזְנִים מִשְׂחָק לוֹ פִּשְׁרוֹ אֲשֶׁר
2 יַלְעִיגוּ עַל רַבִּים וּבָזוּ עַל נִכְבָּדִים בִּמְלָכִים
3 וְשָׂרִים יִתְעַתְּעוּ וְקִלְּסוּ בְּעַם רָב.

iii,17-iv,1 (1:10a) [And they at kings] / will scoff;
and rulers are laughable to them.
2   Its prophetic meaning is that / they will deride the great and will
3   scorn the esteemed. At kings / and commanders they will mock and will
scoff at great armies.

¶13 *Exposition*

iv,1. Note the textual variant in the first word, where the MT reads יתקקלם. This is doubtless the *pi⁽ᶜ⁾ēl*, as also appears at iv,3. See *Text*, §19. Apart from this word, the commentary employs synonyms for the verbs of the Biblical citation.

iv,2. As Stanislav Segert observes (§612) one could read here either the *qal* ילעוגו or the *hif⁽ᶜ⁾îl* ילעיגו. In Job 9:23 the pausal vocalization (preserving old pronunciation), however, is יִלְעָג. The "kings" seem to be interpreted as *rabbîm*, here "great," not "many"; yet below they are interpreted literally. Quite unsuitable to the context is the rendering "rabbins" of del Medico (*Riddle*, p. 111), with reference to the title of exegetes in use since the founding of the schools of Hillel and Shammai (p. 122).

iv,3. The mocking of "kings" points to a world conqueror who subdues the kings of the Near East. *Wĕśārîm* ("and commanders") interprets *wĕrōzĕnîm* ("and rulers") of iv,1. The term *śar* is used of many different high government posts; but was particularly used of generals.

"At great armies" or "at great peoples." The singular "army" (or "people") is probably a generic usage. The plural ⁽ᶜ⁾*ammîm rabbîm* ("many peoples") would convey the wrong meaning. For ⁽ᶜ⁾*am* as "army," see I Sam. 4:17; 15:15, 21, 24; 17:27; 18:13; 26:7, 14; 30:21; II Sam. 1:4; 10:10; 11:7; 12:28; 15:24; 17:8f.; 19:3; I Kings 20:10. Note especially I Sam. 18:13: "So Saul removed him from his presence, and made him a commander (*śar*) of a thousand; and he went out and came in before the army (*hā-*⁽ᶜ⁾*ām*)." For ⁽ᶜ⁾*am rav* = "great army," see Deut. 20:1; Isa. 13:4; Ezek. 17:15; 26:7; also 1Q p Hab iv,7 (¶14). A more general usage is found in Gen. 50:20; Josh. 17:15, 17; II Sam. 13:34; II Chron. 30:13; 32:4. The census of the "people" in II Sam. 24 was military, and as in the Book of Numbers was probably of "every male from twenty years old and upward, all who were able to go forth to war" (Num. 1:20, 22, *passim*). On ⁽ᶜ⁾*am* see also Martin Noth, "Die Heiligen des Höchsten," *NTT*, Vol. 56 (1955), pp. 146-161. See also Brekelmans in *Oudtestamentische Studiën*, XIV, pp. 305-329. Note the comment on 1Q p Hab iv,3 by Delcor (p. 30).

Thus Dupont-Sommer at first translated "armée nombreuse" (*RHR*, pp. 133, 141); and yet the English translation (*Essene Writings*, p. 260) reads "a multitude (of people)," so Burrows (p. 366). My first understanding "at a numerous people" (*BASOR*, 112, p. 11) is that of most interpreters; but Delcor (pp. 23, 30) followed the correct rendering of Dupont-Sommer's French version, as also did Barthélemy (*RB*, 1952, p. 209), Lambert (p. 292), Bardtke (p. 128), and Vermés (*DSSE*, p. 237). We now have confirmation in the so-called Temple Scroll, of which Y. Yadin has published a portion concerning the statutes of the kings in *New Directions in Biblical Archaeology*, Fig. 56, facing p. 121. There the army is repeatedly called ⁽ᶜ⁾*am*; and ⁽ᶜ⁾*am rav* occurs twice, on lis. 4f. (Temple Scroll lviii, 6f.).

Silberman's observation on iv,2f. is noteworthy ("Riddle," p. 340):

> The comment on these words is unusual in that it is a perfect bi-cola with chiastic
> parallelism and could be a quotation from some as yet unknown source.
> 'They scoff at multitudes
>   and despise honored men.
> With kings and princes they trifle
>   and deride a mighty people.'

This was the passage to which Millar Burrows referred (p. 13) in his diary
entry of Feb. 28, 1948, in recording the discovery of "a text of Habakkuk with
midrashic material in verse."

THE MIDRASH PESHER OF HABAKKUK

¶14 (iv, 3-9)

וְהוּא 3

לְכָול־מִבְצָר יִשְׂחָק נ צְבּוֹר עָפָר וַיִּלְכְּדֵהוּ 4

פִּשְׁרוֹ עַל מוֹשְׁלֵי הַכִּתִּיאִים אֲשֶׁר יִבְזוּ עַל 5

מִבְצָרֵי הָעַמִּים וּבְלַעַג יִשְׂחוֹקוּ עֲלֵיהֶם 6

וּבְעַם רַב יַקִּיפוּם לְתָפוֹשָׂם וּבְאֵמָה וָפַחַד 7

יִנָּתְנוּ בְיָדָם וַהֲרָסוּם בַּעֲווֹן הַיּוֹשְׁבִים 8

בָּהֶם 9

3-4 (1:10b) And they will laugh at each fortress
   and will heap up earth and take it. /

5   Its prophetic meaning concerns the generals of the Kittim who
6   will scorn / the fortresses of the peoples and with derision will
7   laugh at them. / With a great army they will surround them to
8   take them; and with dread and terror / they will be given into
     their hand; and they will tear them down, because of the guilt of
9   those dwelling / in them.

¶14 *Exposition*

iv, 3f. On the textual variants, see *Text*, §§20-23.

iv,4. The original scribe doubtless intended יבצור; but the effect of the placement of the supralinear *Yôd* is to lead to the reinterpretation of the initial *Yôd* as a *Wāw*.

iv,5. "The generals of the Kittim." The term *mōšĕlî(m)*, etymologically "those ruling," means according to Dupont-Sommer (*RHR*, p. 156) and van der Ploeg (*Bi Or*, viii, p. 6) "les commandants." Delcor (p. 30) explains: "*Mošelim* désigne ici les tyrans comme en Isaïe XLIV, 7." Dupont-Sommer states (*Essene Writings*, p. 260, n. 2):

> This expression . . . designates the Roman chiefs, the pro-magistrates *cum imperio* whom Rome sent into the provinces and who commanded the armies.

Carmignac (*Textes*, p. 99, n. 2) states:

> The term . . . would be rather curious, if the author made allusion to the Seleucids, whose army was generally commanded by the king in person (except when he was fighting on another front with another army); but it applies perfectly to Roman generals.

The previous pericope (iv,2f.) has already stated that the Kittim "will laugh at *kings* and commanders." They would seem therefore to be a world conquering power, subjecting territories which possess their own kings and commanders. Among such territories are Syria, Judah, and Egypt.

iv,6. The verb ישחוקו is a characteristically uncontracted form still current at Qumrân (*yišḥôqû* for *yišḥĕqû*). Such forms survive in the Massoretic text only in pausal position. Yet the pausal form of the MT (as noted by Segert [§§ 608-609]) is יִשְׂחָקוּ (Ps. 52:8). Curiously, a corrector has found fault with the long *o* vowel and has placed a dot above and below the *Wāw*. As Enoch Yalon argues (in a review of Burrows, *The Dead Sea Scrolls of St. Marks' Monastery*, Vol. I, in *Kiryat Sefer*, XXVII, 1951, p. 173*a*), it is not likely that a corrector would object to the uncontracted form here; he rather preferred to read the *piʿēl* for the *qal*. In Rabbinic Hebrew, according to him, there is a preference for the *piʿēl*.

iv,7. "They will surround them." Delcor (p. 23) read this as "They will strike them" (*ils les frappent*) deriving the word from √ נקף I rather than II. The reference to fortresses, however, favors the meaning "surround" (cf. Barthélemy, *RB*, 1952, p. 209, n. 1) — as Delcor himself also now believes. The language says nothing distinctive of siege tactics. R. P. Gordon (*RQ* 31, pp. 426f.) interprets ʿ*am* as an allegorical interpretation of ʿ*āfār*, citing Rashi, Kimchi, and one Targum manuscript. See ¶13 on ʿ*ām* = "army."

As Yalon observes, "It is possible that 'לתפושם' is an error and should be corrected to 'לתופשם'." However, he calls attention to an analogous reading in Ps. 38:21, where the Massoretes vocalize *rodfî*, but the *kĕtiv* seems to indicate *rĕdôfî*. Usually, the Scrolls support the Massoretic vocalizations of the infinitive. Yet one might read, as Segert (§619 suggests, a noun *tippûś* ("for their capture.").

Cf. iii,4: "whose terror and dread are upon all the peoples." Fear is itself an omen of defeat (Ex. 15:14-16) and a source of infection for others in the holy wars of the Old Testament. Consequently, the fearful were excluded from participation in battle (Deut. 20:8; Jud. 7:3).

iv,8. "Because of the guilt." Originally (*BASOR*, 112, pp. 11, 17) this was read בעיין rather than בעוון, recalling *ʿiyyîn* ("ruins") of Mic. 3:12, but cited as *ʿiyyîm* in Jer. 26:18. J. van der Ploeg, Michel (pp. 10, 20), Edelkoort (p. 55) and Elliger followed me in this. Most critics have read *ba-ʿªwôn*, following Dupont-Somner (*RHR*, pp. 133, 140-41) and Ratzaby (*JQR*, XLI, 1950, p. 157). Others who adopt this reading are Delcor (p. 23), Burrows (p. 366), Bardtke (p. 151), Gaster (p. 250), van der Ploeg, van't Land, Lambert (p. 292), van der Woude (*Bijbelcommentaren*, p. 32), Vermès (*DSSE*, p. 237), Baer (p. 8). P. R. Weis (*JQR*, XLI, 1950, pp. 133f.) read the word as בעין ("in the presence of"); but this is spelled with only one *Yôd* and pronounced *bĕ-ʿên*, in view of the construct. For the use of this idiom, he cited the Arabic. All three possibilities were recognized by G. Molin (*ZKTh*, 1952, p. 58); but in his translation (*Die Söhne des Lichtes*, p. 12), he rendered: "von den Augen ihrer Bewohner," as similarly, Sutcliffe, *Monks*, p. 74. The preposition *Bêt* is frequently used in the sense "because" in Qumrân literature.

THE MIDRASH PESHER OF HABAKKUK

¶15 (iv, 9-16)

אָז חָלַף רוּחַ וַיַּעֲבֹר וַיָּשֵׁם זֶה כֹחוֹ 9

לֵאלֹהוֹ   פִּשְׁר[וֹ עַ]ל מוֹשְׁלֵי הַכִּתִּיאִים 10

אֲשֶׁר בַּעֲצַת בֵּית אַשְׁמָ[תָם] יַעֲבוֹרוּ אִישׁ 11

מִלִּפְנֵי רֵעֵהוּ מוֹשְׁלֵי[הֶם זֶ]ה אַחַר זֶה יָבוֹאוּ 12

לַשְׁחִית אֶת הָאָ[רֶץ וַיָּשֶׂם זֶ]ה כוֹחוֹ לֵאלֹהוֹ 13

פִּשְׁרוֹ [אֲשֶׁר יָאשִׁימוּ . . . לְאֵ[ל] הָעַמִּים 14

לְ[עָבְדוֹ וּלְהִשְׁתַּחֲווֹת לוֹ . . . .]לְ[15

. 16

9 (1:11a) Then, in accordance with the will, they transgressed,
and passed on and were guilty,
(and each one laid waste);

10 (11b) And this one (appointed) his strength / to be their god.
[Its] prophetic meaning [con]cerns the governors of the Kittim, /

11 who through the counsel of [their] house of guil[t] will pass on, each /

12 from before his fellow. Their governors will come, each one after the

13 other, / to devastate the [land. "And thi]s one [appointed] his strength

14 to be their god." / [[Its prophetic meaning is that they will appoint . . .

15 to be the go]]d of the peoples / to [[worship it and to prostrate

16 themselves to it]]. . . . / . . .

¶15 *Exposition*

iv,9f. For the variants, see *Text*, §§24-27. The Biblical verse apart from the commentary would be translated as follows:

> Then they sweep on like the wind
> and pass through and lay waste —
> they whose strength is their god!

iv,9. "In accordance with the will." The noun *rûaḥ* is interpreted adverbially. Cf. the RSV: "They will sweep by *like the wind.*" The feminine gender of the noun excludes it from being the subject of the verb as in the King James Version: "Then shall his *mind* change." The interpretation given here is in accordance with iv,11 "Who through the counsel of [their] house of guil[t]." The *rûaḥ* is the group will expressed in a decision of the conciliar body, as in Dupont-Sommer's English translation of עצה as "decision" (*Essene Writings*, p. 261), rather than French "parti" (*RHR*, p. 133). For this usage of *rûaḥ*, cf. Isa. 40:13 in the text of 1Q Isa*ᵃ* before its correction:

> Who ever fathomed the mind (*rûaḥ*) of the LORD?
> or, as for His counsel (*ᶜᵃṣātô*), has made it known.

On this verse, see *Meaning*, pp. 220f.

"They transgressed" translates *ḥālaf*. One might interpret the verb as simply a synonym of *way-yaᶜᵃvōr*: "swept by," "rushed onward," or the like. However, the interpretation "transgressed" suits the commentary at iv,11 that the counsel by which they acted was that of the "house of guilt." Cf. further at iv,11.

"Were guilty, (and each one laid waste); And this one (appointed) . . ." This is a conflated translation which takes the text three different ways, instead of choosing one as the sole rendering. First of all this translation reads *wĕ-yāšēm* = *wĕ-ʾāšēm* of the MT. With the same meaning it might be vocalized as an imperfect, with an elided ʾ *Ālef* (Habermann, *Megilloth*, p. 44, reads *way-yešem*). Second, it reads *way-yaššēm zèh* (The *Wāw*-cons. *hifᶜîl* imp. of *ŠMM*, plus subject), the view of Gaster (p. 251 and n. 11 on pp. 265f.). Third, it reads (in line with li. 13) *way-yāśem zèh* (the *Wāw*-cons. *qal* imp. of *śîm*, plus subject), the preference of nearly all since 1948. Thus in my conflated translation the verb is used three ways and the demonstrative pronoun is used twice. The translation places within parentheses all but one use of each word, thereby indicating the extent of the conflation. On the reasons for this conflated translation, see the following commentary.

iv,10ff. The *mōšĕlîm* of the Kittim appear to be governors and proconsuls who were appointed annually by the "house of guilt" (which is probably the Roman senate, as is ably argued by Mrs. K. M. T. Atkinson, *JSS*, IV, 1959, p. 243.). J. G. Harris (p. 38) paraphrases, "Their Council House is full of guilt." For the expression "house of guilt" there is the idea of transgression which could have been derived from *ḥālaf* and *way-yaᶜᵃvōr*, but it stands even more directly connected with the reading *wĕ-yāšēm* in the text of Habakkuk. It may be that √ *YŠM* = √ *ƆŠM*. See *Text*, §24. This meaning could be derived from verbal play and not from knowledge of the Massoretic reading.

iv,11f. "Will pass on, each from before his fellow." Instead of the *qal* imperfect, the verb might be vocalized (as by Habermann) a *hifᶜîl (yaᶜᵃvîrû)*, a reading followed by Gaster (p. 251). The full vowel for the *qal* imperfect is characteristic of Qumrân orthography. In either case, the sense is much the same, the reference being to an interchange of governors, as one succeeds another. The idea may have been inferred in part from the verb *ḥālaf*, which can mean "to change" — but not intransitively (and there is no expressed object for this verb in the Biblical verse.) This verb may, nevertheless, have influenced the meaning attached to the √ ᶜ*BR*, which is used of one man passing from his post to make room for his successor. In Rabbinic Hebrew, the *nifᶜal* of *ḥālaf* is employed for succession in office. The same root in Arabic gave rise to the designation *khalifa*, caliph, "successor." "Each" (Ɔ*îš*) interprets *zeh* of Hab. 1:11. Likewise, "each one after the other" (*zeh Ɔaḥēr zeh*) also interprets *zeh*, which is given a reciprocal meaning, as also in the preceding phrase, "each from before his fellow."

iv,12. Dupont-Sommer's initial restoration was מושלי[ם וז]ה (*RHR*, pp. 133, 143). Despite the conjunction, his translation indicates the beginning of a new sentence with *môšĕlîm*; and apparently Michel (p. 10) and Molin (p. 12) followed him here. The restoration adopted in the present study (that of Lambert, p. 292) has been followed by Burrows (p. 366), Bardtke (p. 126), Dupont-Sommer (*Essene Writings*), Lohse, Maier, I (p. 151), Carmignac (*Textes*, p. 100), Vermès (*DSSE*, p. 237), Driver (*Judean Scrolls*, p. 127), and Baer (p. 9).

iv,13. "To devastate *the [and]*" was completed originally (*BASOR*, 112, pp. 11, 16) by העמים, "the peoples" — a restoration followed by Dupont-Sommer (*RHR*, pp. 133, 143), but who later adopted the reading given here (*Essene Writings*, p. 261). Others who followed the first restoration are Michel, Lambert, Edelkoort (p. 55). The second letter, upon close inspection, is certainly an Ɔ*Ālef* and not an ᶜ*Ayin*. Hence, the restoration הארץ is sure. This is the reading of Dupont-Sommer; Molin; Habermann; Burrows; Elliger; del Medico, *Riddle*, p. 248; van der Woude, *Bijbelcommentaren*, p. 32; Driver; Vermès; Maier; Baer.

"To devastate the land" interprets וישם as *way-yaššēm* — the *hifᶜîl* inf. of *šāḥat* (*lašḥît* contracting *lĕ-hašḥît*) being employed as synonymous in meaning with the *hifᶜîl* of *šāmēm*. Thus a second reading of the Biblical text was *way-yaššēm zeh* ("and each one laid waste"). With this S. Talmon agrees in *Textus*, IV, 1964, pp. 130f.

"And *this one* appointed his strength to be *their* god." The Hebrew could be more properly translated: "And these appointed their strength to be their own god." The singular (as constantly in Habakkuk) is a collective reference to the Chaldean nation. The commentary, however, doubtless continues the reference to the Kittim, who have in some way appointed "their strength" to become the god of other "peoples" whose mention is preserved at iv,14. One is certainly to restore after Elliger, van der Woude, and Maier the verb *way-yāśem* in the lacuna of this line, there not being room for the introductory phrase *kîʾ hûʾ ʾašer ʾāmar* ("for that is what He said"), which frequently precedes second quotations. The insertion of *way-yāśem* gives thereby a third interpretation of this verb through a different punctuation from that implied in the preceding interpretation.

iv,14. The restoration with *ʾašer* (cf. iv,1) is required by necessity of the relative brevity of this lacuna. For the end of the line, one thinks instinctively of the combination *kôl hā-ᶜammîm* as I originally read (followed by others, such as Dupont-Sommer and Michel); but space will not permit the insertion of *kôl* after *ʾēl*, which the Biblical verse suggests may fall here.

This partial restoration is sheer speculation, and it is impossible to know what object the Kittim appointed as their god; only, one would suppose that it was an interpretation of *kôhô*, and not a wooden repetition such as *kôhām* ("their strength"). Space-wise, no briefer restorations seem likely than מלכם ("their king") or רומם ("their haughtiness"). The former restoration would imply emperor worship, as of Antiochus Epiphanes or of the later Roman emperors. General chronological considerations would probably exclude this term from any probability. The latter term, *rûmām*, would make an apt sarcastic reference to *Roma*, a name of both the city and its patron goddess. Mrs. Atkinson (pp. 259f.) discusses an altar at Dura-Europos, of the early 3rd century A.D., which portrays the worship of Roman signs and bears in poor Greek the inscription by Bar Hadad: Σημιη μν[ήσθη] ʿΡουμας [Β]αραδαδης. She suggests:

> that we have here the names of two deities called respectively *Semeia* (or possibly a masculine *Semeios*) and *Rouma* (Roma!) . . . The deities are surely the standards (σημεῖα) and the goddess Rome.

Since the cult of the standards figures below in ¶18, there is a bare possibility that the goddess *Rouma* was referred to here as *rûmām* ("their haughtiness").

iv,15. "To [worship it and to prostrate themselves to it]" restores after xii,13f.: "to worship them (the idols) and to prostrate themselves to them." Not knowing the gender of the missing noun, one does not know whether to supply masculine or feminine pronominal suffixes; but any treatment of the missing text at all is simply educated guessing. The suggestions given here are of no historical value. Even these tenuous proposals do not fill the large lacuna, which contained about one more line of the text before the next Biblical quotation begins.

THE MIDRASH PESHER OF HABAKKUK

¶16 (iv, 16-v,8)

16 [הֲלוֹא אַתָּה מִקֶּדֶם]

17 [וְהוָה אֱלוֹהַי קְדֹשִׁי לוֹא נָמוּת וְהוָה]

v,1 לְמִשְׁפָּט שַׂמְתּוֹ וְצוּר לְמוֹכִיחוֹ יְסַדְתּוֹ טָהוֹר עֵנַיִם

2 מֵרְאוֹת בְּרָע וְהַבֵּט אֶל עָמָל לוֹא תוּכַל

3 פֵּשֶׁר הַדָּבָר אֲשֶׁר לוֹא יְכַלֶּה אֵל אֶת עַמּוֹ בְּיַד הַגּוֹיִם

4 וּבְיַד בְּחִירוֹ יִתֵּן אֵל אֶת מִשְׁפַּט כּוֹל־הַגּוֹיִם וּבְתוֹכַחְתָּם

5 יֶאְשְׁמוּ כָּל־רִשְׁעֵי עַמּוֹ אֲשֶׁר שָׁמְרוּ אֶת מִצְווֹתָו

6 בַּצַּר לָמוֹ כִּיא הוּא אֲשֶׁר אָמַר טָהוֹר עֵינַיִם מֵרְאוֹת

7 בְּרָע   פֵּשְׁרוֹ אֲשֶׁר לוֹא זָנוּ אַחַר עֵינֵיהֶם בְּקֵץ

8 הָרִשְׁעָה

iv,16-17
(1:12)   [Art Thou not from of old, / O LORD?
           My God, my Holy One, we shall not die!

v,1   O LORD], / for judging has Thou appointed him;
           and to suffer has Thou established him, as their chastiser –

2 (1:13a) him who is too pure of eyes / to look upon evil;
           for to countenance oppression Thou art unable. /

3   The prophetic meaning of the passage is that God will not destroy
4   His people by means of the nations; / but into the power of His elect
           God will give the judgment of all nations. It is through *their*
5   chastisement / that all the wicked of His people will undergo
6   punishment, since *they* (God's elect) have kept His commandments /
           in their time of suffering; for that is what he said: "too pure of eyes to
7   look / upon evil." Its prophetic meaning is that they have not
8   followed the lust of their eyes in the time of / wickedness.

¶16 *Exposition*

iv,16f. This distribution of the Biblical citation is that of Elliger, except for his numbering of the lines as 17 and 18. The Tetragrammaton, which appears twice in the last line, would require more space than four average letters, since it was written in paleo-Hebrew. For the textual variants, see *Text,* §§28-32.

iv,17. "We shall not die." Rabbinic tradition concerning the "emendations of the scribes" *(tiqqûnê haṣṣôp̄ĕrîm)* declares that the original reading was "Thou shalt not die." This would provide a fitting antithesis to "Art Thou not from of old, O LORD?" Despite this, the Habakkuk Midrash (as also the Septuagint before it) must have read "We shall not die," for this is implied by v,3.

v,1f. If one ignores the construction placed upon the text by the commentary, he may translate:

[O LORD], as a judgment hast Thou appointed them;

O Rock, as their chastiser hast Thou ordained them–

(Thou) too pure of eyes to look upon evil

and (Who) art unable to countenance oppression.

For a discussion of this, see *Text,* §§28-32, also further discussion below.

v,3. "God will not destroy His people" interprets "We shall not die" (Hab. 1:12*b*) and "to countenance oppression Thou art unable" (1:13*b*). It seems probable (as Silberman, "Riddle," pp. 341f. suggests) that לוא תוכל ("Thou art unable") was punned by the interpreter as לוא יכלה אל ("God will not destroy"). He suggests translating Hab. 1:13 as follows: "Him who was too pure of eyes to gaze upon evil and to look upon perverseness Thou wilt not destroy." The first phrase of the verse was indeed transferred to God's people in the commentary (v,6f.); but the phrase והבט אל עמל is not quoted there, and so presumably it could still apply to God as in the translation presented here. Silberman goes beyond the assertion of a pun to that of proposing an actual reading. Until one can find some evidence for legitimate confusion of the roots יכל and כלה, it seems preferable not to alter the Biblical translation to the extent of Silberman.

Curiously the pronominal suffix of ʿammô was originally omitted and was later inserted above the line. H. E. del Medico (*Deux Manuscrits,* p. 112) makes the interesting speculation: "It seems that in the mind of the scribe (or the author) those whom God had decided to destroy had ceased to be 'His' people. Had the corrector wished to weaken this expression?"

v,4. "But into the power of His elect God will give the judgment of all the nations." This is antithetical to the preceding clause and the two might be rather rendered: "God will not destroy His people *by means of* the nations; but *by means of* His elect God will give the judgment of all the nations." In support of this, one might cite x,3, "whose judgment God *will give* in the midst of many peoples." However, the idiom נתן ביד normally means "to give into the power of." God is not here giving judgment, but delegating judgment.

"His elect" is ambiguous in English, where it is either singular or plural. In *BASOR*, 112, p. 17, n. 34, I wrote: "The word 'His elect' (בחורו) may be singular, but it is probably the plural imperfectly written. The plural construct (בחירי אל) occurs in 10:13." Since then a battle has raged over this word. Initially, Dupont-Sommer (*RHR*, p. 134) read this as a singular and applied the reference to the Righteous Teacher. Y. M. Grintz ("אנשי'היחד'-איסיים-בית(א)סין," *Sinai*,) XVI, 32, p. 28) and del Medico (pp. 112, 123) interpreted the singular as referring to the future Messiah. Yalon (*KS*, XXVII, p. 175*b*), K. Schubert (*ZKTh*, 1952, pp. 1-62, with attention here to p. 21), F.A.W. van't Land and A.S. van der Woude (*ad. loc.*) have argued for a defective spelling here. K. G. Kuhn (*ZThK*, XLVII, 1950, pp. 192-211, with attention here to p. 198), M. Delcor (*RSR*, Tome 94, 1952, p. 365) and J. Carmignac (*Textes*, p. 101, n. 3) have recognized the possibility of either reading. Finally, Dupont-Sommer (*Essene Writings*, p. 261) came to apply the word to the sect itself. Yalon listed the following examples of the scribe's writing simply *W* for the plural *YW* (*âw*): סוסו (iii,6), פרשו (iii,7), מצוותו (v,5), עלו (viii,7), אלו (viii, 5, twice); but of these examples, all but v,5 are in citations of the Biblical text, not in the commentary itself—as was pointed out in *Text* (p. 105). That the last syllable of *miṣwôtāw* should be spelled defectively is not surprising, since the full spelling of the preceding syllable already marks the word as a plural. Twice where the Biblical word is written *defectiva* in the citation, the same word is written *plene* in the commentary. Thus one finds ויעבר at iv,9, but יעבורו at iv,11, and עלו at viii,7, but עליו at viii,12. Since בחירו occurs in the commentary rather than in the Biblical citation, the balance of probability favors reading the singular *bĕḥîrô*.

The singular noun *bĕḥîrô*, however, should be interpreted as a collective, "His chosen [people]." As Carmignac (*Textes*) observes, it appears as a synonym of *ʿammô* of the preceding line. In favor of the collective meaning is also the literary allusion to Isa. 42:1, which in 1Q Isa*ᵃ* reads:

Behold, My envoy whom I uphold,
Mine elect (*bĕḥîrô*) whom My soul accepts;
I have put my spirit upon him,
and *his* judgement (*mišpāṭô*) he brings to the nations.

Here one is confronted with a whole series of singulars; yet this same passage is interpreted as referring to Israel by the Septuagint, and as referring to the Qumrân Community (and/or its leaders) in 1QS viii,5-10 (in the revised translation of *BASOR*, 135 [Oct., 1954], pp. 34 f.):

5   When these things come to pass in Israel,/the Council of the Community
    will have been established in truth:
    As an eternal planting, a holy house of Israel,
6   A/most *holy institution* of Aaron,
    True witnesses with regard to religion (*mišpāṭ*),
    And the chosen of divine acceptance to atone for the land,
7   And to render/to the wicked their desert.

That is the tried wall, the costly corner bulwark,/
8   Whose foundations shall not be shaken asunder,
        Nor be dislodged from their place!
9   A most holy abode/belongs to Aaron in the knowledge of them all that
        they may be a covenant of religion (*mišpāṭ*) and offer up an agreeable
10a   odor; and a house of perfection and truth is in Israel / to establish a
9½   covenant with eternal ordinances. /These will be acceptable to make
        atonement for the earth and to decree the condemnation (*mišpāṭ*) of
        wickedness that there may be no more perversity.

In 1QS viii, 6, one finds the phrase *ū-věḥîrê râṣôn* ("and the chosen of divine
acceptance") which echoes *běḥîrî rāṣětāh nafšî* ("My chosen whom my soul
accepts") of Isa. 42:1. This chosen community is to make atonement as the
Servant does in Isa. 53; but there is no clearly universal aspect to it, unless it
appear in the word *hā-ʾāreṣ*, which despite the allusion to Isa. 42:1, is best
interpreted in 1QS viii as "the land," not "the earth." The role of judgment
(*mišpaṭ*) of this community is first of all instructional ("witnesses of truth with
regard to religion [*mišpāṭ*]," li, 6; "a covenant of religion [*mišpāṭ*]," li. 9; "a
covenant with eternal ordinances," li. 10); but it is punitive ("to render to
the wicked their desert," "to decree the condemnation [*mišpāṭ*] of
wickedness," 1QS viii, 7 and 9). In contrast to this passage of the Society
Manual, 1Q p Hab v,3 ff. has a solely punitive concept of *mišpāṭ*; and the
nations, not simply the wicked of Israel, are the object of this punishment. Still
this passage gives an independent interpretation of the Servant (or envoy) of
Isa. 42:1 as a chosen community exercising *mišpāṭ,* and this reinforces the
plural reference in "His elect" of 1Q p Hab v,4. That the "judgment of all the
nations" will be given "into the power" of God's elect accords well with the
reading *mišpāṭô* ("his judgment") in Isa. 42:1, 1Q Isaᵃ, for it is *theirs* (the
servant's) to administer. The Targum, in contrast, renders "My judgment,"
interpreting this as God's judgment. The two readings are not in
contradiction, however, for 1Q p Hab interprets this judgment as in any case
the gift of God.

        v,4. "Through their chastisement" (*û-vě-tôkhaḥtām*) is grammatically
ambiguous–meaning either "*in connection with* the chastisement of the
nations," or "*through* the chastisement inflicted by God's elect," according to
the antecedent of the pronominal suffix, which in turn determines whether
there is an accusative or subjunctive genitive. The latter alternative is
doubtless correct; for this interpretation accords with the reading *lě-môkhîḥô*
of v,1 ("as their chastiser hast Thou established him.") The first clause "as a
judgment [for judging] hast Thou appointed him" was interpreted as the role
of the elect with regard to the nations; but the second is explained as denoting
their role toward the wicked of Israel. J. Carmignac (*Textes,* p. 101, n. 3), who
argues that the word "chastisement" always has an educative purpose also
argues that the objects of this chastisement must be Jews, not Gentiles, and

that the pronominal suffix must therefore refer to God's elect who administer it. Van't Land and van der Woude (*ad loc.*) stress the fact that the plurality of the suffix indicates also the plurality of "His elect."

v,5. "All the wicked of His people will undergo punishment." This certainly refers to all Jews who stand opposed to the sect, who belong to the "sons of darkness." Whether it also refers to all those outside the sect, whether actively opposed or not, is open to question; but the sect seems to draw sharp lines which make impossible a position of neutrality. The verb *ye'šĕmû* ("shall be punished for their guilt") reminds one of the fact that the Servant of the Lord in Isa. 53:10 is to be made a "guilt offering" ('āšām) vicariously on behalf of others; but here the wicked suffer for their own guilt.

"Since they have kept His commandments in their time of suffering." The subject of the verb must be "His elect," not "the wicked of His people"— although tentatively one might consider the interpretation: "who kept His commandments *only when* they were under duress." See J. G. Harris, p. 38. What militates against this interpretation is the following clause: "For that is what *he said:* 'Too pure of eyes etc.' " Dupont-Sommer, followed by Delcor (*Midrash,* p. 24) and Reicke (*Handskrifterna,* p. 32) at first took 'ašer as the beginning of the sentence (p. 134): "Those who have kept His commandments will be as a rock for them." Aside from the improbability of a sentence starting with 'ašer, there is the difficulty of the reading בצר, which Dupont-Sommer read initially as *bĕ-ṣūr* ("in the role of a rock" = "as a rock") in agreement with the reading of *ṣūr* as "rock" in Hab. 1:12*b*—with the designation, however, transferred from Yahweh to the sect. For this interpretation one would expect the *plene* spelling בצור. For this reason, in his later translation (*Essene Writings,* p. 261), Dupont-Sommer translates "in their distress"; but inconsistently he retains the divine title "Rock" in the Habakkuk Text, as do nearly all translators. The idiom *bēṣ-ṣar lē* is frequently attested in the Old Testament (Deut. 4:30; II Sam. 22:7; Isa. 25:4; Hos. 5:15; Pss. 18:7; 66:14; 106:44; 107:6, 13, 19, 28; II Chron. 15:4). In most of these passages men turn to the Lord for succor in their time of affliction. The first reference is most suggestive for the present context: "*When you are in tribulation,* and all these things come upon you *in the latter days,* you will return to the LORD your God and obey His voice" (*RSV*). However, under the duress of persecution, distress may deter from adherence to the Law; and this meaning is more suitable to the present context.

The interpretative relationship of בצר למו כיא הוא to וצור למוכיחו is intriguing. I have previously suggested (*BA,* Sept., 1951, p. 66) a verbal play which broke up למוכיחו and punned this in the form of למו כיא הוא. Silberman also has noted the pun. The poetic form of the pronominal suffix appears with the very words בצר למו in 4Q 178, frg. 1, 1i. 2. Therefore, the whole may be an accidental correlation of words and letters—unless 4Q 178 shows literary dependence. The scroll's variant reading of Habakkuk replaces להוכיח with למוכיחו. One might with Yalon (*KS* XXVII, p. 173*b*) try to equate the readings by explaining the latter as an Aramaized infinitive; but actually the commentary of v,4 f. implies the participial interpretation. When I first treated the hermeneutical connection of this passage, I regarded the interpretation as solely arbitrary on the part of the ancient commentator; but I later observed that the Biblical word far from being universally interpreted as "Rock," was taken as a verb by the Septuagint (*kaì ᾿éplasén me*); and the Syriac read similarly וגבלתני למכסותה ("and thou hast formed me to rebuke him."). For the Greek and Syriac one might derive this word from *ṣūr* IV, which like *yāṣar* means "form, fashion." The Qumrân sect, however, derived the word from *ṣûr* II, or III, with such common meanings as "bind, besiege, show hostility, be troubled." The word in the Scroll could be spelled with a *Yôd* in order to obtain the imperfect of the verb *ṣārar*. However, the infinitive seems preferable, for "fashion" and "be troubled" could be derived from this. Thus the commentator was following tradition in interpreting *ṣûr* as a verb.

If one insists upon the use of the exact idiom at lis. 1 and 6, he may translate as follows: (li. 1) "It will be *distressful* to their chastiser (whom) Thou hast ordained" and (1i. 6) "in the *distress to* them." Silberman renders, respectively: "And the distressed one hast thou established as admonisher" and "in their distress." This interprets *ṣûr* as a passive participle, which is entirely possible. This calls for a merely resumptive suffix for יסדתו, as this harks back to צור. In the translation adopted here, the suffix is not redundant, and in this respect agrees with שמתו. In any one of the three constructions, the Hebrew would be pronounced the same; and each corresponds to the midrashic interpretation.

v,7 f. "They have not followed the lust of their eyes in the time of wickedness." This interprets the Biblical words "too pure of eyes to look upon evil," which referred originally to the LORD, not as here to the faithful elect. The reference to "lust" is probably metaphorical; but it should not be limited to idolatry — as interpreted by Barthélemy (*RB*, 1952, p. 210), who cites Num. 15:39 and Ezek. 6:9. Similarly, Michel (p. 20, n. 6) thinks that this probably refers to idolatry, despite the Rabbinic interpretation that it may refer to impurity as well. Note, however, the broader application to all loyalties rivaling devotion to God in 1QS i,6-7: "with lustful eyes to do every evil."

The reading ברע, which adds the preposition, enabled the commentator to take the word in two senses: "to look (1) *upon* evil, (2) *in* an evil time." The simple accusative would permit only the first interpretation. This "time of wickedness" is the same as the preceding "time of suffering." The Scrolls use the word *qēṣ* in the sense of "time," rather than "end." The rendering "end-time" is tempting, since the eschatological overtone would accord well with this particular document. However, the word is used of all sorts of times in the Qumrân Scrolls, even where no eschatological idea is relevant at all. Cf. the English word "term," which derives from the Latin word "terminus." It seems doubtful that the word *qēṣ* ever means simply "time" in the Old Testament.

"The time of wickedness" is one of the precursors of the end. **K. G. Kuhn** (*ZThK*, 1950, p. 208) has compared קץ הרשׁ(י)ע of CDC vi,10 (=8:9). See likewise CDC xii,23 (=15:4); xv,7 (=19:7); xx,23 (=9:47). Kuhn also cites appropriately Barnabas 18:2, καιροῦ τοῦ νῦν τῆς ἀνομίας — Satan being there "the ruler of the present time of lawlessness," in a passage with a Qumrân-type of dualism. Cf. the "time of trouble" ($^c\bar{e}t$ $ṣārāh$) of Daniel 12:1 and the "last days" with the "times of stress" (καιροὶ χαλεποί) in II Tim. 3:1. Cf. also 4Q p Pss^a ii, 10 (¶11); where one reads of the "poor who will accept the season of affliction" ($m\hat{o}^c\bar{e}d$ hat-$ta^{c}\bar{a}n\hat{\imath}t$). The last days will be a time of "great tribulation" according to Matt. 24:21 (cf. Mark 13:19; John 16:33). The "days are evil" according to Eph. 5:16; and the last time will be a period of apostasy and immorality, according to I Tim. 4:1-3; II Tim. 3:1-8, 12 f.; 4:3 f.; II Peter 3:3; I Jn. 2:18; Jude 18. Cf. CDC iv, 12-18 (=6:9-12). That the saints are to judge the world is asserted by Paul (I. Cor. 6:2); and that they must suffer first is implied by Luke 17:24-25; 22:28-30; Rom. 8:17; II Thes. 1:5; Rev. 2:26-28. The "judgment" assigned God's "elect" in 1Q p Hab. is not the "last judgment" in the Christian sense, but that of the eschatological war described in 1Q M. Cf. Jean Carmignac, *Christ and the Teacher of Righteousness*, pp. 61-63.

THE MIDRASH PESHER OF HABAKKUK

¶17 (v, 8-12)

לָמָּה תַבִּיטוּ בּוֹנְדִים וְתַחֲרִישׁ בְּבַלַּע 8

רָשָׁע צַדִּיק מִמֶּנּוּ   פִּשְׁרוֹ עַל בֵּית אַבְשָׁלוֹם 9

וְאַנְשֵׁי עֲצָתָם אֲשֶׁר נָדַמּוּ בְּתוֹכַחַת מוֹרֵה הַצֶּדֶק 10

וְלוֹא עֲזָרוּהוּ עַל אִישׁ הַכָּזָב אֲשֶׁר מָאַס אֶת 11

הַתּוֹרָה בְּתוֹךְ כּוּל־עֲ[דָ]תָ[ם 12

8 (1:13b) Why, O traitors, will ye look on,
  or thou keep silent? —
9   While / a wicked man *overwhelms*
  one more righteous than he!
10   Its prophetic meaning concerns the house of Absalom / and the men
 of their council who kept quiet at the time of the reproof by the Teacher
11 of Right / and did not help him against the Man of Lies who had rejected
12 / the Law in the midst of their whole c[ongregatio]n.

¶17 *Exposition*

v,8. On the textual variants, see *Text*, §§ 32-34. Already in the Biblical citation, the plural verb of the first clause indicates the transposition of the expostulation from one addressed to God to one addressed to a human party. It would be possible, as many have done, to translate the first clause: "Why will ye look on traitors?" The interpretation, however, indicates that the traitors" (*bôgĕdîm*) are "explained as specifically referring to. . .the house of Absalom and the men of their council who kept quiet"(Silberman, "Riddle," p. 342). Dupont-Sommer (*Essene Writings*, p. 261), Vermès (*DSSE*, p. 238) and Carmignac (*Textes*, p. 100) translate correctly with a vocative.

v,9f. "The house of Absalom" has received two major interpretations. Some wish to identify Absalom with an historical figure, of whom there were several in 200 B.C.-A.D. 100. Others (including Gaster, p. 266, n.16 and van der Woude, *Bijbelcommentaren*, pp. 33f., n. 7) follow my suggestion of 1948 (*BASOR*, 112, p. 17, n. 36) in seeing here a cryptic reference to a religious party: "The commentator does not give us the real name of a rebel leader. He refers to a party which lived up to the name of Absalom who rebelled against his own father." Contrast, however, Paul Winter (*PEQ*, 1959, pp. 38f., 42) and D. N. Freedman (*BASOR*, 114, pp. 11f.). The latter insisted that "this particular house of Absalom" is not rebelling — still, this is what the text itself says, when compared with the Biblical citation. It is guilty of what we commonly call in English "a conspiracy of silence," reminding one of the malicious silence of Absalom before he slew his brother (II Sam. 13:22). J. L. Teicher ("The Habakkuk Scroll," *JJS*, V, 1954, pp. 47-59, esp., p. 57) wrote perceptively:

> This at least seems to be clear:. . . the expression, "House of Absalom," was suggested to the author of the Scroll by the verb *taharish* . . . For the same verb occurs also in the story of Absalom (II Samuel xiii,20), who, when he heard about the outrage to his sister Tamar, said: "Now my sister, hold thy peace" (*haharishi*). Absalom thus connived, although only temporarily, at an iniquity. I suggest that the author of the Scroll used the term, the "House of Absalom," as a symbol for those who connive at, and do not oppose, injustice. Indeed, the best translation of this expression in modern idiom would be "appeasers."

Gert Jeremias (*Der Lehrer*, p. 86) has noted correctly that there is no reference here to Absalom as a person, but only to a party designated "the house of Absalom."

v,10. "And the men of their council" are probably not identical with "the house of Absalom"; but they stand related to it. In his preliminary translation, Dupont-Sommer (*RHR*, p. 134) rendered this phrase "et leurs partisans." "Their partisans" did not belong to the House of Absalom according to him (p. 158) since they did not belong to the family of Absalom. Yet they were members of the same religious party. The second phrase would therefore place the "house of Absalom" within a larger context. In his later translation (*Essene Writings*, p. 261), however, Dupont-Sommer renders the phrase "*et les membres de leur conseil"* ("and the members of their council"), with the Sanhedrin in mind. The house of Absalom (even if there had been an Absalom, so named) is probably the Pharisees; and the members of "their council" would be the Pharisaic dominated Sanhedrin. Between these two diametrically opposite interpretations by Dupont-Sommer lay the publication of the Manual of Discipline which revealed that ᶜ*ēṣāh* may mean "council" and not solely "counsel." At Qumrân, however, the ᶜ*ēṣāh* was coextensive with the sect. See, however, John Worrell in *VT*, XX, 1970, pp. 65-74; and my rebuttal in *Biblica*, LII, 1971, pp. 328f., n. 3.

"At the time of the reproof by the Teacher of Right." Because here the *môrēh haṣ-ṣedeq* stands in antithesis to the "Man of Lies," we translate "the Teacher of Right" (meaning "the Teacher of Truth" as J. L. Teicher argues in *JJS*, II, 1951, p. 97). See ii,2, where however the Hebrew varies. The "one more righteous" of the Hab. text is a matter of relative righteousness, Israel being less wicked than the Chaldeans; but as applied to the Teacher, one understands an inspired spokesman who is wholly right.

bĕ-tôkhahat môrēh haṣ-ṣedeq. The noun *tôkhēkhāh* (or *tôkhahat*) has two possible meanings: "chastisement" or "reproof." A further ambiguity arises from the subjective and objective genitive. Thus there are four possibilities of interpretation: (1) the reproof received by the Teacher, (2) the reproof given by the Teacher, (3) the chastisement received by the Teacher, (4) or the chastisement given by the Teacher. No. 1 was favored in 1948 (*BASOR*, No. 112, p. 17, n. 38), since the Teacher was a persecuted figure. Others who have favored No. 1 are: Sutcliffe (*Monks*, p. 174), Elliger (p. 185, n. 8), Gaster (p. 251). The latter two have given the noun a different nuance by their translations, respectively: "*Anklage*" (i.e., "accusation") and "charges levelled against." Dupont-Sommer (in *VT*, V, 1955, p. 121) has argued against Elliger's rendering, having in mind legal charges in a court case. According to him, no such meaning appears elsewhere. No. 2 has been favored by Delcor (p. 31), Barthélemy (*RB*, 1952, p. 216, n. 2), Lambert (*NRTh*, pp. 267f., 293), Maier (I, p. 152), and probably Michel (pp. 11, 182f.). No. 3 has received the support of Dupont-Sommer, Bardtke (p. 127), Molin (p. 13), Edelkoort (p. 56), Burrows (pp. 147f.), Vermès (*DSSE*, p. 235). No. 4 has been favored by Reicke (*Handskrifterna*, pp. 32, 48f.), having in mind military action against Alexander Jannaeus—the silence of the followers of Absalom (Queen Alexandra's brother) being in their failure to participate in this. For the sense and active character of the noun he appealed to v,4 and argued: "In both cases the righteous executes the sentence."

Two considerations serve to eliminate most of these possibilities, one of these is the apparently disputational context in which both "reproof" and silence find their natural place. The other, as argued by Carmignac (*RQ*, No. 12, pp. 507-510), is that elsewhere in both the Old Testament and the Qumrân literature the noun *tôkhahat* and the related verb are employed always in accord with true justice, the righteous being the subject and the wicked being the object. The only real argument for the objective genitive is the Biblical text which asserts that "a wicked man swallows up (בלע) one more righteous than he." If the action of the verb "swallow" is represented by the noun "reproof," then the objective genitive is called for. Yet, as I argued in 1952 (*BASOR*, 126, p. 17):

> However, it is just as likely (it seems to me now) that what we are to understand is that it was the Teacher's reproof of the Man of Lies which involved him in trouble and that, because the house of Absalom 'did not help him,' the Teacher was 'swallowed up.'

In this case, the nature of the injustice suffered by the Teacher is not referred to at all, the focus rather being on the historical context of the guilty silence. Because of this, we do not know how best to translate the verb BL^c, which apparently represents two different roots with their varied meanings: (1) "swallow, destroy" and (2) "daze, confound." The translation "overwhelms" (as given above) allows for either interpretation.

v,11. "The Man of Lies" appeared earlier in ii,1f. (¶7) where he is leader of the first group of *bôgĕdîm*. In the present passage he is still among these "traitors," of whom it was said earlier that "they [did] not [believe in the words of] the Teacher of Right (which he spoke) from the mouth of God."

"They did not help him against the Man of Lies." Is this defensive action or offensive action which they failed to take? Did the Teacher take the initiative by way of a rebuke of the Man of Lies in which the House of Absalom and the members of its council failed to join? Did this then leave the Teacher at the mercy of the Man of Lies? Or, contrariwise, did the Man of Lies attack the Teacher, and quite successfully, because the House of Absalom failed to come to his rescue? Either seems possible. In any case what was meant by the "swallowing up" of the Teacher is not spelled out. This commentary was not written to tell us history but to interpret a history already known.

v,11f. "Who had rejected the Law in the midst of their whole c[ongregatio]n." If, as seems probable, the "Man of Lies" was a prominent Jewish leader, his rejection of the Law would be the repudiation of a special interpretation. To members of the sect, the Teacher spoke words of God; but those outside the sect did not believe this (ii,2). My initial restoration of this lacuna was "in the midst of all peo[ple]s"; and this was followed by Dupont-Sommer (*RHR*, pp. 134, 144), Lambert (p. 293), van der Ploeg (*Bi. Or.,* VIII, p. 6), Michel (p. 11), H. H. Rowley, Delcor (p. 24) and van't Land. This reading was used repeatedly by Rowley as an important clue for locating these events in the time of Antiochus IV (so in *ETL* 1952, pp. 257-276 and *ALBO*, II, fasc. 30, p. 264; *ET*, Sept., 1952, p. 382; *The Zadokite Fragments and the Dead Sea Scrolls*,1952, p. 43, n. 5.) The Epiphanian persecution would put this repudiation of the Law in an international context, if the Man of Lies is none other than Antiochus. Silberman ("Riddle," p. 343) who also adopts this restoration interprets it to mean simply "publicly."

The first to question this restoration is S. Talmon (*VT*, 1951, p. 35), who suggests that the final *Mêm* is the possessive pronoun and that we should restore either עדתם or עצתם, with allusion to the same body referred to in lines 9f. Close scrutiny of the vestiges of the word reveals clear traces of the upper left and lower left of the *Tāw;* so that ᶜ*ammîm* is excluded as a possible restoration. The very slight remains of the upper right of the second letter, to my eyes, more probably suggest a *Dālet,* rather than a *Ṣādê.* On that ground alone I prefer ᶜᵃ*dātām* (their congregation) to ᶜᵃ*ṣātām.* Habermann (ᶜ *Edah,* p. 48; *Megilloth,* p. 45), Burrows (p. 367), Vermés (*Discovery,* p. 127; *DSSE,* p. 238), Gaster (p. 251), van der Woude (*Bijbelcommentaren,* p. 33), Carmignac (*Textes,* p. 102), and G. Jeremias (*Der Lehrer,* p. 85) read the former; Elliger and Dupont-Sommer (*Essene Writings,* p. 261, n. 4) read the latter.

An important question is the antecedent of "their" (in "their congregation"). Most probably it is to the entire "house of Absalom" of which "the men of their council" would be a special body.

In other passages, the Man (or Prophet) of Lies leads astray those who should follow the Teacher of Right (¶¶7, 29). This may mean (as van der Woude, pp. 42f., n. 7 holds) that we have to do here with a rift within the sect. Perhaps, however, this rift should be seen within a larger context such as the Hasidim, so that what we have referred to here is the origin of the sect—in which those who followed the Man of Lies were regarded as apostate from Israel and so were dubbed "traitors," "the house of Absalom," and "unbelievers" (¶7). To the Man of Lies, however, the apostate would be those who turned aside to follow the Righteous Teacher.

An Historical Excursus

Persons identified as the Man of Lies have included the following: Antiochus Epiphanes, Bacchides or Demetrius (associated with Alcimus), John Hyrcanus, Alexander Jannaeus, Simon ben Shetach, Herod the Great, Jesus, Paul, Menahem son of Judah, Simon bar Giora, John of Gischala, and Bar Kokhba. Any attempt to deal adequately with the subject of these identifications must be postponed until a later volume.

Since the identity of the Man of Lies affects also the identity of the Righteous Teacher (the question of whose personal name arises at xii,4f.), I am constrained to mention here a narrative concerning John Hyrcanus I which will be referred to again in ¶33. In April, 1952, both D. Barthélemy (*RB,* LIX, pp. 207-18) and I (*BASOR,* 126, pp. 10-19) dealt with the historical allusions of this scroll and suggested that the event referred to in the present pericope is actually mentioned by Josephus and by Rabbinic tradition (Barthélemy, pp. 213-17; Brownlee, pp. 12, 17f.).

Josephus records how a growing disaffection between Hyrcanus and the Pharisees (*JA,* XIII, x,5, §§288ff.) led the former to invite his critics to a banquet where he made a speech declaring his intention of being righteous; but "at the same time he begged them, if they observed him doing anything wrong or straying from the right path, to lead him back to it and correct him."

All who responded joined in praising him as virtuous, except for one man who arose to rebuke him (§§290-92):

> However, one of the guests, named Eleazar, who had an evil nature and took pleasure in dissension, said, "Since you have asked to be told the truth, if you wish to be righteous, give up the highpriesthood and be content with governing the people." And when Hyrcanus asked him for what reason he should give up the highpriesthood, he replied, "Because we have heard from our elders that your mother was a captive in the reign of Antiochus Epiphanes." But the story was false, and Hyrcanus was furious with the man, while all the Pharisees were very indignant.

If here is portrayed the Teacher's rebuke of the Man of Lies, then the identity of the three parties is clear: the Teacher is Eleazar, the Man of Lies is Hyrcanus, and the House of Absalom is the Pharisees. The latter were silent in that none of them spoke up to support the Teacher. Others, evidently, were outspoken in their indignation against the rebuker—but not necessarily all.

Later, Jonathan (a Sadducean friend of Hyrcanus) accused the Pharisees of complicity in the outspokenness of Eleazar and urged Hyrcanus to test the Pharisees on the matter by having them decree the penalty to be imposed upon Eleazar. (Evidently, it was a question of the Council or Sanhedrin, which was dominated by the Pharisees.) When "they replied that Eleazar deserved" only "stripes and chains," their leniency was taken as proof that they approved of Eleazar's defamatory rebuke. Consequently Hyrcanus deserted the Pharisees, joined the Sadducees, and began to punish those who followed the Pharisaic interpretations of the Law (*JA*, XIII, x,6, §§ 293-300). The consequence of this is evidently referred to by Josephus in *JW*, I. ii,8; §299 states, "he quieted the outbreak" ($\pi\alpha\acute{\upsilon}\sigma\alpha\varsigma\ \tau\grave{\eta}\nu\ \sigma\tau\acute{\alpha}\sigma\iota\nu$). Although earlier Hasmonean high priests had suppressed the Hellenizers and political dissidents, Hyrcanus is the earliest known persecutor of other Jewish parties. In *Jewish Antiquities*, Hyrcanus' opponents are referred to in general terms as Pharisees; and yet, despite their supposed judicial leniency, they did not approve of Eleazar and so "did not help him against the Man of Lies who had rejected the Law in the midst of their whole congregation," but they sentenced him to flogging and imprisonment. In *Jewish Wars*, Josephus does not identify Hyrcanus' opponents as Pharisees.

Actually, as Barthélemy has argued, Pharisees of the second century B.C. may have been simply separatists. It was only later under the leadership of Simon ben Shetach and Hillel that Pharisaism achieved fully its classical character. Thus "the Pharisees" of Hyrcanus' rule may have included the Hasidim generally, with the complete break between the Pharisees and Essenes not arising until the time of Hyrcanus. Yet, so interpreted, the different schools of thought preceded this rupture, so that the incipient divisions were older. Thus, even before this event, Eleazar was known as one "who took pleasure in dissension" ($\sigma\tau\acute{\alpha}\sigma\epsilon\iota\ \chi\alpha\acute{\iota}\rho\omega\nu$), *JA*, XIII, §291. He was already a sectarian in temperament and practice, although the rupture was not complete. In this connection, it may be noted that Ralph Marcus ("Pharisees, Essenes, and Gnostics," *JBL*, LXXIII, 1954, pp. 157-61) suggested that the Essenes were "gnosticizing Pharisees." Chaim Rabin

(*Qumran Studies*, 1957) has gone too far in identifying the Qumrân Community with the Pharisaic Ḥaburah, as has also Leah Bronner (*Sects and Separatism during the Second Jewish Commonwealth*, pp. 134-49). Nevertheless, they have established a certain affinity between the parties which points to a common rootage of both the Pharisees and the Essenes in the Hasidic movement of early Hasmonean times. If Hyrcanus proceeded violently against the moderate Pharisees, how much more would he be inclined to persecute extremists like the Essenes.

The variant form of the story as recorded by Rabbinic tradition (Ḳiddushin, 66a) makes Jannai (i.e., Jannaeus) the ruler, Judah son of Jedidiah the man who rebuked him, and Eleazar son of Poᶜirah the Sadducean spokesman. Jannai and John Hyrcanus were evidently confused in this tradition; but Berakot 29a rightly records that (according to Rabba) "Jannai was originally a wicked person, but John was originally a righteous person." If one assumes that the Rabbinic tradition is correct as to the name of the rebuker, then there arises the possibility that Judah son of Jedidiah is the same person as Judas the Essene who figures in a legend relating to Hyrcanus' son and successor, Aristobulus I (*JA*, XIII, xi,2 §§311-13; *JW*, I, iii,5, §§78-80). This in turn raises the question as to whether these are the same as "Judah the Law Doer" mentioned in 1Q p Hab xii,4 (¶33).

For the chronology of the sect these identifications would be important, for Judah son of Jedidiah was described as *zāḵēn* ("an elder" or "old") in about 108 B. C. and Judas the Essene was described for the year 104 as ὁ γέρων ("the old man"). Thus with either man identified as the Teacher, there would be no difficulty (if the evidence warranted it) to push the beginning of his career back to the rule of Jonathan (161-143) or Simon (143-135). J. T. Milik has identified the Wicked Priest with Jonathan (*Ten Years of Discovery*, pp. 61-73) and has considered Hyrcanus to be the Prophet of Lies (pp. 88f.). Frank M. Cross, Jr., (*Ancient Library*, pp. 127-60) chose Simon as the Wicked Priest and likewise identified the Prophet of Lies with Hyrcanus. Neither Milik nor Cross has discussed the narrative treated here in that connection. To each, the ascription of a mantic role to Hyrcanus by Josephus (*JA*, XIII, x,7, §§299f.; *JW*, I, ii,8, §§68f.) was a major consideration in identifying Hyrcanus with the False Prophet. Although both scholars insisted that there was only one Wicked Priest and that he was not to be identified with the Man of Lies, Milik believed that the author of the *pēšer* sometimes got these men confused, so that what is said of the Wicked Priest in ¶25 actually fits better Hyrcanus and what is said of the Prophet of Lies in ¶29 suits only Jonathan. Since ¶25 marks the alienation of the sect from the Hasmoneans, perhaps one should begin the story of Qumrân conflict with the Hasmoneans with Hyrcanus, who was both one of the Wicked Priests in my interpretation of 1952 and also the False Prophet. Then one should continue the history through Aristobulus I down into the reign of Jannaeus, who was perhaps the primary Wicked Priest. Cyril Detaye ("Le cadre historique du Midrash d'Habacuc," *ETL*, XXX, 1954, pp. 323-43) made Jannaeus the

Wicked Priest, but he ascribed to Hyrcanus the role of the Man of Lies. Mrs. Bronner (p. 133) agreed with Milik and me that ¶25 only really fits Hyrcanus, and so she identified him with the Wicked Priest of that passage. Yet "Jannai, the son of Hyrcanus, was the notorious 'wicked priest'. . ."

One of the problems which has vexed the identification of the Wicked Priest is the assumption that the requirement of the Zadokite lineage for the Chief Priest disqualifed, at the outset, any Hasmonean. Hence the Qumrânites are said not to have objected to the secular authority of the Hasmoneans, but to their assumption of the highpriesthood. This would fit the language of the rebuke of Hyrcanus, "Give up the highpriesthood and be content with governing the people." The reason given, namely that Hyrcanus' mother as a captive was disqualified through her loss of virginity (cf. Lev. 21:7, 13-15), has nothing to do with the question of Zadokite lineage. According to the Talmud, Judah's rebuke was: "O King Jannai! Let the royal crown suffice thee, and leave the priestly crown to the seed of Aaron." There is no mention of the necessity of his being of the line of Zadok. However, the published manuscripts make no distinction between Zadokite and Aaronic lineage; and the Hasmoneans were of the line of Joarib (I Macc. 2:1), the Jehoiarib who according to I Chron. 24:7 was of the first order of Aaronic priests, by the choice of the lot cast in the presence of Zadok. In 1Q S v,2, 9, the highest authority in the Qumrân Community was vested in the sons of Zadok; but in viii,9 and ix,7, the same authority is ascribed to the sons of Aaron. Until evidence can be found to the contrary, Zadokite lineage as distinct from Aaronic should not be regarded as a factor in the Qumrân rejection of the Hasmonean chief priests. It seems only to have been a matter of objection to their religious policies, together with the charge that Hyrcanus had a non-Jewish father, or at least a disqualified mother.

The present discussion of the identity of the leading foes of the Righteous Teacher and his Community serves simply as an illustration of the kind of data to be studied more broadly and more precisely in the future. Meanwhile, one must recognize that all identifications are only theoretical. In the present passage one may object that nothing really proves that we actually have in Josephus and the Talmud parallels to the Teacher's rebuke of the Man of Lies. Nothing proves that the two or three Judahs brought into the discussion were the Righteous Teacher, or that his name was Eleazar. One may maintain that the Teacher is still unknown to us by name and that the story of Hyrcanus' banquet is just one of many occasions in which he (or some other Hasmonean ruler) suffered rebuke from a Jewish leader. One should not, however, conclude that identifications of this kind are to be excluded *a priori*. When all lines of historical inference are put together, many conclusions may seem reasonable. Whatever their identity, both the Wicked Priest and the False Prophet were public figures concerning whom we have written history, so that one should not forsake the task of their identification.

THE MIDRASH PESHER OF HABAKKUK
¶ 18 (v,12-vi,8)

12	וַתַּעַשׂ אָדָם כִּדְגֵי הַיָּם
13	כָּרֶמֶשׂ לְמָשֹׁל בּוֹ כּוּ[ל]וֹ בְּחַכָּ[ה יַעֲלֶ]ה וִיגֹרֵהוּ בְחֶרְמוֹ
14	וַיַּסְפֵהוּ בְּמִכְ[מַרְתּוֹ עַל כֵּן יְזַבֵּ]חַ לְחֶרְמוֹ עַל כֵּן יִשְׂמַח
15	[וְיָגִיל וִיקַטֵּר לְמִכְמַרְתּוֹ כִּי בָהֶם] שָׁמֵן חֶלְקוֹ
16	[וּמַאֲכָלוֹ בָּרִי פִּשְׁרוֹ עַל מוֹשְׁלֵי הַכִּתִּיאִים אֲשֶׁר]
17	[יִכְבְּשׁוּ הָעַמִּים וְרָדוּ בָהֶם וְנִתְּנוּ עָרֵיהֶם בְּיַד חֵיל]
vi,1	הַכִּתִּיאִים וְיֹוסִיפוּ אֶת הוֹנָם עִם כּוּל־שְׁלָלָם
2	כִּדְגַת הַיָּם וַאֲשֶׁר אָמַר עַל כֵּן יְזַבֵּחַ לְחֶרְמוֹ
3	וִיקַטֵּר לְמִכְמַרְתּוֹ פִּשְׁרוֹ אֲשֶׁר הֵמָּה
4	זֹבְחִים לְאֹותוֹתָם וּכְלֵי מִלְחֲמוֹתָם הֵמָּה
5	מוֹרָאָם כִּיא בָהֶם שָׁמֵן חֶלְקוֹ וּמַאֲכָלוֹ בָּרִי
6	פִּשְׁרוֹ אֲשֶׁר הֵמָּה מְחַלְּקִים אֶת עֻלָּם וְאֶת
7	מִסָּם מַאֲכָלָם עַל כּוּל־הָעַמִּים שָׁנָה בְשָׁנָה
8	לַחֲרִיב אֲרָצֹות רַבֹּות

12	(1:14)	Thou hast made man as fishes of the sea, /
13		as gliding things over which to rule.
	(1:15a-c)	They will bring [them] all up [with a hook],
		and fish them out with their net, /
14		and gather them with [their] sei[ne].
	(1:16a)	[Therefore, they will sacri]fice to their net;
15	(1:15d)	Therefore they will rejoice / [and exult]
	(1:16b-d)	[and burn incense to their seine,
		For thereby] their ration will be [lib]eral, /
16		[and their food abundant].

17   [[Its prophetic meaning concerns the rulers of the Kittim who / will tread down peoples and subdue them; and their cities will be given into

vi,1   the power of the army of]] / the Kittim, who will gather their wealth

2   with all their loot / as fish of the sea. And as for what he says,

3   "Therefore they will sacrifice to their net / and burn incense to their

4   seine," its prophetic meaning is that they / sacrifice to their standards

5   and (that) their weapons of war are / their objects of veneration. "For

6   thereby their ration will be liberal, and their food abundant." / The

7   prophetic meaning is that they will distribute their yoke and / their tax

8   burden, their food, upon all the peoples, year by year, / in order to lay waste many lands.

¶18 *Exposition*

v,12ff. On the textual variants see *Text*, §§35-44. V,12 "Fishes" renders a plural form, whereas in vi,2 "fish" is a collective. Both uses are known to English, although the collective singular is more common.

v,13. "As gliding things *over which to rule*" (Hab. 1:14). The MT reads rather, "over which is no ruler." The idea is that subhuman creatures have no ruler. Cf. concerning the ant, Prov. 6:7; and concerning the locusts, Prov. 30:27. According to Habakkuk, human society without a ruler is not fully human and lies open to exploitation by men who do have rulers, just as the animal world is normally subject to man. In the reading of the scroll, the perspective is different. It is the viewpoint of Gen. 1:26, 28 and Psalm 8:7-9 (Heb., English 8:6-8), in which all animals, including fish and *remeś* (either crawling or gliding things) were placed under the rule of man by the Creator, a rule which permits exploitation and appropriation. However, there is an implied limit to man's exploitation of nature in Hab. 2:17. It is the exploitation of men of which the Kittim are accused. The word for "man" in this verse is *ʾādām*, precisely as in Genesis. According to the reading of 1Q p Hab, man under the Chaldeans loses his role of dominance among the creatures and is himself reduced to an animal status. Such exploitation of man by man is a denial of human dignity. In the reading of *limšōl* for *lōʾ mōšēl*, the commentator (or the text he cites) has assimilated Hab. 1:14 to Gen. 1:26, 28 and Psalm 8:7-9.

v,16f. This daring restoration of the wholly missing lines is without merit except as a dramatic way of presenting the probable nature of their contents. So persistently are peculiar readings of the Habakkuk quotations integral to the interpretation of the document, we may feel certain that *limšōl* (v,13 = 1:14) dominated the interpretation of 1:14 which appeared here. The "rulers of the Kittim" (cf. iv,5,10) may well have been referred to here, along with appropriate verbs describing their rule. The two verbs chosen to represent this idea are those of Gen. 1:28, which together with Ps. 8:7-9 influenced the reading. As applied to men √ כבש means to subdue, or to bring into slavery. √רדה means to rule, or dominate, and the idea of oppressive rule is brought out in Lev. 25:43, 46, 53 by the addition of בפרך, a term which might have appeared here. The last word of this column (li, 17 or 18) may well have been *ḥayil*; for a reference to the "army of the Kittim" (cf. ix,6 f.) would suit well in connection with the implements of fishing mentioned in 1:15; for these are explained in connection with 1:16 (at vi,4 f.) as military "standards" and "implements of war." If there were eighteen rather than seventeen lines to this column, as Elliger posits, there would be room for some additional elements. Since the implements of fishing are explained later, it is not likely that this subject received attention here. Similarly, one might expect mention of particular instances of oppressive rule; but, again, this element appears at vi,6 ff. and might have been reserved for that point.

vi,1. The fishing operation is explained as loot taken in war. This loot may be that of the subjected nations (cf. viii,12, but with reference to the Wicked Priest) or that of their rulers. Cf. ix,4 ff. where the wealth of the "last priests of Jerusalem" "will be given into the power of the army of the Kittim." Schoeps (*ZRG*, 1951, p. 326) believes that the plundering referred to in vi,1 is also that of the Hasmonean wealth.

vi,2. "As fish of the sea" (with a slight difference in the Hebrew) echoes Hab. 1:14. It is clear that the fish are interpreted as "wealth" and "loot." However, Ethelbert Stauffer (*ThLZ*, 1951, col. 671) compares Test. Judah 21:7 where men are seized as well:

> For the kings shall be as sea monsters.
> They shall swallow men *like fishes:*
> The sons and daughters of freemen shall they enslave;
> Houses, lands, flocks, money shall they plunder.

He interprets the reference to fish as a bit of "anti-Syrian polemics." For allegorical interpretation, see Betz, pp. 77 ff.

vi,2f. The citation of Hab. 1:16*a-b* is in proper order here, in contrast with the confusion of the major quotation at v,15f. For the problem see *Text*, §41.

vi,3f. "The meaning is that they sacrifice." The personal pronoun *hēmmāh* appears in lieu of the ever present Kittim, or more specifically, "the army of the Kittim." The emphatic pronoun, however, is required as the subject of the participle *zōvĕḥîm*.

vi,4f. "They sacrifice to their standards and their weapons of war are their objects of veneration." *Môrā'ām*, here rendered "their objects of veneration," is equivalent to "their god." Cf. Isa. 8:12*b*-13:

> Do not fear their [this people's] object of fear [*môrā'ō*]. Yahweh of Hosts, Him alone shall you sanctify. Let Him be your object of awe [*ma'ariṣĕkhem*].

Similarly, *môreh* (teacher) of Hab. 2:18 should perhaps be read *Môrāh* = *môrā'*, as in Ps. 9:21 (=9:20). Barthélemy (*RB*, 1952, p. 210) notes that *môreh šāqer* of 2:18 is rendered *dahªlat šĕqār*, "false object of fear" = "false divinity" by the Targum. (Yet, *hû' yôreh* in 2:19 is probably a gloss implying the meaning "teacher" in vs. 18.) Isaac's God, according to the common interpretation, was called *paḥad yiṣhāq* ("the Fear of Isaac") in Gen. 31:42, 53. However, according to W. F. Albright (*From the Stone Age to Christianity*, 2nd ed., 1957, p. 248) the original meaning of the Hebrew here was "the Kinsman of Isaac." In Rabbinic Hebrew, as M. H. Segal observes (*JBL*, 1951, p. 133), the noun יראה means idol. See Jastrow, *Dictionary*, p. 593b.

The cultic interpretation which is given of the words of Habakkuk appears also in the Targum of Jonathan, but with a transposition of the order: "Therefore, they sacrifice to their weapons (*lĕ-zênêh*) and burn incense to their standards (*lĕ-sēmāwātêh*)." This led N. Wieder ("The Habakkuk Scroll and the Targum," *JJS*, IV, 1953, pp. 14-18) to suggest that one should correct the text of 1Q p Hab, by transposing its interpretative equivalents to agree with the Targum; but is would be brash to correct either to agree with the other. See the critique in *JSS*, VII, 1956, pp. 176ff.

Considerable debate has developed over the cult of the *signa*, whether it was practiced at all by the Seleucids (making them eligible for the role of the Kittim), or by the Romans only. If the Kittim are the Romans, how early was their observance of this cult, as early as the Roman republic or only later under imperial Rome? Actually, the Targum is concerned only with the practice among the Chaldeans; and as Delcor has observed (p. 42, n. 3; also *RB*, LVIII, 1951, p. 527), the cult did exist among the ancient Egyptians, Assyrians, and Persians. Even if one concluded that this cult was not characteristic of the Seleucids or early Romans, all that is required for this interpretation to arise in the Targumic tradition prior to 1Q p Hab is that this interpretation have begun no later than the Persian period. Even so, the *pēšer* would not have taken this up, if its author had not believed it also applied to the Kittim of his own day. Yet in this he may have stretched a point; for it was probably the exegetical tradition rather than any specific event which suggested the interpretation. Yet Mrs. Atkinson (*JSS*, IV, 1959, pp. 246-263) has argued from numismatic evidence that the worship of military standards was current in republican Rome and was not Seleucid practice. For the literary evidence see Roger Goosens, "Les Kittim du Commentaire d'Habacuc," *NC*, IV, 1952, pp. 138-70.

vi,5f. ברי = בריא, replacing the Massoretic בראה which is erroneously in the feminine gender. Cf. *Text*, §44.

vi,6f. "They distribute their yoke." עולם can only be Ꞔ*ullām* ("their yoke"), not Ꞔ*ôlām* (= Rabbinic "world"); but cf. del Medico, *Deux Manuscrits*, p. 113; *Riddle*, p. 250): "ils se paragent l'univers," "they divide out the world." The meaning of the word is determined by its parallel *missām*.

vi,7f. "and their tax burden" = מסם. In the Old Testament *mas* always means "forced labor, the corvée," the meaning adopted by: van der Ploeg, *Bi Or*, VIII, p. 7; del Medico; G. Molin, *Die Söhne des Lichtes*, p. 13; Bardtke, p. 127; Elliger; Dupont-Sommer, *Essene Writings*, p. 262; van der Woude, *Bijbelcommentaren*, p. 33; Maier, I, p. 152; Carmignac, *Textes*, p. 104; and Lohse. However, the translation "tax-burden" (*BASOR*, 112, p. 12) based upon Rabbinic usage, was followed by: Dupont-Sommer, *RHR*, pp. 135, 159; Schoeps, *ZRG*, 1951, p. 331; Lambert, p. 293; Stauffer; and Burrows, p. 367; Edelkoort, p. 57; Vermès, *DSSE*, p. 238; Sutcliffe, *Monks*, p. 174. This meaning is supported by the parenthetical "their food" (*maꟄᵃkhālām*); for not only were taxes more directly convertible into nourishment than forced labor, they were often collected in the form of grain. (See Mrs. Atkinson, pp. 244f.) The annual assessment, also, favors the imposition of taxes. Also there was good midrashic ground for equating *maꟄᵃkhāl* ("food") with "tax," for in Rabbinic Hebrew and Aramaic (*leḥem* and *lĕḥēm*, respectively) mean not only "food, bread," but also "tribute, tax, a salary." For the whole passage, cf. (after Yalon, *KS*, p. 173b) Ben Sira 40:1.

vi,8f. "To lay waste many lands." Although the verb was first translated as a *qal* infinitive, the decision to read לחרוב in *DDS*, I, was that of Millar Burrows; for I had already adopted the *hif⁽ᶜ⁾il* reading לחריב with its elided *Hē*. (See Ratzaby in *JQR*, XLI, 1950, p. 157; Lehmann, in *PEQ*, 1951, p. 51).

Taxes by ancient nations were often oppressive. Such language would seem justified of the Ptolemies, Seleucids, and Romans. A self-styled Roman benefactor like Cicero (who was contemporary with 1Q p Hab) found considerable fault with Roman administrators who preceded him for the exacting of heavy taxes and for the charging of 48% interest on back debts (Atticus V, 21; VI, 1). Such practices, according to him, contributed to the devastation of a country. Concerning Cilicia (where he was proconsul and successor to Appius Claudius) he wrote:

> You must know that my arrival in this province, which is in a state of lasting ruin and desolation was expected eagerly. . . Everywhere I heard the same tale. People would not pay the poll tax; they were forced to sell out their investments; groans and lamentations in the towns, and awful conduct of one who is some kind of savage beast, rather than a man. All the people are, as you may suppose, tired of life.
> Atticus V:16 (208:2)

> I had taken upon myself to relieve the miseries of ruined states, ruined mainly, too, through the action of their own magistrates, it was impossible that, in the matter of that unnecessary expenditure, I should show no concern.
> Familiares III:8 (222:2-5), §5

Philo also wrote of ruinous taxation (*Special Laws*, I, ¶143):

> The cities pay under compulsion and reluctance and groan under the burden. They look askance at the tax collectors as general agents of destruction.

Josephus, even, speaks of ruinous taxations as the virtual destruction (ἀπώλεια) of Palestinian cities (*JW*, I, xi,2 [§222]). If the charge by the ancient scroll that the Kittim "lay waste many lands" in their collection of taxes is a slight exaggeration, it was a rather common one. The New Testament also reveals the hatred of the publican by the Palestinians, particularly when the tax agents were Jews, to be classed as "publicans and sinners."

THE MIDRASH PESHER OF HABAKKUK
¶19 (vi, 8-12)

עַל כֵּן יָרִיק חַרְבּוֹ תָּמִיד   8
לַהֲרוֹג גּוֹיִם וְלוֹא יַחְמֹל   9
פִּשְׁרוֹ עַל הַכִּתִּיאִים אֲשֶׁר יְאַבְּדוּ רַבִּים בַּחֶרֶב   10
נְעָרִים אֲשִׁישִׁים וּזְקֵנִים נָשִׁים וָטַף וְעַל פְּרִי   11
בֶּטֶן לוֹא יְרַחֵמוּ   12

8 (1:17) He shall therefore draw his sword continually, /
9   to slay nations, and that without showing pity. /
10   Its prophetic meaning concerns the Kittim who will destroy many
11 with the sword: / youths, mature men, and old men, women and (even)
12 children; "for upon the fruit of / the womb they will show no pity."

¶19 *Exposition*

vi,8 ff. For the variants, see *Text*, §§47-50. The omission of the *Hē* interrogative probably makes the sentence declarative. The scroll reads "sword" (*ḥerev*) for the MT "net" (*ḥerem*). The different placement of the *Wāw* makes for a different emphasis. The MT places it before *tāmîd* of 1:17*a* ("and that continually"); but the scroll, before *lôʾ yaḥmōl* ("and that without showing pity"). The entire interpretation focuses upon the lack of pity, ignoring completely the idea of *tāmîd*.

vi,11. "Mature men." The noun ʾ*ašîšîm* (or, ʾ*ašîšôt*) occurs in the Bible only as "raisin cakes" (II Sam. 6:19; I Chr. 16:3; Song of Songs 2:5; Hos. 3:1), unless it be in Isa. 16:7, where (as Lehmann, *PEQ*, 1951, p. 36 noted) the Targum renders Heb. ʾ*ašîšê qîr ḥªreśet* as ʾ*anāš kĕrākh* ("men of the city" or "of Kerak"). The parallel Jer. 48:31 reads ʾ*anšê qîr ḥereś* and receives the same translation as Isa. 16:7. Either the Targum presupposes the same reading in each place, or else it equates ʾ*ašîšîm* with ʾ*anāšîm* (the plural of ʾ*îš*). The use of ʾ*ašîšîm* by 1Q p Hab seems to attest the latter as a designation of "mature men" lying between "youths" (*nĕʿārîm*) and "old men" (*zĕqēnîm*).

vi,11f, "*For* upon the fruit of the womb they show no mercy." This rendering assumes that *pĕrî beṭen* is only a poetic figure for *ṭaf* ("toddlers, small children"). As Carmignac observes (*Textes*, p. 105, n. 9), "Le 'fruit des entrailles' désigne les enfants en bas âge." Other scholars, however, have seen in this a reference to atrocities committed against pregnant women, even though women as victims have already been mentioned. Delcor (p. 59) and Barthélemy (*RB*, 1952, p. 210) have suggested this understanding, which appears in the usual German translation "der Frucht im Mutterleibe" (Bardtke, p. 127; Molin, p. 13; Lohse). This is expressed in greater explicitness in Reicke's Swedish rendering (*Handskrifterna*, p. 33); "aven med fostret i moderlvet sakna de forbarmande" ("even toward the fetus in the womb they lack pity"). It is expressed succintly by Roberts (*BJRL*, 1952, p. 379): "and will not spare the unborn." However, no evidence for this interpretation has been presented. In the Old Testament it even explicitly refers to the body of the father (Ps. 132:11; Mic. 6:7; cf. Ps. 127:3). Actually, the whole clause is a quotation of Isa. 13:18 in the reading of 1Q Isa*ᵃ* (which differs from the MT by the double occurrence of the preposition *ʿal*):

> Bows will mangle youths (*nĕʿārîm*),
> *and upon the fruit of the womb*
> *they will show no pity,*
> and toward children their eye
> will not be sparing.

This verse has provided the word *nĕʿārîm* for 1Q p Hab and the whole of the second clause. *Bānîm* ("children") is in parallelism with *pĕrî beṭen*, and is probably synonymous. For crimes against pregnant women, the Old Testament uses a different expression *biqqēaʿ hārôt* (II Kings 8:12; 15:16;

Hos. 14:1 [=13:16]; Amos 1:13). The first of these provides the best parallel to the present passage:

> . . . you will slay their youths (*baḥūrêhem*) with the sword,
> and mangle their infants (*ʿolělêhem*),
> *and rip open their pregnant women.*

This passage seems not to have influenced the author of 1Q p Hab. The only real coincidence is "with the sword," which is a variant reading of Habakkuk. The greatest lack of pity according to the *pēšer* is toward children. Crimes against women had already been mentioned. On the general sense, cf. Deut. 28:50 (concerning the Chaldeans, which in our scroll are the Kittim). Note that vs. 29 correlates well with iii,10 f.

Parallels to 1Q p Hab include Jubilees 23:23 (concerning the Syrians):

> And He will wake up against them the sinners of the Gentiles, who have neither mercy nor compassion, and who shall respect the person of none, neither old nor young, nor any one . . .

Psalms of Solomon 17:13 (concerning Pompey):

> The lawless one laid waste our land
> so that none inhabited it,
> They destroyed young and old
> and their children together.

Cf. also what Herod's troops did in the taking of Jerusalem in 37 B.C. (Josephus, *JA*, xviii,2 [§352]): "No quarter was given to infancy, to age, or to helpless womanhood."

THE MIDRASH PESHER OF HABAKKUK

¶ 20 (vi, 12-vii, 5)

עַל מִשְׁמַרְתִּי אֶעֱמוֹדָה 12

וְאֶתְיַצְּבָה עַל מָצוֹרִי וַאֲצַפֶּה לִרְאוֹת מַה יְדַבֶּר 13

כִּי וּמָ[ה אָשִׁיב עַ]ל תּוֹכַחְתִּי וַיַּעֲנֵנִי יְהוָה 14

[וַיֹּאמֶר כְּתוֹב חָזוֹן וּבָאֵ]ר עַל הַלֻּוּחוֹת לְמַעַן יָרוּץ 15

[הַקּוֹרֵא בּוֹ   פֵּשֶׁר הַדָּבָר אֲשֶׁר] 16

[חֲבַקּוּק יִתְפַּלֵּל לְדַעַת הַנִּהְיוֹת בְּאַחֲרִית הַיָּמִים] 17

אֶל

vii,1 וַיְדַבֵּר אֶל חֲבַקּוּק לִכְתּוֹב אֶת הַבָּאוֹת עַל

2 עַל הַדּוֹר הָאַחֲרוֹן וְאֶת גְּמַר הַקֵּץ לוֹא הוֹדִיעוֹ

יָרוּץ

3 וַאֲשֶׁר אָמַר לְמַעַן הַקּוֹרֵא בוֹ

4 פִּשְׁרוֹ עַל מוֹרֵה הַצֶּדֶק אֲשֶׁר הוֹדִיעוֹ אֵל אֶת

5 כּוֹל־רָזֵי דִּבְרֵי עֲבָדָיו הַנְּבִיאִים

12 (2:1)   At my watch I will stand,/
13   and at my post I will keep my station.
14   I will stay alert to see what He will say/ to me
     and h[ow I should respond t]o His reproof of me.
15 (2:2)   Then the LORD answered/ [and said:
     "Write the vision
       but leave it vague (?)] upon the tablets,
16   that/ [he who reads it] *may run (may divulge).*
17   [The prophetic meaning of the passage is that/ Habakkuk][[prayed
that he might know the things which would happen in the last days,]]/
vii,1 Then God told Habakkuk to write the things that are coming upon/
2 upon (sic.) the last generation; but the fulness of that time He did not
make known to him./
3   And as for that which He said, "for the sake of him who reads it" (or,
4 "that he who reads it may run [may divulge])," / its interpretation
5 concerns the Righteous Teacher to whom God has made known / all
the mysteries of the words of His servants the prophets.

¶20 *Exposition*

vi,12-16. For the variants of the Biblical verses, see *Text*, §§ 51-54.

vi,14. We do not know whether the text read with the MT אשיב, or whether it gave support to the emendation ישיב ("and how *He will respond* to my complaint"). The latter reading (which is supported by the Peshitto) is appealing because of the parallelism with both the preceding and following clauses. For the translation of *tôkhaḥtî* (lit., "my complaint [or reproof]"), cf. Delcor (p. 24): "et (ce que je répondrai) á la remonstrance qu'il me fera." This makes the best sense of the unemended text. Van der Woude (*Bijbelcommentaren*, p. 34) translates similarly.

vi,15. Unfortunately, we do not know whether the manuscript read באר ("engrave, make plain, explain") or בער ("make empty, leave fallow"); but see the commentary below.

vi,15f. "That he who reads it may run" is a suitable translation, once one understands fully what "run" in Habakkuk means. However, it would seem to have been given by the commentary an additional meaning (cf. below). The phrase has been interpreted by many scholars to mean that the text is to be written so plainly that one may read it on the run. Another explanation takes "run" figuratively for fast reading: "that he who reads it may read it quickly." This figurative sense for *rûṣ* is unattested. See J. M. Holt in *JBL*, LXXXIII, 1964, pp. 298-302. In taking "run" as the main verb and in giving it a spiritual significance he is correct; but his interpretation "live obediently" misses the point here, for one must not lose sight of the imagery of the watchman, whose message would be carried by a runner. "Run" in the sense of serve as a royal messenger is attested in II Sam. 18:21-26; and it is used of the prophets as running on a divine mission in Jer. 23:21:

> I did not send the prophets,
>   yet they ran;
> I did not speak to them,
>   yet they prophesied.

Cf. God's hypostatized "word" running on a mission in Ps. 147:15. The participle *rāṣ* means a courier, or messenger, in Jer. 31:31; Est. 3:13, 15; 8:10. In II Chron. 30:6, 10, these royal couriers proclaim a religious message. It seems probable that what the divine command to Habakkuk means is "that any one who reads it may carry the message to others, the same as you." Probably a minority of the population could read; but those who could not read would be informed of the prophetic message by those who could. A curious crowd would gather about those who could read in order to learn what the text said. Such reading aloud was "running," an extension of Habakkuk's own prophetic mission.

vi,16 f. Elliger (p. 36) restores on li. 16: פשרו על חבקוק אשר of which he thinks he detects slight traces of the *Qôf* of *ḥᵃbaqqûq* and the *ᵓĀlef* of *ᵓašer*. What he takes to be the top of the *Qôf*, unfortunately, can only be a *Rêš*, that belonging to הדבר. He was probably on the right track, however, in suggesting a reference to the prophet. If we restore the longer introductory formula (that found in v,3), li. 16 will be sufficiently filled that the name "Habakkuk" must have appeared at the beginning of li. 17.

vi,17. There is no need to doubt that 2:1 could be treated sufficiently in the remainder of this line, although Elliger as always supposes an eighteenth line. The restoration of li. 17 given here (and it is *only* illustrative) shows that it is reasonable to suppose that 2:1 was treated much more briefly, as a mere background of prophetic prayer which was followed by God's command "to write." Cf. "Habakkuk's prayer" (3:1), Nebuchadnezzar's desire to know "what would be hereafter" (Dan. 2:29, 45), and Daniel's assurance (vs. 28): "But there is a God in heaven Who reveals mysteries, and He has made known to King Nebuchadnezzar what will happen in the last days." For *han-nihyôt* ("the things that will happen"), cf. my discussion in *The Dead Sea Manual of Discipline*, pp. 54 f. For the use of this participle for future events, see the following passages: Ben Sira 42:19, 25 (both in Hebrew and in Greek); 1Q S iii,15; xi,11; CDC ii,10 (2:8); 1Q *26* I: 1, 4; *27* I: i,3, 4.

vii,1 f. That "God told Habakkuk to write the things that are coming upon the last generation" interprets the command "Write the vision." (The dittograph of ʿ*al* was cancelled by two supralinear dots; so, Elliger and Martin, §24.). This definition of the "vision" is important for the entire book, since the superscription of 1:1 designates the whole as a "vision." In fact, all prophetic literature was viewed by the people of Qumrân as primarily concerned with the last days. See Eva Osswald, "Zur Hermeneutik des Habakuk-Kommentars," *ZAW*, LXVIII, 1956, pp. 243-256, esp. pp. 248-51.

"But the fullness of that time He did not make known to him" interprets the verb *bāʾēr* or *bāʿēr*. The former verb (according to Gesenius) meant "engrave" (both here and in Deut. 27:8); but the LXX and the Targum interpret all references (including Deut. 1:5) as meaning "make plain" or "explain." Such an interpretation would contradict the presuppositions of Qumrân; for if the meaning had been written with full clarity, the ingenious interpretations of Qumrân would be an imposition. Consequently, the text had to be made to say just the opposite. The interpretation may have punned *bāʾēr* as *bāʿēr*, through very little straining, since the letters ʾ*Ālef* and ʿ*Ayin* are often interchanged in Qumrân orthography. Jastrow (*Dictionary*, p. 182*b*) gives as one of the meanings of the *qal* stem "to be empty." The *piʿēl* stem of this could mean "make empty" (in Jastrow "to clear, remove"). Related to this verb is the √ בוז which means "to be empty, waste, uncultivated" (Jastrow, *Dictionary*, p. 148*b*). In the *hifʿîl*, it means "to let lie waste; to neglect." Since the *piʿēl* (the form in Habakkuk) may also be treated as a causative (or permissive), one assigns that meaning to this stem in interpreting the scroll. In the literary realm, "to leave empty or uncultivated" should mean something like "to leave vague or obscure." The *piʿēl* form of this root is *biyyēr*; but, by analogy with Aramaic, it could theoretically be written with ʾ*Ālef* rather than

Yôd as its middle radical. Hence it is not necessary to suppose that the Biblical text read *bā^cēr* in order to obtain the Qumrân meaning. In Jer. 10:14 the Hebrew text *niv^car kol ʾādām mid-da^cat* ("every man is stupid, without knowledge") is rendered according to one reading of the Targum *ʾittabbārû kol ʾamměmayyāʾ mil-lěmida^c ḥokhmāʾ* ("all peoples are emptied from [devoid of, too stupid for] knowing wisdom"). It is this emptiness (or vagueness) of the prophetic text, which the Teacher fills with meaning through his inspired interpretations.

"The fullness of that time" (*gěmar haq-qēṣ*) contrasts with the emptiness (or vagueness) of the last time as depicted in the literal words of Habakkuk. Originally, I translated this as "the final phase of the end" (*BASOR*, No. 112, p. 12). Not only had I not realized at that time that *qēṣ* means "time," but I was unduly influenced by the definition of *gāmār* given by Jastrow (*Dictionary*, p. 255b): "finishing, last touch, consummation." Dupont-Sommer's "la consommation du temps" and Fitzmyer's "consummation of the period" (*Essays*, p. 29) were no great improvements; for this knowledge was revealed to Habakkuk, though not fully. That which was not made known was the entire content to which the enigmatic words really relate, for they contain mysteries not disclosed. Knowledge of these was reserved for the Righteous Teacher. It was not mere chronological knowledge which Habakkuk lacked, such as when the consummation would come or how long the period of the last days would last (so B. J. Roberts, *BJRL*, March, 1952, p. 379); but it was an understanding of the specific events to which his words made veiled and enigmatic allusions. Eva Osswald (p. 249) has compared this expression with τελείωσις χρόνων (Test. Reuben 6:8), συντέλεια τῶν αἰώνων (Test. Levi 10:2; Heb. 9:26), συντέλεια τοῦ αἰῶνος (Matt. 13:40, 49; 24:3; 28:20); καιρὸς συντελείας (Test. Zebulon 9:9). The expression which would most fully correspond with these Greek phrases is *ʾaḥarît haq-qēṣ*, "the close of time" (4Q p Nah. iii,3 [¶10]; 4Q p Pss^b, frag. 1, li. 5). The importance of this last phrase is its correspondence with the more usual *ʾaḥarît hay-yāmîm*, for the abstract use of the concrete "days" has given way to the fully abstract term "time." Thus it would be possible to translate *gěmar haq-qēṣ* as "the fullness of time" (discarding the specificity of a particular time). This suggests that the real Greek equivalent is τὸ πλήρωμα τοῦ χρόνου (Gal. 4:4), where "the fullness of time" is something which *comes* when the Christ appears. Although *The Jerusalem Bible* translates this as "the appointed time," its footnote states: "Lit. 'fullness of time'; the phrase indicates how when the messianic age comes it will fill a need felt for centuries, rather than filling up a jug." Delcor (in a private communication) agrees with my interpretation.

The prophets did not know all that the messianic age would contain. According to the Babylonian Talmud (Yalk. ii, 368, Eccl. Rabbah i,8) only part of the future glory was shown to the prophets. According to Midr. Shoḥer Ṭob to Ps. 90:1, "With the exception of Moses and Isaiah, none of the prophets knew the content of their prophecies." Cf. also I Peter 1:10-12. Philo went even further. In Special Laws I, 65, he asserted that the prophets were so completely under the control of God that they did not even know what they were speaking.

vii,3. "For the sake of him who reads it." The verb *yārûṣ* was first omitted and then inserted between the lines by a different hand. The omission alters the sense of *lĕmaᶜan* from the purposive conjunction "that" to the preposition "for the sake of." Even though the first citation (vi,15) certainly reads the word *yārûṣ*, the omission here is probably not accidental. For a divergent second citation, cf. xii,6 f. The omission emphasizes "him who reads it" — the Righteous Teacher.

"That he who reads it *may run*." Although the verb is not original, it is at least implicit (since it occurs in the earlier quotation). The meaning of Habakkuk seems to have been "that any one who reads it aloud may 'run' as a prophetic messenger in so doing." This meaning of the verb is not to be abandoned in the scroll; but the reference is restricted to an especially gifted reader, whose running performs a special interpretative task. For Habakkuk there was a direct revelation from God; and for the Teacher there was an inspired interpretation as he read.

Yārûṣ, according to Silberman ("Riddle," pp. 344 f.), was understood to mean "that in the future he who reads his [Habakkuk's] words may shatter (=interpret) them." For this idea he appealed to the Babylonian Talmud (Sanhedrin 34a) where Jer. 23:29 is interpreted to mean " 'And like the hammer that breaketh the rock in pieces,' *id est*, just as the rock is split into many splinters, so also may one Biblical verse convey many teachings." Here the verb is פצץ; but by analogy Silberman argues the same meaning may have been applied to *yārûṣ* as derived from the √ רצץ ("crush, shatter"). He also saw a possible verbal play on the √ תרץ, which in Yebamot 11b-12a means "interpret." This does not exhaust the midrashic possibilities. One may compare also the √ רצה, which in the *hifᶜil* stem may mean "to arrange subjects for debate, to discourse" (Jastrow, *Dictionary*, p. 1493b). In order to give the root *rûṣ* the same meaning as the root *rāṣāh*, the interpreter would need to read *yārîṣ* (which through the ambiguity of the *Wāw* and the *Yôd* is quite possible). This in turn might have been punned as *yālîṣ* ("he may interpret"). In 4Q Pss[a] i,27 (¶7), the Teacher is called the *mēlîṣ daᶜat* ("the interpreter [or spokesman] of knowledge"). A verbal play on the letters רץ might also yield the suggestion for *rāz* ("mystery"), for the Teacher's interpretations divulge mysteries unknown to Habakkuk. Cf. the non-disclosure to Isaiah of the mystery concerning the time of the Messiah's coming in the Babylonian Talmud (Sanhedrin 94a), in which the Lord answers with a *bat qôl* from heaven with the words of Isa. 24:16 רזי לי רזי לי ("My secret is my own; my secret is my own.") to which the prophet responds: "Alas for me, alas for me! How long?" Silberman observes: "According to the commentator, it is such a secret as this the Moreh ha-Zedek does know."

vii,5 f. "All the mysteries of the words of His servants the prophets."

הנבאים (han-nĕvî'îm) is spelled defectively, so K. Stendahl (*School of St. Matthew*, p. 119, n. 1); but Habermann at first (*Edah*, p. 49) took this as *han-nibbā'îm* ("the prophesying ones"). The Righteous Teacher was to read and interpret as divine "runner" all the prophets, of whom Habakkuk is representative. Cf. ii,7-10; vii,1f. "All the mysteries of the words" is probably equivalent to *gĕmar haq-qēṣ* of vii,2. For the Teacher's role in relation to divine mysteries, see the following passages of 1Q H which may be by the Teacher himself, as translated by Menahem Mansoor, *The Thanksgiving Hymns*:

ii,13   Thou hast made me a banner to the righteous elect
and an interpreter of knowledge by wondrous secrets,
to test [the men] of truth,
and to try the lovers of correction.   (p.106)

iv,   And through me Thou hast illumined the faces of many
27ff. and Thou hast become mighty infinitely,
for Thou hast made known to me Thy wondrous mysteries,
and by Thy wondrous secret
Thou hast wrought mightily with me.   (p.128)

vii,   And Thy marvelous mysteries Thou hast made known to me,
27   and Thy lovingkindness (Thou hast made known) to a [wicked] man,
[and] Thy abundant mercies to him of distorted understanding.   (p.151)

Frg. Thou hast revealed the [won]der of Thy mysteries.
6,5

Note also the probable parallel in 4Q p Pss*ᵃ* iv,25 ff. (¶31). Concerning the first passage above, Mansoor comments:

> This is clearly an exceptional, supernatural, wondrous knowledge, of which the speaker boasts and of which not every member of the covenant does partake directly. It is probably a man in an eminent leading position, possibly the teacher of righteousness himself . . . but it is incumbent upon him to influence the community through this teaching. Only such a man could say about himself something as bold as in this passage.

Nothing in these passages limits these mysteries to "the mysteries of the words of God's servants the prophets." However, the claims made by the Teacher are consistent with those made for him in 1Q p Hab. Cf. also Matthew 13:35 in its use of Ps. 78:2 and Krister Stendahl, *op. cit.*, pp. 116f. Cf. also Luke 24:27.

In his interpretive role, the Righteous Teacher is like Daniel, who in the interpretation of Nebuchadnezzar's dream was called upon to disclose its hidden meaning which constituted a *rāz* (Dan. 2:18, 19, 27, 30, 47; 4:6[=4:9]), an Aramaic word of Persian origin. God is the "revealer of mysteries" (2:28f., 47) and has disclosed them to Daniel, so that he can make them known. According to I Enoch, mysteries are known to angels only in so far as God has revealed them (10:6f.; 16:3). The disobedient watchers revealed to men only the worthless mysteries, since the greater mysteries which concern the future history of salvation had not yet been disclosed. Noah explained his knowledge of the future (106:19), stating: "for I know the mysteries of the holy ones; for He, the Lord, has showed me and informed me, and I have read (them) in the heavenly tablets." On the "tablets" of Habakkuk the divine mysteries were not plainly written as in the "heavenly tablets." They required a gift to which Noah did not lay claim, the power of inspired exegesis (or, really, eisegesis). According to I Peter 1:10-12, the supreme revelation has not been made to angels in heaven, but to men on earth through the saving work of the Christ. Cf. Eph. 1:7-10. Otto Betz, pp. 82-88, stresses the historical character of the mysteries of Qumrân.

THE MIDRASH PESHER OF HABAKKUK

¶21 (vii,5-8)

כִּיא עוֹד חָזוֹן   5

לַמוֹעֵד יָפִיחַ לַקֵּץ וְלוֹא יְכַזֵּב   6

פִּשְׁרוֹ אֲשֶׁר יַאֲרִיךְ הַקֵּץ הָאַחֲרוֹן וְיֶתֶר עַל כּוּל־   7

אֲשֶׁר דִּבְּרוּ הַנְּבִיאִים כִּיא רָזֵי אֵל לְהַפְלֵה   8

5-6 (2:3a) For the vision is yet / for the appointed time;
   but at the end it will speak and will not disappoint. /
7   Its prophetic meaning is that the last time will be long in coming but
8   will excel all / that the prophets predicted, for the mysteries of God are
to be surpassingly wonderful.

¶21 *Exposition*

vii,5 f. For the textual variants, see *Text*, §§55-61.

vii,6f. "But at the end it will speak." So renders the King James Version of 1611 A.D. This suits admirably the commentary of 1Q p Hab. *Pûḥ* in connection with "lies" means "to utter." Cf. Prov. 6:19; 14:5, 25; 19:5, 9. So also, in connection with "truth" (Prov. 12:17). A considerable sapiential influence has been detected in the vocabulary of Habakkuk. (See Paul Humbert, *Problèmes du Livre d'Habacuc*, 1944.) Other alternatives are: "It will speak of the end;" "It hastens to the end." The last alternative (that of the Revised Standard Version) contradicts the preceding clause, which the RSV correctly paraphrases as "For still the vision *awaits* its time."

"And will not disappoint" (*wĕlô' yĕkhazzēv*). This is a better rendering than "and will not lie," which in the RSV could be easily misunderstood as meaning "will not lie still," since it is *hastening* on its way. However, for this passage one might render "will not deceive" (as Dupont-Sommer, *RHR*, p. 135; *Essene Writings*, p. 262). The verb may mean "It will not be falsified by events;" and this lies close to the idea "will not disappoint." Similarly, Job 41:1 is rendered by the RSV (41:9): "Behold, the hope of man is disappointed." *BDB* (p. 469b) ascribes the same meaning to Isa. 58:11b, which in the RSV is rendered:

> And you shall be like a watered garden,
> like a spring of water
> whose waters fail [*yĕkhazzĕvû*] not.

Qēṣ in Habakkuk meant "end," though not in an eschatological sense. To make the meaning "end" unambiguously clear, the commentary needed to say "the last *qēṣ*," for the word had come to mean simply "time." "Will be long in coming" — for this verb read either *ye'erôkh* (*qal* imperfect) or *ya'arîkh* (*hif'îl* imperfect), but preferably the latter. Generally the verb in the Old Testament means to "prolong, last (or make last) a long time." But in Isa. 48:9 and Prov. 19:11, it means "to postpone or to defer" anger. Cf. Ezek. 12:22. Jastrow (*Dictionary*, p. 121a) lists for this meaning Y. Taan. II, 65 bot., "When collecting debts (punishing) מאריך וגובה he is slow in collecting (punishes in long intervals, gives extensions)." An alternative rendering is that of Fitzmyer (*Essays*, p. 22): "The last period extends over and above all that the prophets said." Yet, the phrase "for God's mysteries will be surpassingly wonderful" shows that this cannot refer to the period of suffering in which the sect is now living — though Elliger would equate the term with "the time of wickedness" in v,7f. It is not even identical with the "last generation" (of ii,7 and vii,2); but it refers to the grand fulfillment which the last generation awaits (vii,12). If we interpret, "Will be long [or delayed] in coming" (with Talmon [*VT*, I, p. 35], van der Ploeg [*Bi Or*, VIII, p. 27], and Isaac Rabinowitz [*VT*, III, p. 179]), the protracted fulfillment does not necessarily relate simply to the history of deferred fulfillment during the Second Hebrew Commonwealth, but it includes within its scope the long time since the prophet spoke. Note particularly that this follows a pericope concerning the prophet Habakkuk himself, and that "the prophets" are referred to here also.

vii,7f. "But will excel all that the prophets predicted." C. Rabin (*VT*, V, pp. 159f.), standing among a long list of scholars who have interpreted this to mean "will be longer than the prophets told," has alone seen the problem with this interpretation; for it would seem to contradict the Biblical text "and will not lie." To assert that the prophets were right as to their hopes, but wrong as to their chronology, would be a surprisingly modern idea. Rabin (noting the internal contradictions) has transposed the interpretations of ¶21 and ¶22, except for the last statement of ¶22, in order to make the interpretations consistent with the Biblical verses cited. He translated Hab. 2:3*a*: "For the vision is yet for an appointed time, he shall be in despair for the end *to come*, but he shall not disappoint." "Despair," would not even suit vii,10f. with which he connects it; for the opposite is asserted of "the men of truth, . . . whose hands *do not slack* from the service of the truth." This no doubt implied that others did despair; but only these latter would be the persons one would expect to be discussed, if the interpretation found in vii,10f. referred originally to *yāfêah* taken in the sense suggested by Rabin. However, he was right in finding the idea of not disappointing in *lôʾ yĕkhazzēv*; for that is precisely what vii,7f. is dealing with. The verb "will not disappoint" is interpreted as litotes for "will more than satisfy."

The exact reading of ויתר is uncertain. One might think of the *qal* active participle *wĕ-yōtēr*, or of the *hifʿîl* imperfect *wĕ-yōtîr*; but against both these readings is the defective spelling, especially in the latter case. Yalon states that יתר על is common in Rabbinic Hebrew, and sometimes יותר occurs. Apparently the former would be vocalized as *yeter*, a noun, which is used adverbially in Dan. 8:9. The usage is even closer to the Jewish *kĕtûbbah* cited by P. Benoit in *DJD*, II, p. 253. The latter, however, would favor a *qal* active participle. Also a *piʿēl* (perfect *Wāw*-consecutive *wĕ-yittēr*), is attested in Rabbinic literature. In any case, the initial *Wāw* is needed and is to be translated "but." The reading יותר = יותיר (favored by Ratzaby, *JQR*, XLI, p. 157) is therefore to be excluded, unless one is to read ויתר, arguing that one letter has suffered haplography. The context favors the meaning "surpass in quality" (which Michel, p. 21, n. 7, notes as an alternative).

vii,8. "For the mysteries of God will be surpassingly wonderful." להפלה = להפלא. Martin, at §26, noted that hand A corrected an ʾĀlef to a Hē. For this spelling, see Pss. 17:7; 31:22. These "mysteries" are not just secret meanings; for they are to be marvellous in their own right, especially in the denouement of the messianic age. This clause reinforces the interpretation of the preceding as not referring to the duration of that time. The word often carries with it in the Old Testament the idea of a marvellous manifestation of divine activity (Deut. 28:59; Isa. 28:29; 29:14; Joel 2:26). Such marvels are beyond human comprehension (Zech 8:6; Deut. 17:8; 30:11; Ps. 118:24 [=118:23], 139:6,14).

For this reason the prophets could not perceive all the wonders of the age to come. Cf. I Pet. 1:10-12; but esp., I Cor. 2:8-10.

It is also possible that the meaning of we-yāfēah may be illumined by the infinitive lĕ-haflēh. In Job 10:16 (hitpāᶜēl) and probably also in Judges 13:19 (hifᶜîl), the meaning of the latter verb is to "show oneself marvellous." Cf. also II Chron. 2:8 (= 2:9) where the temple is "to be great and wonderful." If yāfēah could mean "to manifest itself," this would correlate very well. In fact, the Septuagint translates Hab. 2:3:

> διότι ἔτι ὅρασις εἰς καιρὸν
> καὶ ἀνατελεῖ εἰς πέρας
> καὶ οὐκ εἰς κενόν

> For the vision is for an appropriate time
> and at the end it will arise (or dawn?)
> and not in vain.

The Syriac rendered, "The end is coming." One may compare ᶜad še-yāfûah hayyôm (Cant. 2:17; 4:6), which was translated by the King James Version "until the day dawn," but was rendered by the LXX as ἕως οὗ διαπνεύσῃ ("until the day revive"). Actually, this expression refers to the evening, when very often in Palestine there are cool coastal breezes blowing in from the Mediterranean. This time of day is called rûah hay-yôm in Gen. 3:8. According to the usual reckoning, the day began in the evening; when "the day breathes," the new day is manifesting its life. We may conjecture, therefore, that in Habakkuk we should translate: "But at the end it will *manifest itself* and will not disappoint." If, however, we translate pûah as "speak," the meaning will be much the same; for the "speaking" of the vision "at the end" will be its manifestation in event. Although this has seemed obscure to modern interpreters, the idea was well expounded by the old classical commentary of Matthew Henry:

> At the end it shall speak and not lie. We shall not be disappointed of it, for it will come at
> the time appointed; nor shall we be disappointed in it, for it will fully answer our
> believing expectations. The promise may seem silent a great while, but at the end it shall
> speak; and therefore, *though it tarry* longer than we expected, yet we must continue
> *waiting for it*; being assured it will come, and willing to tarry until it does come.

Henry's interpretation is precisely in line with that of 1 Q p Hab. It may be that the translation of Reicke (*Handskrifterna*, p. 34) is to be understood similarly: "Its meaning is that even if the last time delays, it will surpass all that the prophets said; for God's secrets will be wonderful."

THE MIDRASH PESHER OF HABAKKUK

¶22 (vii,9-14)

9 אִם יִתְמַהְמַהּ חַכֵּה לוֹ כִּיא בוֹא יָבוֹא וְלוֹא

10 יְאַחֵר   פִּשְׁרוֹ עַל אַנְשֵׁי הָאֱמֶת

11 עוֹשֵׂי הַתּוֹרָה אֲשֶׁר לוֹא יִרְפּוּ יְדֵיהֶם מֵעֲבוֹדַת

12 הָאֱמֶת בְּהִמָּשֵׁךְ עֲלֵיהֶם הַקֵּץ הָאַחֲרוֹן כִּיא

13 כּוּל־קִיצֵי אֵל יָבוֹאוּ לְתכּוּנָם כַּאֲשֶׁר חֲקַק

14 לָהֶם בְּרָזֵי עָרְמָתוֹ

9 (2:3b)   If it seems slow, wait for it:
10   for it will surely come and will not / be late.
11   Its prophetic meaning concerns the men of truth, / the doers of the
12   Law, whose arms will not be relaxed from the service of / truth, when to
13   them the last time seems to be delayed; for / all God's times will come in
14   their measured sequence, just as He decreed / for them in the mysteries of
      His providence.

¶22 *Exposition*

vii,9f. On the textual variants, see *Text*, §§58-60.

vii,10f. "The men of truth, the doers of the Law." Cf. also "the men of truth" in 1Q H ii,14; xiv,2; 1Q M i,16. This expression could also mean, "men of faithfulness," or "faithful men" (as van der Ploeg, *Bi Or*, VIII, 7; and Reicke, *Handskrifterna*, p. 34 translate); but, at vii, 11f., ʾᵉ*met* is the object of service. Cf. (after Delcor, p. 32) the similar appelations "the sure house" (CDC iii,19 [=5:5]) and "house of faithfulness (or truth)" (1QS v,6; viii,9). Actually, "doers of the law" is epexegetical to "men of truth;" and "truth" is something one does in Qumrân terminology. Cf. 1QS i,5; v,3; viii,2; also Test. Reuben 6:9; Test. Benjamin 10:3. Therefore, "truth" is a synonym for *Tôrāh*, or Law. Cf. also the expression "sons of truth" or "sons of His [or Thy] truth" (1Q M xvii,8; 1Q S iv,5f.; 1Q H vii,29f.; ix,35; x,27; xi,11). God too has "His deeds of truth" (1Q S i,19; 1Q H i,30; 1Q M xiii,1, 2, 9; xiv,12, "his deeds of faithfulness"). Actually, "men of truth" is in this context a pregnant expression meaning both; for their unflagging labor shows that they are "faithful men" and this labor is in the "service of the truth." In 4Q p Pssᵃ iv,4f. (¶26), "the men of truth" are known for what they say. Cf. Test. Dan 5:2. One is to "love the truth" in Test. Dan 2:1; 6:8; to "follow the truth" in Test. Asher 6:1; to "keep the truth" in Test. Issacher 7:5.

"The doers of the Law" may stand in antithesis with those who only preach the Law. Cf. James 1:22-25; Matt. 7:21-27; Luke 6:46-49. In any case, the verb "do" (ᶜ*āśāh*) is constantly in use in the Society Manual (1Q S) to express the purpose of the Qumrân Community (i,2,5,6f.,16; v,3,20,22; viii,2,15; ix,13,15,20,23); and the members undergo annual examination as to their progress in "understanding and deeds" (v,21,23; vi,17f.). One of the numerous etymologies for Essene is "doer." This would be especially appropriate to explain ancient spellings of Essene with *Omicron* rather than *Epsilon* in the first syllable, as in Hippolytus, Philosophumena 9:4 (18*a*-28*a*). Cf. also Philo's derivation of the name from ὅσιος (Every Good Man is Free, ¶12), which (instead of being a translation of *ḥāsāʾ* = *ḥᵃsîd* ["pious or faithful"]) might be a verbal play on ᶜ*ōśēh*. In Rabbinic Hebrew, the plural of this is often ᶜ*ôśîn*, rather than ᶜ*ôśîm*. It is also possible that the different, though similar, spellings of the term Essene do not all reflect the same etymology. In any case, if one considers the designation "Doer" as one of the underlying Hebrew terms, it could be an abbreviation of "Doer of the Law." Such an appelation would find a close parallel in the Samaritan interpretation of their own name as meaning "those keeping the Law in truth," for which see Moses Gaster, *The Samaritans*, 1925, p. 5.

The expression "doer(s) of the Law" occurs also in vii,1; ix,2; xii,4. Cf. also 4Q p Pssᵃ ii,14, 22. In 4Q p Pssᵃ ii,5 (¶5), one finds the expression "the doers of His will" (ᶜ*ôśê rᵉṣônô*). The "Law" in 1Q p Hab is not to be thought of as restricted to the Pentateuch; for 1Q S viii,15f. joins the doing of the Law of Moses with performance of the teachings of the prophets.

vii,11f. "Whose arms (or hands) will not be relaxed from the service of truth." One should probably vocalize *yirpû* (*qal*), rather than *yarpû* (*hif⁻íl*); although the latter, which is employed by Habermann (*Megilloth*, p. 46), is also possible. The closest parallel seems to be 1Q S iv,9, in which one of the first steps toward Hell taken by the sons of darkness is "indolence of the hands in *the service of righteousness*." A dozen or so vices later, this issues in "ways of pollution in *the service of uncleanness*" (iv,10). According to 1Q S i,11, when one joined the sect he "volunteered [or dedicated himself] to His truth." "Truth" and "righteousness" are nearly synonymous. Cf. John 3:20-21; I John 1:6.

vii,12f. "When to them the last time *seems* to be delayed." This subjective connotation is suggested by ᶜ*alêhem* and is required by the next statement which gives assurance that all God's appointed times come on schedule. At this point, we truly see reflected the sense of delay in fulfilment which belonged to the last century and a half before Christ. This delay was only as men perceived it; for God's own purpose as announced in Scripture knows no delay beyond the decreed time. Even the Talmud deals with the subject of delayed fulfilment, for Rabbinic Judaism faced a crisis of non-fulfilment in connection with Bar Kokhba. Sanhedrin 96*a* cites Habakkuk 2:3 in dealing with this problem.

vii,13f. "All God's times will come in their measured sequence." This verse was at first (*BASOR*, no. 112, p. 13 and n. 54 of p. 18) incapable of a correct understanding, since it contained two Hebrew words of unknown meaning. קיצי (or קיצו, as first read), does not refer to "summer fruit" (*qayiṣ*) despite the *Yôd* in it, but to *qēṣ* which appeared here in the unexpected sense of "time." Since the noun is of double ᶜ*Ayin* derivation, the vocalization is *qiṣṣē*, and the *Yôd* stands for *Ḥireq*; but this spelling is found only here. The noun *tikkûn* was previously unknown and an attempt was made to relate it to the noun *tĕkûnah* of Job 23:3, and the meaning "storehouse" was proposed as appropriate for "summer fruit." These mistakes were soon corrected (*BASOR*, 114, p. 10; 116, p. 15). The only important question is whether this noun is to be derived from the √תכן in the sense of "regulate" or in the sense of "measure." (See M. Z. Kaddari, in *RQ*, No. 18, 1965, pp. 219-24.) Within the Qumrân Community each man had his assigned place, but it was also the measure of his rank. The word seems even to be used in the sense of ordinance or regulation; for *tikkûn* in 1Q S ix,12 is closely parallel to CDC xii,21 (=15:2), where *mišpāṭ* is employed instead. (On "Measure" see II Esdras 4:36f. On the measure of time, see S.B. Frost, "Apocalyptic and History," in *The Bible and Modern Scholarship*, pp. 98-113.) However, in 1Q S ix,12,18, the word is employed with ᶜ*ēt* ("time"); and in other contexts it has an astronomical meaning (1Q S x,5; 1Q M vi,12f.; 1Q H xii, 8). Thus the proper calculation of the holy seasons is bound up with the use of this word. Here, however, the "times of God" are not calendric, but those of divine providence.

Doubtless the basic meaning is that of measurement, which is all-important both for calendar and for eschatology.

vii,13f. "Just as He decreed for them in the mysteries of His providence." "All God's times" of intervention into human affairs were foreordained and there has never been any deviation from the divine time schedule. So also will it be in connection with the "last time." "In the mysteries of His providence" suggests that God has His own reasons for His schedule. Note that ᶜormah, which is generally translated "prudence," is best translated "providence" in the present context; for the latter word means not only "foresight," but also "skill or wisdom in management; prudence." See *Webster's New Twentieth Century Dictionary of the English Language*, 1968, p. 1450. Both "prudence" and "providence" go back to the Latin *providentia*. Such words as "prudence," "shrewdness," "cunning," and "astuteness" are properly human attributes. "Wisdom" would be appropriate here, but should not this rendition be reserved for *ḥoqmāh*?

THE MIDRASH PESHER OF HABAKKUK

¶ 23 (vii,14-17)

הִנֵּה עֻוּפְּלָה לוֹא יָוֹשְׁרָה 14

[נַפְשׁוֹ בּוֹ] פִּשְׁרוֹ אֲשֶׁר יִכָּפְלוּ עֲלֵיהֶם 15

[חֲטָאֵיהֶם וְלוֹא יֵֽ]רָצוּ בְּמִשְׁפָּטָם [כִּיא יְכַלֶּה] 16

[אֵל אֶת כָּול־הָרְשָׁעִים] 17

14 (2:4a) Behold, how heavy-burdened
15 (and) not acquitted is / [his soul within him]!
16 Its prophetic meaning is that / [their sins] *will be doubled upon
them;* and they will not be pardoned at the time of their jud[g]ment, [[for
17 / God *will destroy* all the wicked.]]

¶23 *Exposition*

vii,14f. See, *Text*, §§62-64. The Scroll presents us with two verbs in the *puᶜal*: ᶜ*uppĕlāh* and *yuššĕrāh*. The former is usually interpreted as a denominative derived from the noun ᶜ*ōfel* ("mound") and meaning "to be made into a mound, be swollen, puffed up." However, the ancient commentator assigned it the meaning "to be heaped upon." The latter verb in the context of Habakkuk should (in contrast with the "puffed up, or proud") mean "made level, humbled." For the original text and its meaning, see "The Composition of Habakkuk," pp. 264f. The commentary gives the verb quite a different sense. Cf. li. 16. Ps. 119:128 may be corrupt in the MT, but it provides a clue for the meaning of the intensive of *YŠR*:

על־כן כל־פקודי כל ישרתי כל־ארח שקר שנאתי

Therefore, I wholly approve the precepts of all [Thy law];
I hate every false way.

The reading of the first clause in 11QPssᵃ ix,1 is: "Therefore, I approve [Thy] precepts in all things." The King James Version translated the verb *yiššārtî* as "I esteem . . . to be right." From this understanding of the verb to that of "I approve" (suggested by the antithesis "I hate") is an easy step. This development of meaning could explain the LXX rendering of Hab. 2:4*a*: ἐὰν ὑποστείληται, οὐκ εὐδοκεῖ ἡ ψυχή μου ἐν αὐτῷ. The Hebrew *Vorlage* was probably *lôᵓ yiššerāh nafšî bô*, which may be translated: "My soul does not approve him." For the use of the preposition *bĕ*, cf. by analogy רצה and מאם. Since the *puᶜal* is the passive of the *piᶜēl* (both being intensives), the reading of 1Q p Hab could mean "not deemed right, not approved." However, the interpretation of the scroll is one of legal judgment rather than subjective judgment, indicating the sense "not acquitted."

By analogy, one may appeal to the *piᶜēl* of certain other words which may take the declarative sense: *ṭihar* (cleanse, declare clean), *timmēᵓ* (defile, pronounce unclean), *ṣiddēq* (pronounce righteous, vindicate, acquit). So, similarly, one may posit the meaning of "pronounce upright" ("acquit") for *yiššar*, the passive of which would be "not acquitted." Unexpectedly, this shows a history of the theme of justification being associated with Hab. 2:4 in pre-New Testament times!

vii,15f. "[Their sins] are doubled upon them." Silberman ("Riddle," p. 347) has rightly seen in the use of the √*KPL* a pun upon ᶜ*PL*; but more than this, I believe there to be the attribution of a special sense to ᶜ*uppĕlāh*, "to be heaped upon." The semantic equivalent in Greek is σεσωρευμένα ἁμαρτίαις ("heaped up [burdened, or overwhelmed] with sins"), II Tim. 3:6. Although the verb might be pointed as the active *yikhpĕlû* ("They double [their sins] upon themselves"), this would most probably be spelled *plene* in the scroll's orthography, and hence יכפולו (*yikhpôlû*). Since the *nif^cal* (*yikkāfĕlû*) is passive, it corresponds with the *pu^cal* of the Biblical text. For this reason, one should not introduce the subject at the beginning of li. 16, although Elliger (pp. 195f.) has suggested either הרשעים ("the wicked") or הבוגדים ("the traitors"); and van der Woude (*Bijbelcommentaren*, p. 35) reads the former. The subject could have been left indefinite, or the subject deferred until later, as below in the restoration of li. 17. The language adopted here is suggested by Isa. 40:2:

> Speak tenderly to Jerusalem
>   and cry out to her
> that her term of service is completed,
>   that her guilt is *pardoned* (*nirṣāh*),
> that she has received from the LORD's hand
>   *double* (*kiflayim*) for all her *sins* (*ḥaṭṭōtehā*).

Gaster (p. 267, n. 27) has noticed the allusion to this verse; and Habermann (*Megilloth*, p. 46) restores חטאתיהם, in close agreement with this passage; but the word is too long for the space. One might propose the briefer plural form חטואתם despite the feminine gender of the noun, for the masculine verb sometimes functioned as a common gender. The thought of the *pēšer* is developed in antithesis to Isa. 40:3. Note the close correspondence of *yērāṣû* with *nirṣāh*.

The usual translations of vii,15f. agree approximately with Dupont-Sommer (*Essene Writings*, p. 263): "The explanation of this is that [the wicked] will receive two-fold to themselves [and will be treated] with[out loving] - kindness at the time of their judgment." Vermès has done better with his rendering: "Interpreted, this means that [the wicked] shall double their guilt upon themselves [and it shall not be forgiven] when they are judged." Gaster's translation (p. 253), with its strong forensic element, comes the nearest to the interpretation given here: "This refers to the fact that they will pile up for themselves a double requital for their sins, and shall not be quit of judgment for them."

vii,16. "At the time of their judgment." This recognizes the forensic element in the interpretation of Hab. 2:4*a*. The note is eschatological, but it is not certain whether the judgment referred to is that which is to be administered by God's elect (v,4f. [¶16]), or that of God Himself on the Day of Judgment (xiii,2f. [¶35]). Cf. also the following phrases in the Hymns: "shall be condemned in judgment" (1Q H vii,12) and "Who will be righteous in Thy sight when he is judged?" (vii,28).

vii,17. "For God will destroy all the wicked" is supplied after xiii,3f. Cf. also x,3ff. (¶28). Nevertheless, this restoration is placed within double brackets, as too speculative to be of any value, except to suggest the general nature of the lost contents and to test the feasibility of limiting the column to seventeen lines.

THE MIDRASH PESHER OF HABAKKUK

¶24 (vii, 17-viii, 3)

[וְצַדִּיק בֶּאֱמוּנָתוֹ יִחְיֶה]   17
פִּשְׁרוֹ עַל כָּול־עוֹשֵׂי הַתּוֹרָה _בְּבֵית יְהוּדָה אֲשֶׁר   1
יַצִּילֵם אֵל מִבֵּית הַמִּשְׁפָּט בַּעֲבוּר עֲמָלָם וֶאֱמָנָתָם   2
בְּמוֹרֵה הַצֶּדֶק   3

vii,17 (2:4b)   [But the righteous through their steadfast faith will live.] /
viii,1   Its prophetic meaning concerns all the doers of the Law in the
2   house of Judah whom / God will deliver from the house of
                  damnation, because of their patient suffering and their steadfast
3   faith / in the Teacher of Right.

¶24 *Exposition*

vii,17. The *Vorlage* of the Septuagint was ᵓᵉmûnātî, "My faithfulness," instead of ᵓᵉmûnātô, "his faithfulness, or faith." The commentary implies the Massoretic reading. The translation "steadfast faith" affirms the meaning of *faith*, without surrendering the idea of *faithfulness*. The Biblical text of the first chapter is full of singulars which are collectives for the Chaldeans, which are naturally rendered as plurals in English. The present singulars ("The righteous [one] through his faith will live") are generic and are correctly interpreted by plurals in the commentary.

viii,1. "All the doers of the Law in the house of Judah" identifies the "righteous" of Hab. 2:4. That those destined to live are "doers of the Law" accords with Lev. 18:5; Ezek. 20:13,21; cf. Luke 10:28; Rom. 10:5; Gal. 3:12. They are declared to be "in the house of Judah," rather than "in the house of Israel," perhaps because in the history of Kings and Chronicles the house of Judah was shown to be more loyal (cf. also Hos. 1:7; 4:15; 12:1 [=11:12]), or by contradistinction from the Samaritans who claimed to be "the house of Israel," or again, to designate the party of the Teacher whose name may have been Judah. Certainly all true doers of the Law were believed to be within the sect alone. Del Medico (*Riddle*, p. 252) found in "the house of Judah" a name for the sect. Also C. Rabin (*VT*, V, p. 157) allowed that "house of Judah" may sometimes designate the sect, but not here. On the pronunciation of *BBYT*, see ᵓ*BYT* at xi, 6. One needs to consider here 4Q p Pssᵃ ii,13-15 (¶8), which interprets Ps. 37:12f. as follows:

> Its prophetic meaning concerns the violators of the covenant in the house of Judah, who will plot to destroy the doers of the Law who are in the Council of the Community; but God will not abandon them into their hand.

"The house of Judah" and "the Council of the Community" are not mutually exclusive, in as much as 1Q p Hab locates "the doers of the Law" as "*in* the house of Judah." A violent schism once ripped "the house of Judah" apart, so that the "violators of the covenant" were regarded as traitors (as in ¶7, above). In retrospect "the house of Judah" had once included all the Hasidim; but after the schism, the emerging "Council of the Community" regarded itself as the only true "house of Judah."

To this schism, CDC vii,10-14 (=9:3f.) and xiv,1 (=16:11) may allude in quoting Isa. 7:17 concerning "the day that Ephraim departed from Judah." Thus, according to 4Q p Nahum iii,3-5 (¶10), "Ephraim" is the party of "the expounders of smooth things." "When Judah's glory is revealed, the simple ones of Ephraim . . . will abandon their beguiling teachers and join Israel." Thus the sect constituted both the true Israel and the true Judah. Gaster's rendering of "the house of Judah" as "Jewry" (p. 253) is too inclusive.

viii,2. *Bêt ham-mišpāṭ,* "the house of judgment," probably means "house of damnation" in the sense of place of punishment in Sheol, as G. Lambert interpreted already in 1952 (p. 271). Cf. x,3 and the discussion of ¶28. However, Dupont-Sommer (*RHR*, p. 145) took this to mean "the house of Israel as guilty and damned." Yet, in *Essene Writings* (p. 263, n. 3), he interpreted "house of judgment" as "the Tribunal before which mankind will be judged at the end of time"—implicitly correlating it with "the Day of Judgment" (xii, 14; xiii, 2f.).

However, according to most scholars "the house of judgment" has been thought of as designating a religious party doomed to punishment with fire and brimstone. See Hastings' *Dictionary of the Bible* (rev. ed., p. 356*b*). The Sanhedrin could be referred to here, with the idea that they were persecutors of the righteous. So Barthélemy (*RB*, 1952, p. 210) and G. R. Driver (*Judean Scrolls*, p. 272). The antithesis with the preceding pericope, at vii,17, suggests that the meaning here is not merely that the righteous will escape their persecutors on the scene of present history, but that they will also escape their eschatological doom. Cf. the Wisdom of Solomon 5:15 whose promise "the righteous will live forever" stands immediately before a description of God's intervention against their foes.

"Because of their patient suffering" (*ba^cavûr ^camālām*) alludes to the sect's persecution. Apart from the literary allusions, the word *^cāmāl* would be of ambiguous meaning: "labor, painful toil, or suffering." Lambert (p. 294) renders "á cause de leur affliction." I have introduced the qualification "patient" in giving the interpretation the connotation of faithfulness which belongs both to the Biblical text and the interpretation of the commentary. J. van der Ploeg (*Bi Or*, VIII, p. 7) and J. Carmignac (*Textes*, p. 106) have translated with *peine*, which seems also to be ambiguous (meaning either "pain" or "labor"). Cf. the English "pains." Molin's *Mühe* (p. 14) might also capture this ambiguity. In *ZKTh*, 1952, p. 60, n. 18, Molin asks whether this may be a matter of "works and faith." Yalon (*KS*, XXVII, p. 174a) argues that only "good works" can explain the meaning of *^cāmāl*. A linking of works and faith would find an interesting parallel in James 2:14-26. K. Schubert (*ZKTh*, 1952, p. 22) interpreted 1Q p Hab to mean that justification by works is not enough, that "those loyal to the Torah will be saved from the judgment only if they put works and faith in the Teacher of Righteousness side by side." However, more probably *^cāmāl* does not refer here to works of the Law alone, but also to perseverance under persecution.

Note the influence of Deutero-Isaiah upon the interpretation of Hab. 2:4. The interpretation of 2:4*a* (discussed at vii,15 f.) denied that there would be any expiation for the sins of the wicked, despite the affirmation of Isa. 40:2 that temporal suffering can atone for sins. We are now prepared for the opposite statement with regard to the righteous: *their* suffering will atone. The word *^cāmāl* (as Dupont-Sommer believed) may allude to Isa. 53:11*a*, which in 1Q Isa^*a* and 1Q Isa^*b* reads: "Because of [or, after] his suffering of soul [*mē-^camal nafšô*] he will see light." In *Meaning*, pp. 226-233, I explored the meanings of the expression "will see light." The two meanings which seemed most relevant to Isa. 53:11 were "will experience deliverance" and "will live." Both of these ideas fit admirably here; for deliverance is explicitly referred to, and this in turn also interprets the verb "will live" of Hab. 2:4! The influence of the Servant Songs has already been noted in v,2 ff. (¶16). In 1Q S viii,3 f., the leaders (or founders) of the Community are "to expiate iniquity through practicing justice and through the anguish of the refining furnace."

viii,2f. "And their steadfast faith in the Teacher of Right." The defective spelling ואמנתם made possible Habermann's vocalization wa-ᵃmānātām. The noun ᵓᵃmānāh (ᶜEdah, p. 50; Megilloth, p. 46) occurs twice in the Old Testament: Neh. 10:1 (= 9:38) and 11:23. In the former verse it means "a pledge of faith" (RSV, "firm covenant"); and in the latter, "support, fixed provision." The first of these meanings seems to be well supported in Rabbinic usage, and Jastrow (Dictionary, p. 78) lists also the definition "faith in Providence." Thus, whichever reading one may prefer, the question still arises whether the word means faith, or faithfulness. Carmignac (Christ and the Teacher, p. 67) reads the same as Habermann, but notes that the "meaning is hard to determine precisely. One hesitates between belief, confidence, assurance." But all these are shaded synonyms, none of which stresses faithfulness. But in the French (Textes, pp. 106 f.) he translated "leur fidélité."

The meaning of "faithfulness" was adopted by van der Ploeg (Bi Or, VIII, p. 7), Delcor (p. 25), Molin (p. 14), Reicke (Handskrifterna, p. 35), Bardtke (p. 128), Raymond E. Brown (CBQ, XVII, 1955, p. 417, n. 54), Sherman Johnson (HThR, XLVIII, 1955, p. 165), van der Woude (Bijbelcommentaren, pp. 35, 43), Carmignac (Textes, p. 106), Lohse, and J. G. Harris (p. 39). Johnson, however, allowed for the meaning "faith," which would give an important background for the use of the passage with reference to the Christ in the New Testament. That the reference is to faith is supported by Dupont-Sommer, Barthélemy, del Medico, Kurt Schubert, and Millar Burrows (p. 335). Taking issue with Delcor, Barthélemy has argued that foi (faith) was better than fidélité (faithfulness) for the following reasons: (1) The Teacher is considered an inspired exegete in whose interpretations one must believe (ii,6). (2) The use of the preposition B suggests "faith in," rather than "faithfulness to." However, in ¶7 the meaning of the verb האמין (in each case complimented with ב) seems to shift from the sense "being faithful to" (ii,4) to "believing in" (ii,6), and yet the former meaning suits better at ii,14. In ii,2, the enemies of the sect are charged with lack of faith in the Teacher. Because both faith and faithfulness are required for the endurance of persecution, I have translated "because of their steadfast faith." Cf. Gerhard von Rad, Old Testament Theology, II, 1965, p. 267, concerning Hab. 2:4: "It speaks of the promise that accrues to perseverance in faith on the part of the righteous."

It is because of the nature of the faith in the Righteous Teacher that we here translate "Teacher of Right;" for faith in him is not due to his personal righteousness, but to rightness of this teaching, which if followed will bring salvation. At this point, Gaster's rendering "who teaches the Law aright" is about right. One may compare II Chron. 20:20: "Believe in the LORD your God, and you will be established; believe His prophets, and you will succeed." Cf. Exod. 19:9, which concerns believing in Moses. Like the prophets, the Qumrân Teacher interprets God's will, and one believes him while trusting in the LORD alone for salvation.

All this contrasts sharply with faith in Christ as a redemptive figure, as G. Jeremias has strongly insisted in *Der Lehrer der Gerechtigkeit*, pp. 145 f. See also W. Grundmann in *RQ*, No. 2, 1960, pp. 237ff.; Brownlee, "Habakkuk," Hastings' *Dictionary of the Bible* (rev. ed., 1963), p. 356*b*; *Meaning*, pp. 126f. A contrast between faith and works was impossible at Qumrân, for faith itself was a meritorious work. See R. Bergmeier in *RQ*, No. 22, 1967, pp. 253 ff.; Matthew Black, *The Scrolls and Christian Origins*, 1961, pp. 160 f.

That the idea of faith is not to be excluded from the passage is reinforced by the Targum which seems to represent a stage of interpretation behind 1Q p Hab: "Behold, the wicked say in their heart all these things are not [to be]; but the righteous, because of their truth (קושטהון), shall survive." Since the "truth" of the righteous stands in antithesis to the denial of the prophetic message on the part of the wicked, it seems probable that the Targum interprets *ᵓemûnāh* as an affirmation of the prophetic message. The next development beyond faith in the prophets would be faith in the inspired interpreter of the prophets. This is the stage of understanding reached by 1Q p Hab. After this, the next development in the evolution of interpretation would be faith in the one who fulfils all prophecy. This last stage is represented by the New Testament.

Although the perspective of 1Q p Hab is that of a works-righteousness, as is also the assumed position of much of 1Q S, Qumrân also knew the concept of the need for an infused righteousness from God. See esp. 1Q S xi,14 f.; 1Q H iv,25-37; xi,30 f. and my discussions in *BASOR*, No. 121 (Feb., 1951), pp. 12 f., also "Anthropology and Soteriology in the Dead Sea Scrolls and in the New Testament," pp. 221-25. This gift of righteousness as a divine force for good is solely one of election and it appears isolated in Qumrân thought from all connection with righteousness as merit and with salvation through obedient faith in the Righteous Teacher. Neither is it in any way connected with the messianic hope. The implicit contradiction between these opposite poles of Qumrân thought remained, never being resolved except by Paul who identified God's righteousness with Jesus the Christ and who made salvation wholly a matter of grace by faith in him. The Scriptures were filled with exhortations to obey the Law that one may live (Lev. 18:5; Deut. 4:10; 12:1; Ezek. 20:11, 13, 21; Neh. 9:29; cf. Luke 10:28). Paul, who was as much concerned with the heart as with outward performance, found the idea of perfect obedience an impossible one. He, therefore, advanced the thought of a righteousness bestowed as God's gift through faith in the Christ (Rom. 1:16f.; 3:19-30; 10:4-10; Gal. 3:6-14). Nothing at Qumrân hints of this theological "breakthrough."

Kurt Schubert asserted that both works and faith stand side by side here as the way of salvation. By works, Schubert understood "laboring in the Torah in the Pharisaic sense." Such works, however, were not sufficient, faith in the Teacher being necessary as well. In the light of the above discussion it seems that "good works" as such do not enter the picture at all, but only a steadfast faith which makes possible the endurance of suffering. It is not wholly clear whether the righteous will be justified through their own suffering, or also through faith in their persecuted Teacher. Such faith in any case would involve faithfulness to the Law as the Teacher expounded it; for it is precisely the "doers of the Law" who are the righteous. So argues Carmignac (*Christ and the Teacher*, pp. 99f.), who cites CDC xx,27-34 (9:50-54). Likewise in *Textes*, p. 107, he stresses: "The context which speaks of the practice of the Law indicates sufficiently that it is a question of fidelity to the directives of the Teacher of Righteousness on the observation of this Law."

Significantly, in 1Q p Hab, "the doers of the Law" would seem (from implications above) to have sins to be atoned for through suffering — this also being an aspect of righteousness through obedience. This may stand related to the theme of refining through suffering (Dan. 11:35; 12:10; 1Q S viii,3f., 9½). See *BASOR*, No. 132 (Dec., 1953), pp. 12 ff., No. 135 (Oct., 1954), pp. 34f.; *Meaning*, pp. 211f.; "Whence John," pp. 174-76 (but remove all dots under the *h*'s, which were inserted by the publisher!); H. L. Ginsberg, "The Oldest Interpretation of the Suffering Servant," *VT*, III, 1953, pp. 400-04; Delcor, *Le Livre de Daniel*, p. 256.

THE MIDRASH PESHER OF HABAKKUK

¶ 25 (viii, 3-13)

וְאַף כִּיא הוֹן יַבְגִּיד גֶּבֶר יָהִיר וְלוֹא 3

יִנְוֶה אֲשֶׁר הִרְחִיב כִּשְׁאוֹל נַפְשׁוֹ וְהוּא כַמָּוֶת לוֹא יִשְׂבָּע 4

וַיֵּאַסְפוּ אֵלָו כּוֹל־הַגּוֹיִם וַיִּקְבְּצוּ אֵלָו כּוֹל־הָעַמִּים 5

הֲלוֹא כוֹלָם מָשָׁל עָלָיו יִשָּׂאוּ וּמְלִיצֵי חִידוֹת לוֹ 6

וְיוֹמְרוּ הוֹי הַמַּרְבֶּה וְלוֹא לוֹ עַד מָתַי יַכְבִּיד עָלָו 7

עַבְטִט   פִּשְׁרוֹ עַל הַכּוֹהֵן הָרָשָׁע אֲשֶׁר 8

נִקְרָא עַל שֵׁם הָאֱמֶת בִּתְחִלַּת עוֹמְדוֹ וְכַאֲשֶׁר מָשַׁל 9

בְּיִשְׂרָאֵל רָם לִבּוֹ וַיַּעֲזוֹב אֶת אֵל וַ[יִּ]בְגּוֹד בַּחוֹקִים בַּעֲבוּר 10

הוֹן וַיִּגְזוֹל וַיִּקְבּוֹץ הוֹן אַנְשֵׁי חָמָס אֲשֶׁר מָרְדוּ בָאֵל 11

וְהוֹן עַמִּים לָקַח לוֹסִיף עָלָיו עֲוֹן אַשְׁמָה וְדַרְכֵי 12

תּ[וֹעֵ]בוֹת פָּעַל בְּכוֹל־נִדַּת טֻמְאָה 13

3 (2:5) Wealth, alas, will make a traitor
    of the man in high office,

4   and he will not / stay home in the fold;
For it has made his soul feel big as Sheol;
    and he, like death, cannot be sated. /

5 All nations have been gathered to him,
    and all peoples have been amassed to him. /

6 (2:6) Will they not all intone a burden concerning him?
    and its composers taunt him with riddles /

7   as they sing:
"Alas for him who heaps up what is *not his own*
    (*nor his to own*)!

8 How long will he bring over himself / the *glory*
    clouds (nay, *gory clods*) of dirt?"

9   Its prophetic meaning concerns the Wicked Priest who / was
considered a member of the Truth Party (and called by the NAME

10 of Truth) at the beginning of his rule; but while he bore rule / over
Israel, his heart became haughty and he abandoned God and

11 became a traitor to the statutes because of / wealth; and he
robbed and amassed the wealth of the apostates who had rebelled

12 against God; / and the wealth of the peoples he took, so as to
increase the guilt of transgression upon himself; and /

13 a[bom]inable *behavior* he committed, with every kind of defiling
impurity.

131

¶25 *Exposition*

viii,3-8 (Hab. 2:5-6). For the variants, see *Text*, §§ 65-84; "The Composition of Habakkuk," pp. 259, 264-266.

viii,3. The Scroll reads *hôn* (wealth) where the MT reads *hay-yayin* (wine). "Wealth" makes more sense in the Biblical context than "wine," and hence this reading was adopted in the Jerusalem Bible and the New American Bible. However, the original reading is probably that implied by the Septuagint and Syriac renderings, namely, *hawwān* or *hayyān*, meaning "presumptuous;" and this is followed by the New English Bible. Indeed the word might be so read in 1Q p Hab, but the commentary interprets the word as "wealth." For a study of the word in connection with Hab. 2:4-5, see *JBL*, LXXXII (1963), pp. 323f.

Either we must read *yavgîd* ("make a traitor") or give a comparable meaning to *yivgôd* (which, after *DSS*, I; Habermann [*ᶜEdah*, p. 50; *Megilloth*, p. 46], Elliger and Lohse, might also be read), if we are to see the relationship of the Biblical quotation to the following interpretation. The latter reading is the usual understanding of the text; but see the discussion in *Text*, §67, pp. 46, 48f. Delcor's translation (p. 25), "la richesse *conduira à la trahison* l'homme orgueilleux," supports the reading of the *hifᶜîl*, which unfortunately is unattested elsewhere. The translations of Dupont-Sommer (*RHR*, p. 136), Lambert and del Medico (*Riddle*, p. 252) are similar. Contrast Michel's rendering (p. 13) of the verb as *trahira*.

Gever yāhîr in the original context probably means the "arrogant man;" but Driver (*Judaean Scrolls*, p. 128) translates "a wealthy man (?)." Jastrow, *Dictionary*, p. 567a, however, attests the post-Biblical meaning of "aristocratic." The rendering "in high office" is nearly this, and it fits the interpretation which follows. If, however, by "aristocratic" one means one who is high born, this would be possible for any one of the descendants and successors of Simon, who headed a new dynasty of rulers.

viii,4. The verb *yinweh* of Hab. 2:5 is a *hapax legomenon*, generally explained as a denominative verb derived from the noun *nāweh* (abode, or sheepfold). The idea would then be "to remain in the fold," or, losing the denominative character, "to abide, to remain," as most have translated. The Targum interpreted it to mean "survive"—employing the same verb (the *ᵓithpaᶜēl* of *qûm*) to translate also *yihyeh* of Hab. 2:4; and indeed it seems best to interpret the two verbs in the original context as synonyms. The denominative meaning would be possible, however, if the wicked party were Judean rather than a foreign foe. In that case the fold would be the Holy Land and the thought would be similar to Ezek. 20:37f. If, however, the *nāweh* be thought of as the temple (as in II Sam. 15:25), then the charge of not abiding in the fold in 1Q p Hab might mean a turning away from service at the temple to engage in worldly activity. This is quite appropriate to the present passage. Dupont-Sommer (*Essene Writings*, p. 263) has given the word a moral sense, "he does not remain (faithful)." Similar would be the notion, "he does not remain (an adherent of the truth)," or "remain (close to God)." The fulsome rendering "stay home in the fold" is intended to allow for various applications. Cf. the King James Version, "neither keepeth at home." Certain renderings like that of Lambert (p. 294) "et il ne s'arrête pas" and Maier (I, p. 153) "nicht kommt er zur Ruhe" probably misread the verb as *yānûaḥ*.

viii,4. "For it has made his soul feel big as Sheol." In context this means rather, "who enlarged his appetite as Sheol." Instead of "appetite," a number of scholars interpret it as "throat." In either case Sheol (and its parallel, "death") is personified as an insatiable beast. In the scroll, however, one must notice the correlation with li. 10, "his heart became haughty." From this we infer that the *nefeš* is interpreted as "soul" = "heart," and not as "appetite" (or "throat"). Thus the enlargement of the *nefeš* is construed as a figure for pride. This interpretation may derive from an equation of *rĕḥav lēv[āv]* (Ps. 101:5; Prov. 21:4) with *rĕḥav nefeš* (Prov. 28:25), both of which are translated as "proud heart" in the King James Version. The synonymity is supported also by Hans-Joachim Kraus, *Psalmen*, Vol. II, p. 101. R. B. Y. Scott in *Proverbs*, p. 167, suggests as alternatives to "greedy" at Prov. 28:25, "ambitious," "arrogant." Sheol is a better figure for insatiableness than for pride; but in the present context it could simply express the superlative. See D. Winton Thomas, in *VT*, III (1953), pp. 222 ff.

viii,6. "Will not they all intone a burden concerning him?" "Burden" translates *māšāl*, which is punned as "bore rule" at li. 9. Although the Hebrew roots may be distinct (see excursus at end of this pericope), English "burden" and "bore" are related in meaning. It would be possible to read *mōšel* in the Biblical text and thus obtain the forced sense: "Will they not all, because of him, endure a burdensome government?" All this seems unnecessary, however, for the pun can be indicated without changing the sense of the Biblical verse. The verb *yiśśĕ°û* means to lift the voice in solemn utterance. The *māšāl* to be so uttered is a taunt song; thus "intone" is an exactly appropriate rendering. "Burden" also is known to the English Bible reader as "message" or "oracle" (as in the superscription to Habakkuk) where it translates *maśśā°*, which is cognate with the verb *nāśśā°* employed here. As an English word, in the area of music, "burden" can mean "the refrain or chorus of a song." Thus, "burden" (though inexact) is not wholly inappropriate for a taunt song.

"And *its composers* taunt him with riddles" or "And *his taunters* (intone) riddles concerning him." Although one might read *û-mĕlîṣê* ("and interpreters of [riddles]," as read in the first transcription and by Habermann, Elliger, and Lohse, and implied by the rendering of Delcor ("des interprètes d'enigmes"), we follow here the reading *û-mĕlîṣāw* of Segert, §99. Notice the defective spelling of °*ēlāw*, twice, in the preceding line. The new proposal made here is that the antecedent of the pronominal suffix may be the noun *māšāl*. The apparent root meaning of the verb underlying the participle seems to be *to speak fluently, or loquaciously.* Only secondarily did it come to mean "to scoff." Thus the participle would seem to have the basic meaning of "spokesman," in the various senses of "interpreter" (Gen. 42:23), "intercessor" (Job 33:23), "ambassador" (II Chron. 32:31), "prophet" (Isa. 43:27), and "scoffer" (Job 16:20). The conjectured meaning "composers" for the present context has in mind oral composition and rendition. "Its interpreters" in English would suggest the interpreters of the Qumrân Community, which are nowhere in view in the interpretation of the *pešer*. Elsewhere the role of spokesman is related to "knowledge" (1Q H ii,13; 4Q p Pss i,27 [¶7]), "error" (1Q H ii, 14), "lies" (1Q H ii,31; iv, 9-10), and "deceit" (1Q H iv,7). With such abstract nouns in the genitive, one concludes that the *māšāl* is the probable antecedent of "*its* composers."

The "riddles" here, as interpreted in the Scroll, are meanings concealed under the form of sarcastic puns.

viii,7 f. In Hab. 2:6*b*, the first statement may be interpreted either as "heaps up what is not his," or as "heaps up what is not for him." In the latter case, this means that the plunderer will in the end need to abandon his wealth to others who invade his territory; or in the context of the Scroll passage, it "is not for him to own" because according to the rules of holy war such loot should be consecrated to God under a ban of destruction. Cf. below at li. 12. The punning ambiguities are expressed in the translation by "his own," and "his to own."

The second statement among the "riddles" may be translated three ways. The first meaning, probably that of the Bible, is "will he make heavy upon himself pledges" (taken as security for debts). By dividing the word ꜥ*avṭiṭ* (or ꜥ*avṭēṭ* in defective spelling?) into two words ꜥ*āv ṭîṭ* (for which also there is manuscript and versional evidence) we obtain the second and third meanings: (2) "will he make glorious over himself a cloud of mud," and (3) "will he make heavy upon himself a cloud [or, thickness?] of mud." Of these three meanings, only the third is explicitly developed in the commentary. The second, however, as a sarcastic attack upon the Priest's pride was probably not entirely out of view. Instead of having the glory cloud of the Shekinah rest upon him, he was weighed down with a cloud (or mass) of mud (=sin and impurity). On sin being *heavy*, note Gen. 18:20 ("very grave" RSV). The English translation has tried to bring out the last two meanings by punning "glory clouds" as "gory clods." The literal "mud" had to be abandoned for "dirt" because "clods" does not go well with "mud."

viii,9. "Called by the name of truth" is not simply an ambiguous expression, but a pregnant expression, which means at the least three things in the present context:

(1) "Called by the NAME of Truth," i.e., called by the name of Yahweh, or of God Himself. This interpretation was proposed by Dupont-Sommer (*RHR*, p. 145) to indicate that the priest was regarded as a true priest of Yahweh. Del Medico (*Riddle*, pp. 252f.), "who gave himself the Name of the Truthful One," claimed this as "an epithet often used to designate God." 4Q Sᵉ

reads *derekh hā-ʾemet* for "the way of Yahweh" in citing Isa. 40:3 (=1Q S viii, 13). In the Old Testament those who are called by Yahweh's name are claimed by Him as His own. In connection with the high priest, this allusion would be particularly apt, in view of the inscription "Holy to Yahweh" (Ex. 28:36). The title "priest of God Most High" (Gen. 14:18) was reintroduced in Hasmonean times. However, it is not likely that a theophorous personal name was meant, as Del Medico has suggested—for there was nothing distinctive of the priesthood in this. An allusion to the priest being called by God's NAME is the fitting background for the later statement that "he abandoned God."

(2) "Had a name for being true, or faithful." This interpretation, proposed by van der Ploeg (*Bi Or*, VIII, p. 8), has been followed by van't Land and van der Woude (*Bijbelcommentaren*, p. 35). Frank Cross translates "was called by a trustworthy name." Applying the passage to Simon, he says: "To be called by a 'trustworthy name' may mean no more than Simon had a good reputation." (*Ancient Library*, p. 142, n. 142) Similarly, Theodor Gaster (p. 253) translated "enjoyed a reputation for truth." To entertain this meaning in addition to no. 1 is not gratuitous, for it provides a fitting background for the antithetical statement that the Wicked Priest "became a traitor." Furthermore, it may be reinforced by appealing to Ex. 18:21, which enumerates the qualifications of those who administer the Law of Moses. These are: (a) *ʾanšê ḥayil* ("able men"). (b) *yirʾê ʾelôhîm* ("fearers of God"), (c) *ʾanšê ʾemet* ("faithful men"), (d) *śōnĕʾê bāṣaʿ* ("haters of unjust gain"). There is no question about the priest here being an "able man;" but in the commentary he is disqualified on the grounds of all the others. That "he had a name for being faithful" (the thirs attribute) is given prominence because of its importance as an antithesis to *bāgad* ("was a traitor").

(3) "Was considered a member of the Truth party," or "Was reckoned among the adherents of the truth." This presses beyond no. 2 through recognition of the fact that *anšê hā-ʾemet* in Qumrân usage refers not merely to "faithful men," but to the religious party described at vii,10 as "the men [or adherents] of the truth, the doers of the Law, whose arms will not be relaxed from the service of the truth." The word *ʾemet* is a term fraught with great theological import at Qumrân and is not simply to be resolved into the concept of "faithfulness," although that is included. The sect regarded itself to be "a house of truth in Israel," and its members to be "men of truth," and "sons of truth." Their function was to be "witnesses of truth;" and truth was to be the object of their service. According to this interpretation, the priest was recognized at first as belonging to "the adherents of truth" but later defected by "being a traitor to the statutes." This explanation of Lambert (p. 294, n. 121) and Geza Vermès (*ETL*, 1951, p. 75, n. 50) accords well with the Biblical statement "he did not remain in the fold" (viii,3f.). Although this "fold" may have been understood metaphorically of God Himself (as in Jer. 50:7), it was hardly limited to this, since the figure of the "fold" is employed elsewhere for the true society into which God's people are to be gathered (Jer. 23:3; Ezek.

34:14. Cf. John 10:16). God and people belong together as shepherd and flock. The Wicked Priest abandoned both God and His people.

The paraphrastic rendering "reckoned among" (= "considered a member of") calls for validation. Note the following passages:

> Gen. 48:6. "And the offspring born to you after them [Ephraim and Manasseh] shall be yours; they shall be *called by the name of their brothers* in their inheritance." (RSV) ". . . *reckoned as belonging to* these two brothers." (Moffatt)

> I Chron. 23:14. "As for Moses, the man of God, his sons shall be called according to the tribe of Levi." (So literally). ". . . his sons were *reckoned among* the clan of Levi." (Moffatt)

The only difference between this usage and that of 1Q p Hab is that we are not concerned with tribal connection, but with religious affiliation.

Yet, one caution is needed. Since in this passage the "adherents of the truth" antedate the rift between the Wicked Priest and the sect, we should not equate truth's adherents at this stage of history with Essenes. Most probably they are the Hasidim, whose reputation as defenders of the truth was later claimed by the Essenes, who thought of themselves as their true successors.

The above three meanings seem quite sufficient to exhaust the true import of "called by the name of the truth." However, other interpretations have been given and are of interest for the history of scholarly exegesis of this document. They are as follows:

(4) "Summoned against the name [or cause] of truth." This first translation recognized the importance of "truth" to the sect, but saw in this expression just another instance of bad things to be said about the Wicked Priest. This easy assumption was followed by Schoeps (*ZRG*, [1951], p. 329). The interpretation would fit admirably the pre-Hasmonean priests Jason, Menelaus, and Alcimus; but it was erroneous, and with its passing from the scene of serious consideration, the spectre of these Hellenizing priests disappears from any probable connection with the Wicked Priest. *Niqrāᵓ ᶜal* can indeed mean "summoned against" (as in Isa. 31:4); but the phrase is not followed by *šēm*.

(5) "Called in the cause of truth" was Segal's correction (*JBL*, LXX [1951], p. 137). He rightly objected that ᶜal *šēm* in Rabbinic idiom means "for the cause of," not "against the cause of." According to him, "the truth" is the true religion as in nos. 3 and 4. In fact, what he meant may be the same as no. 3. However, the word "called" here seems to have a connotation like "summoned." Instead of being "summoned" by the Seleucids for an unholy cause, he was "called" by God, or by his people, to take up the cause of truth.

(6) "Called by the right title." According to this understanding, the priest was called Chief Priest, or high Priest, and not King. J. Carmignac (*Textes*, p. 107), who lists this alternative (under the translation *nom de vérité*), calls attention to Hyrcanus II who was first of all only high priest, but was later secular ruler.

(7) "Called by the true title." According to this rendering, one could mean "called *kôhen hā-rôʾš* (chief priest), rather than *hak-kôhēn hā-rāšāᶜ* (wicked priest)." That the latter is a perversion of the former on the part of those who denied the legitimacy of the Wicked Priest is clear; but what compelling reason is there to relate this sarcastic surrogate with this particular passage? This interpretation was proposed by Elliger under the translation *"der berufen wurde unter dem rechten Namen."*

(8) "Called by his real name." This would seem to be an alternative suggested by Carmignac under the translation *"s'est appelé du nom véritable;"* for he refers to numerous cases of name substitutions. In contrast with no. 7, this would be a personal name, rather than a title substitution.

(9) "Called by a trustworthy name." According to this view the priest's personal name suggested one who could be counted upon as faithful. As proposed by Delcor (p. 25), this interpretation was applied to Alexander Jannaeus, who was called first of all Jonathan (*Yĕhônātān*) and later Jannaeus (*Yannai*). The name recalled the Biblical Jonathan, who was David's loyal friend, and so it represented faithfulness (p. 64). This is the preferred understanding of Carmignac, whose rendering for this is *nom de fidélité* (the same as that of Delcor). Cross, who suggests this meaning in conjunction with no. 2, above, thinks of Simon, whose name reminded one of the famous Simon II who was eulogized by Ben Sira (Sirach 50:1-21), and/or of Simon the Just. (On this priest, see Ralph Marcus, "The Date of the High Priest Simon the Just," in Josephus' *Jewish Antiquities*, Vol. VII, Appendix B, pp. 732ff.). In the case of Simon, however, what evidence is there that he was ever called anything else? If there is any truth in this position, the allusion may rather be to his being called *ḥᵃsîd* (Hasidean), which certainly would be a "trustworthy name;" but by turning from a personal name to a religious designation, we would be returning to no. 3 above.

viii,9. "At the beginning of his rule" (*bithillat ᶜomdô*). The second word is probably the infinitive employed as a noun. Habermann and Lohse vocalize it as *ᶜômĕdô*, as if we had here the noun *ᶜōmed* listed in Rabbinic dictionaries. *Wāw* for the *Qāmeṣ hāṭûf* (as in the infinitive) is a commonplace in Scroll literature. Since the verb *ᶜāmad* commonly means "to rise to power, to take office," one might render this as "at the beginning of his accession." However, accessions are not normally thought of as being a process, with a period called the beginning. What the passage refers to is the first period of his rule. Thus van der Ploeg interpreted correctly *"au commencement de son office,"* as also del Medico "at the beginning of his ministry," and Bardtke (p. 128) "at the beginning of his work." Some have interpreted this to mean "when he first took office as chief priest," and indeed the verb is attested in connection with the priestly office (I Kings 12:32; II Chron. 11:15; Ezra 2:63; Neh. 7:65); but it is used equally of kings (Dan. 8:23; 11:2-4, 7). The verb is also used of the succession of leaders from Mattathias to Simon in I Maccabees where the primary idea is one of rising to military leadership or to secular rule, although the high-priesthood is associated with this office in some of the passages (I Macc. 2:1; 3:1; 9:30 f.; 13:8, 14, 42; 14:41).

"But while he bore rule over Israel" (or simply, "but while he ruled Israel"). Those who interpret the preceding clause as meaning "took office as chief priest" have tried to give this a different meaning, "but when he became secular ruler over Israel." Hence a sharp distinction is drawn between a period when he was solely a religious leader and when he became temporal ruler. Thus Hyrcanus II was high priest before he became king; and Simon was an important military and spiritual leader before he came to power; but in the latter case, secular rule was joined with his high priesthood from the moment he took office, and I Maccabees does not speak of him "arising" until the death of Jonathan and he was ready to rule the country in his stead. Actually, I Maccabees constructs a dynastic *de facto* rule which began with the elderly Mattathias, to which certain of his sons succeeded one by one (Cf. "The Mattathias tradition" in *IDB*, Vol. K-Q, p. 205*a*).

Elliger, p. 198, states that *māšal bĕ-yiśrāʾēl* was a *terminus technicus* for the exercise of the high priesthood in post-Exilic times. Certainly the verb was used of priestly authority within the sphere of sectarian life, as is shown by the Manual of Discipline (1QS ix,7). Priestly authority is therefore not to be excluded from the meaning of *māšāl*, but the following lines describe a type of rule which involved the ability to conduct war.

Two periods in the career of the Wicked Priest are indicated, an earlier period when he was loyal to God and a later period when he became disloyal; but it is not at all apparent that it was the action of the verb *māšāl* which distinguished the periods. In the case of a man like Hyrcanus II, who was first of all chief priest alone, and later also secular ruler, the term *mālakh* (reigned) would be needed to make the distinction clear.

viii,10. "His heart became haughty." This is not solely *hubris* inspired by the exercise of power, for wealth also played a role here, as shown by the words: "For it [wealth] has made his soul feel big as Sheol" (Cf. above, viii,4). The "soul" is here identified with the "heart." For the idiom *rām libbo* in association with riches, see Deut. 8:11-14. Cf. Ezek. 28:5. The former stresses the danger of riches; the latter reveals that danger in connection with a ruler. Cf. also II Kings 14:10; II Chron. 25:19; 26:16; 32:25; Dan. 11:12; I Macc. 1:3.

"He abandoned God." At this point the priest is accused of ceasing to be a "fearer of God"—the second of the four qualifications for an office holder in Israel (Ex. 18:21). If one keeps within view also the declaration of the Biblical text *wĕlôʾ yinwéh* ("he will not stay home in the fold"), he may compare Jer. 50:7: ". . . for they have sinned against Yahweh, the *fold of righteousness.*" Thus not staying in the fold is an abandonment of God. An important passage which combines the ideas of pride and not staying home is II Kings 14:10 (=II Chron. 25:19), in which King Jehoash of Israel rebukes King Amaziah of

Judah saying: "Your heart has lifted you up. Be content with your glory, and stay at home." According to the Chronicler, Amaziah had indeed abandoned God (II Chron. 25:14-15).

Sometimes in the Old Testament, Jerusalem or the temple seems to be meant by the "fold" (Cf. Ex. 15:13; Isa. 33:20; Jer. 31:23). Therefore, by abandoning God, the commentary might also mean that the wicked priest was neglecting the temple service in order to engage in military exploits. Certainly he was not accused of worshipping other gods, except in the metaphorical sense. Amaziah was rebuked for conducting a military campaign against Israel instead of staying home in Judah.

"And became a traitor to the statutes because of wealth." Like Rehoboam, he also "forsook the Law of the LORD" (II Chron. 12:1), whereas those with Abijah had "not forsaken Him" (13:10). As a traitor he is now outside "the fold" as regards the true community of God's people. For this use of "fold" (or "pasture"), see Isa. 32:18; Jer. 23:3; 25:30; 50:19; Ezek. 34:14. He is no longer among the *ʾanšê ʾᵉmet* ("the adherents of the truth, the doers of the Law," vii,10f.). Thus he has joined the ranks of the *bôgĕdîm* mentioned in ¶7 (ii,1 ff.) and he has ceased to fulfill qualification no. 3 mentioned in Ex. 18:21. Since he did this "because of wealth," he is also disqualified from holding office according to the fourth requirement of Ex. 18:21. Actually, *baᶜᵃvûr hôn* may be interpreted either "because of the wealth he already had," or "for the sake of the wealth he wanted." For the former, cf. Deut. 8:11-14 and Ezek. 28:5; but for the latter note the following clauses in which the plundering of neighboring peoples is referred to. Actually, it is a matter of both. Wealth already claimed has contributed to his arrogance and has whetted his appetite for more. His insatiableness is shown by the fact that after becoming rich he continues to plunder and to amass wealth. (Cf. also Hans Kosmala, *Hebräer-Essener-Christen*, Leiden: E. J. Brill, 1959, pp. 234f.)

This interpretation of the *gever yāhîr* of Hab. 2:5 finds a remarkable parallel in Ps. 52:9 (=52:7):

> So this is the man [gever] who would not
>   consider God his refuge,
> but trusted in his great wealth,
>   relied upon his perniciousness!
>   (Mitchell Dahood, in *The Anchor Bible*, Vol. 17, p. 11)

In contrast with this figure is that described in 1Q H x,22 f.,

> And Thou hast not placed my support in gain,
> [nor does] my [heart delight in riches];
> Thou hast given me no fleshly refuge. . .
> [For the soul] of Thy servant has loathed [riches] and gain,
>   and he has not [desired] exquisite delights.
> My heart rejoices in Thy Covenant
> and Thy truth delights my soul.
>   (G. Vermès, *The Dead Sea Scrolls in English*, p. 184)

In this contrast between 1Q p Hab and 1Q H, we see portrayed the false and true priests. viii,11 f. "He stole . . . the wealth of the apostates who rebelled against God; and the wealth of the peoples he took." The Bible speaks of "all *gôyîm* and all *ʿammîm*" (viii,5), which the commentator interprets respectively as "apostates" and "peoples." The former are Jews or Samaritans and the latter are gentiles. This distinction is already implicit in the translation of J. van der Ploeg who rendered the former vaguely as "hommes injustes," but the latter as "gentils." Gaster's translation which paraphrases: "the kind of wealth usually acquired by *criminals*" and "*public* property" totally misconstrues the passage.

The implied equation of *gôyîm* as apostate Jews is supported by other evidence. (See Aelred Cody in *VT*, xiv, 1964, pp. 1-6.) One possible reference here would be to the Samaritans, since the Bible itself seems to employ this term concerning them. Being allegedly of foreign origin (II Kings 17:24-41; Ezra 4:1 f., 9 f.), they were exiled to Israel from among *hag-gôyîm* (17:33) and so they were designated *hag-gôyîm* (II Kings 17:26), *hag-gôyîm hā-ʾēlleh* (17:41), and *gôy nāvāl* ("the foolish nation that dwells at Shechem," Sirach 50:26*b*). Some scholars find a reference to the Samaritans in "this *gôy*" of Hag. 2:14.

Against this interpretation, Elliger (pp. 199 f.) cites the absence of the article before both *ḥāmās* (in the expression *hôn ʾanšê ḥāmās*) and *ʿammîm* (in the expression *hôn ʿammîm*) which eliminates any reference to specific groups. The grammatical objection, however, is a doubtful one, for as M.H. Segal has observed in connection with Mishnaic Hebrew:

> The article is always omitted with a number of common expressions, especially compounds, which are considered definite in themselves. . . . Conversely, other nouns of the same character are only found with the article . . .; but plur. is without the article [even in the same compound designations].
>
> (*A Grammar of Mishnaic Hebrew*, Oxford: Clarendon, 1927, §378, p. 184.)

In the present case we are concerned with compounds, both of them in the plural. Standing as it does between Old Testament and Mishnaic Hebrew, the Qumrân Hebrew sometimes exemplifies Mishnaic traits.

The phrase *ʾanšê ḥāmās* may be rendered "men of violence" and/or "men of apostasy"—the former meaning brigands in general (as in Sirach 13:13, Heb.) or Samaritans in particular. Cf. the Shechemite slaughter of the sons of Gideon, called *ḥāmās* in Jud. 9:24, and the record of strife between the northern and southern kingdoms. Amos charged the Israelites with storing up *ḥāmās* on the mountains of Samaria (3:9f.). Strife between the Jews and the Samaritans reached its climax when John Hyrcanus destroyed Shechem and the temple on Mt. Gerizim. One might also think of the internecine strife between Hellenizers and Hasidim, or between other Jewish groups. Thus Carmignac (*Textes*, p. 107, n. 12) calls attention to Jannaeus who confiscated the property of the Pharisees. As a Biblical expression, the ᵓîš ḥāmās of Ps. 18:49 is simply a foe. Its parallel, II Sam. 22:49, reads ᵓîš ḥᵃmāsîm.

The meaning "men of apostasy" (or "apostates") may be supported by Mid. Rabbah, I (Genesis translated by H. Freedman), London: Soncino, 1939, p. 241, where ḥāmās has four meanings, including "idolatry" (XXXI, 6):

> Another interpretation: FOR THE EARTH IS FILLED WITH ḤAMAS, etc. R. Levi said: "Ḥamas connotes idolatry, incest, and murder. Idolatry, as it is written, 'for the earth is filled with ḥamas' [Ezek. 8:17]. Incest: 'The violence done to me and to my flesh be upon Babylon' [Jer. 51:35]. Murder: 'For the ḥamas against the children of Judah because they have shed innocent blood' [Joel 4:19]. In addition, ḥamas bears its literal meaning also [robbery].

The meaning "idolatry" (or "apostasy") is very old as shown by Ben Sira. According to Sirach 47:21, "An apostate kingdom arose out of Ephraim" (מאפרים ממלכת חמס), and according to 49:3 it was "in the days of apostasy" that Josiah "achieved fidelity" (ובימי חמס עשה חסד). Here ḥāmās and ḥesed appear as antonyms. The Apostrophe to Zion (11Q Pssᵃ xxii,6f.) is important here:

> Apostasy is purged from thy midst,
> falsehood and error are cut off from thee.

As applied to 165 or 164 B.C., the reference in the psalm is probably to Judas' recovery of Jerusalem from the Hellenizers and his purging of the temple of all sacrilege. (See *Meaning*, pp. 31f. and M. Delcor, "L'hymne à Sion du rouleau des Psaumes de la grotte XI de Qumrân," *RQ*, 21, Feb., 1967, pp. 72-88.) Although in all these passages "idolatry" would be an appropriate rendering of ḥāmās, we cannot be sure whether in Qumrân usage it means solely this, or whether, as the parallelism in the Apostrophe to Zion suggests, it was used more generally as a synonym for "falsehood and error." Most likely, however, the ᵓanšê ḥāmās were heretics of some kind (whether Hellenizers or Samaritans) for they "had rebelled against God." Note 1Q H vi,5 f., where one psalmist declares:

> [Thou hast saved me] from the congregation of iniquity
> and from the *assembly of apostasy*;
> Thou hast brought me into the Council of [Thy holiness]
> [and hast cleansed me of] guilt.

Carmignac (*loc. cit.*) says that this "assembly of apostasy" (but in his translation, "comité de violence") is "without doubt an invective against the Pharisees."

On rebelling against God, cf. Hos. 14:1 (=13:16): "Samaria shall bear her guilt because she has rebelled (*mārĕtāh*) against her God." Joshua constantly warned the Israelites against rebelling against the Lord in building a rival altar to the one central sanctuary west of the Jordan, each time employing the same

verb as our manuscript, *mārad* (Josh. 22:16, 18 f., 29). Ezek. 2:3 in the MT
speaks of "nations rebelling" against the Lord, employing the verb *mārad*.

viii,12 f. "So as to increase the guilt of transgression upon himself; and
abominable behavior he committed with every kind of defiling impurity." For
"guilt of transgression," see Lev. 22:16. Dupont-Sommer (*Essene Writings*, p.
264) translates "the worst iniquities," and it is possible that the expression is
intended as a superlative, which unlike "holy of holies" employs a synonym
rather than the plural of the same word in the genitive position. Here we have
an interpretation of the punning taunt of line 8: "How long will he bring over
himself the *glory clouds* (nay, *gory clods*) of dirt?" For discussion of the pun,
see above *ad loc.* For "cloud" (ᶜ*āv*) as a symbol of sin, see Isa. 44:22. *Ṭîṭ* would
appear to be a symbol of sin, or at least of uncleanness in Isa. 57:20. The
Wicked Priest may have been spoken of by some as worthy that the Shekinah
should rest upon him (a Rabbinic expression); but quite to the contrary, the
ancient commentator declared that he was befouled by all types of impurity.
Wealth as a source of impurity seems to be alluded to first (by context) and
then "abominable behavior" whereby he was contaminated "with *every kind*
of defiling impurity." J. G. Harris paraphrased (p. 40): "he even practised
prostitution, and became immersed in every kind of filth and disgrace."
However, there is no reason to restrict *tôᶜēvāh* to "prostitution." Prov. 16:5
declares: "An abomination to the LORD is everyone of haughty heart" which
is precisely the condition of the Wicked Priest. Sodom, whose sin was so grave
(*kāvĕdāh*) according to Gen. 18:20, "became haughty and committed
abomination" according to Ezek. 16:50. Although *niddāh* (li. 13) was often
used of the menstrual impurity of the female (as Delcor, *Midrash*, pp. 32f.
observes), or even of incest (Lev. 20:21); Ezek. 36:17 employs this as an apt
description of all evil conduct.

The interpretation of the final clause in 1Q p Hab may be compared with
the translation of the Targum: ᶜ*D* ᵓ*YMTY* ᵓ*T MTQYP* ᶜ*LK TQWP*
ḤWBYN ("How long wilt thou burden thyself with a burden of guilts?"). It is
clear that ᶜ*avṭîṭ* was interpreted as etymologically equivalent to ᶜ*av ṭîṭ*
("thickness of mud"), and that therefore "guilts" is the primary meaning of
hôvîn. Yet the meaning "debts" in the root meaning would permit a secondary
allusion to the supposed reference to "pledges" in ᶜ*avṭîṭ* (an intensive of ᶜᵃ*vôṭ*).
The Syriac and the Vulgate versions perpetuated the interpretation "thickness
of mud."

It is therefore not surprising to find the King James Version rendering:
"woe . . . to him that ladeth himself with thick clay!" As long as one
understands ᶜ*av ṭîṭ* in this way, the overall interpretation of the whole passage
as given in 1Q p Hab is assured. Hence, Matthew Henry's early eighteenth
century commentary gave the following comment:

> See here what this prosperous prince is doing: he is *lading himself with thick clay*.
> Riches are but clay, thick clay; what are gold and silver but white and yellow earth? Those

who travel through thick clay are both retarded and dirtied in their journey; so are those who go through the world in the midst of the abundance of wealth of it; but, as if that were not enough, what fools are those that *load themselves with it*, as if this trash would be their treasure! They burden themselves with continual care about it, with a great deal of guilt in getting, saving, and spending it, and with a heavy account which they must give of it another day. They overload their ship with this thick clay, and *so sink* it and themselves *into destruction and perdition*.

Despite the word "wine" at vs. 5, Henry inferred from the general context that vs. 6 referred to "riches" by which men are "dirtied in their journey" and "burden themselves with a great deal of guilt." This similarity to 1Q p Hab should prevent us from being contemptuous of the ancient interpreter.

An Excursus on משׁל

1Q p Hab interpreted the noun *māšāl* with the verb *māšal* in the sense of "rule" (at viii,6,9. Cf. pp. 196 f., 201 f.). The meanings of the words are so different, that one may well posit two different roots; and yet the ancient midrashist probably did not even consider this as punning, but as utilization of different meanings of one and the same word.

משׁל is not without its problems, even, for the modern lexicographer. *BDB*, p. 605, apparently lists three roots; but perhaps they were intended as simply distinctive categories of meaning: I, "represent, be like." II, "use a proverb"— a denominative from the noun *māšāl*. III, "rule, have dominion, reign." The first two categories are clearly divergencies stemming from a common verbal root. The real question is whether this is true of the third also. Gesenius (as translated by Robinson, 1871, p. 627), after referring to previous conjectures by himself and others as to how "to show the point of connection between the two significations, *to rule* and *to liken*," concluded: "But not improbably two roots of different origin have coalesced under this form."

Scholars who explain the root meaning of *māšāl* as "likeness" or "similitude" generally imply no connection with the meaning "rule." Yet A. H. Godbey (in *AJSL*, XXXIX, 1923, pp. 89-108) suggested that the concept of similitude in משׁל arose from sympathetic magic and that from the idea of "pattern-setting" came the meaning "rule." Cf. also A. R. Johnson's article "משׁל." Contrariwise, G. Boström (*Paronomasi*, 1928) argued that the original meaning of the verb was "rule," and that from the power of the ruler *māšāl* derived its earliest meaning, "word of power," or "incantation." Among those adopting his theory are: Bentzen, *Introduction*, p. 311; Hempel, *Althebräische Literatur*, p. 44; Weiser, *Old Testament: Its Formation*, pp. 39 f.

If from either perspective one assigns the meaning of magical power to *māšāl*, he may wish to translate Hab. 2:6a in the Bible as follows:

Shall they not all intone *an incantation* against him,
and a taunt song of him, as they sing?

In this case, the following *māšāl* (vs. 6b) is no mere gloating over the downfall of the oppressor, but an incantation intended to bring about his fall.

THE MIDRASH PESHER OF HABAKKUK

¶26 (viii, 13-ix, 7)

13   הֲלֹוא פִּתְ[אֹ]ם יָקוּמוּ

14   וְנֹ[שְׁכֶ]יךָ וְיָקִיצוּ מְזַעְזְעֶיךָ וְהָיִתָה לִמְשׁ[י]סֹות לָמֹו

15   כִּי אַתָּה שַׁלֹּותָה גֹּויִם רַבִּים וִישָׁלֹּוכָה כֹּול־יֶתֶר עַמִּים

16   [פִּ]שֶׁר הַדָּבָר עַ[ל] הַכֹּוהֵן אֲשֶׁר מָרַד

17   [וַיִּ]עֲזֹו[ב] חֹוקֵּ[י אֵל וַיָּקִים מַלְאֲכֵי חֶבֶל נַיִּתְעַ]לְּלֹו בֹ לְ[מַעַן]

ix,1   נָגֹועֹו בְמִשְׁפָּטֵי רִשְׁעָה וְשַׁעֲרוּרִיֹות מַחֲלִים

2   רָעִים עָשֹׂוּ בֹו וּנְקָמֹות בִּגְוִיַּת בְּשָׂרֹו וַאֲשֶׁר

3   אָמַר כִּי אַתָּה שַׁלֹּותָה גֹויִם רַבִּים וִישָׁלֹּוכָה כֹּול־

4   יֶתֶר עַמִּים   פִּשְׁרֹו עַל כֹּוהֲנֵי יְרוּשָׁלַם

5   הָאַחֲרֹונִים אֲשֶׁר יִקְבֹּוצוּ הֹון וּבֶצַע מִשְּׁלַל הָעַמִּים

6   וּלְאַחֲרִית הַיָּמִים יִנָּתֵן הֹונָם עִם שְׁלָלָם בְּיַד

7   חֵיל הַכִּתִּיאִים   כִּיא הֵמָּה יֶתֶר הָעַמִּים

viii,13 (2:7) Shall it not happen suddenly

14   that / thy own tormentors *shall arise*? Shall not thy own torturers sicken (thee) and thou become prey to them? /

15(2:8a) Because thou plunderedst many nations, all the remaining peoples shall plunder thee. /

16   T[he prophetic meaning of the passage conce]rns the priest

17   who rebelled / [and abroga]ted the ordinances of [[God; but He raised up pain-inflicting angels who attac]]ked him in [[order]] /

ix,1   to plague him. In recompense for (his) wicked laws and

2   abominable acts, / they inflicted evil *diseases* upon him and

3   vengeful acts on his body of flesh. And as for that which / He

4   said, "Because thou plunderedst many nations, all / the

5   remaining peoples shall plunder thee, its meaning concerns the / last *priests of Jerusalem,* who will gather wealth and spoil by

6   plundering the peoples; / but in the last days, their wealth

7   (including their spoil) will be given into the power of / the army of the Kittim—for they are "the remaining peoples."

¶26 *Exposition*

viii,13-15 (Hab. 2:7-8a). For the variants, see *Text*, §§84a-94. Yet, at §85, one should restore with Martin, §30, the dittograph: פתח[א]אום. Martin noted: "The tips of two shafts still exist at the righthand side of the erasure and they suggest an Aleph." They are not apparent in Trever's colored photograph; but they disappeared during the interval between the photographings.

As regards *Text*, §§86-87, one should (with Elliger, p. 54) recognize the initial writing as ויקום ונשכיך, which the scribe subsequently corrected to read with the MT: ויקומו נשכיך. The deletion of the *Wāw* before the second word was indicated by a short stroke above and below. Martin, §31, argues that the second letter of the second word is not a *Nûn*; but its vertical stance agrees with one near the end of viii,2.

viii,13, "suddenly." See David Daube, *The Sudden in the Scriptures*, p. 1, who shows that this word refers to sudden disasters, usually as a divine judgment.

viii,14. "Thy tormentors" ("those biting thee") is a figure of speech for "those exacting payment from thee in fulfilment of a debt." These were probably interpreted in the commentary as the angels of pain which bring disease. By deriving *wĕ-yāqîṣû* from *qûṣ* (feel sick [from dread]), rather than from *qîṣ* (awake), we obtain the meaning "sicken thee," rather than "awake"— for which the parallelism calls. The meaning "sicken" is implied by the reference to "evil diseases" in ix,1f. Cf., after Jastrow (*Dictionary*, p. 1339*b*, קוץ I): *Sifra Qĕdosh*, Par. 4, c. XI, which interprets *wāʾāqūṣ* of Lev. 20:23 as meaning כאדם קץ שהוא ממזונו ("like a man that is sick of his food [and vomits]"). Gaster sensed that "awake" would not suit the present passage, and so he proposed that the verb "is fancifully construed by our author as if it were the very similar *yaᶜkiṣu*, 'sting.'" Such a change in the root seems unnecessary. Silberman ("Riddle," p. 349) was right in deriving the verb from *qûṣ* I, "feel a loathing, abhorrence." But then he obtained the wrong connotation in his rendering "those who shake you will make you loathsome." Even with this understanding of the meaning of the root, the *hifᶜîl* should mean "make you loathe" (or better, "make you feel a sickening dread"), as in Isa. 7:6.

As at ix,16, "the priest" is not described as "wicked", but is so, nevertheless. He was doubtless chief priest. See R. de Vaux, *Ancient Israel, Its Life and Institutions*, 1961, p. 378, who has observed:

> The head of the clergy is usually referred to in the Bible as 'the priest,' without any qualification; he was *the* priest (cf. the list of Solomon's ministers, I K 4:2; Yehoyada 2 K 11:9f.; 12:8f.; Uriyyah, 2 K 16:10f.; Is. 8:2; Hilqiyyahu, 2 K 22:12,14: all these were quite evidently heads of the clergy).

viii,17. Rival restorations of this line are as follows: (1) Dupont-Sommer, "Le Maître de Justice fut-il mis à mort," *VT*, I, pp. 200-215, esp. pp. 202-5: [ויפי]ר חוקי [אל וירדף מורה הצדק ויתע]ללו בו ל[אבות] ("[and he viola]ted the precepts [of God and persecuted the Teacher of Righteousness. And they s]et upon him to smite him"—translation of *Essene Writings*, p. 264); (2) Elliger (citing Job 24:13) [בא[ו]ר חוק[י אל והוא ואנשי עצתו הסתו[לל[ו] בו ל[בלתי] ("who rebelled / [against the ligh]t of the ordinances [of God. Both he and the men of his counsel rose up against Him in order not] / [to]. . ."); (3) Lambert, p. 294: *"et qui a résisté aux préceptes de Dieu; mais il est tombé aux mains de ses ennemis qui se sont érigés en juges et lui ont infligé son châtiment."* This does not seem to be a mere paraphrase of the missing material, for in n. 123 he states: "Line 17 of col. VIII is restored conjecturally, taking into account traces of letters still usable . . ." No matter how one seeks to reconstruct such a Hebrew text, Lambert's restoration is too long. (4) Vermés: [ויפ[ר חוקי [אל ויתנהו ביד אויביו ויתג[ללו בו ל[פקוד] ("who rebelled / [and violated] the precepts of [God; but He gave him into the hand of his enemies, and they atta]cked him to [command] / his chastisement")—following *Discovery*, p. 94, n. 37, but correcting the last verb from [ל[עשות] to agree with *DSSE*, p. 240. The first two scholars suppose that the "tormentors" are the Wicked Priest and his henchmen and that their victim is the Teacher of Righteousness. Dupont-Sommer had found this idea at the beginning of the next column; but it was only in disputation with Barthélemy (in *RB*, 1952, p. 208) that he undertook to restore this line. For purposes of concession only, Dupont-Sommer restored the line, in order to prove that the limit of seventeen lines permitted a shift from the Wicked Priest to the Righteous Teacher who was the sufferer at the top of the following column. He succeeded in making this shift, but not successfully, for the plural verb at the end of the line receives no plural subject. Though Elliger's restoration remedied this defect, it left no room for any mention of the Teacher of Righteousness, whose persecution he left for the supposed missing eighteenth line. Both of these interpreters depart from the Biblical context which identifies the sufferer with the guilty party. The moment the interpretation of viii,16 begins, "Its interpretation concerns the priest who rebelled," the sufferer has been identified! It is not really satisfactory to plead, as Dupont-Sommer and Elliger do, that the commentator often does violence to the Biblical text, for in this case he would have begun his interpretation in some such fashion as: "The interpretation of the passage concerns the Righteous Teacher who was mistreated by the Wicked Priest, who together with his henchmen did so and so." Thus their restorations contradict not simply the Biblical text, but the context of the commentary as well. Therefore, any dexterity in shifting hypothetically the reference from the Wicked Priest to the Righteous Teacher, whether within one, or even two lines, is wholly irrelevent. The third and fourth restorations identify the sufferer with the rebellious priest and draw heavily upon ix, 10 ("whom God gave into the hands of his enemies") for appropriate language to introduce the "tormentors" of the priest. Still these restorations are basically unsatisfactory, for the priest of this passage suffered attacks of illness, which do not come from human foes. Bo

Reicke attributes the priest's bodily plagues to God (see *Handskrifterna*, pp. 50f.) Vermés suggested a plausible circumvention of this difficulty by comparing *maḥᵃlîm* (diseases) with *maḥluyîm* of II Chron. 24:25, "diseases caused by wounds." Yet the nominal forms are not identical; and in 4Q 181 i,1f., one finds the exact phrase in a similar context: "And for great judgments and *evil diseases* in the flesh according to God's mighty deeds."

The first word of viii,17 was initially restored by me as ר[ויעבו]; but, since this is one letter too long, the verb was altered to ר[ויפי] by A. Dupont-Sommer, while Delcor, p. 33, restored ר[בעבו]. The upper portion of the third to the last letter is sufficiently preserved to indicate a horizontal stroke, which excludes both *Pê* and *Bêt*. Closer examination indicates that the vestage is probably the upper left portion of a *Sāmekh*. This leads us to the restoration *way-yāsîr*, "and he set aside, or abrogated." On this verb, see Joshua 11:15b; Isa. 31:2; Dan. 11:31. The Wicked Priest is charged with setting aside and not administering the "ordinances of God" which had previously been in force. On these "ordinances," cf. iii,5 and viii,10, also the restoration of ii,15.

"But He raised up pain-inflicting angels." This restoration identifies the "tormentors" and "torturers" of viii,14 with disease-bringing angels. For the *malᵒᵃkhê ḥevel* (literally, "angels of pain"), cf. 1Q S iv, 12: "And the visitation of all who walk by it [i.e., by the spirit of perversity] consists in a multitude of plagues [*něgîm*, or *něgûᶜîm*] by the hand of all pain-inflicting angels." Cf. also 1QM xiii,12 and CDC ii,6 (=2:4). Cf. also the Rabbinic *malᵒakh ḥabbělāᵒ* (angel of destruction). Note also Job 36:14f. in the LXX, which is difficult, but probably means:

> Hence they are put to death, their soul [being yet] in youth,
>   their life being mortally wounded by angels,
> in as much as they afflicted the weak and powerless;
>   yet judgment on behalf of the meek He will make clear.

The text (or at least the interpretation) varies considerably from the Hebrew, but one point is clear: the LXX supports *qědôšîm* ("holy ones") rather than *qědēšîm* ("male prostitutes," or, as in the Rabbinic targum, "keepers of brothels"). In the 11Q Targum of Job, וחיתם בקדשים is rendered ומ[דינתהון בממתין] "and their [c]ity (perishes) through executioners." (See J. P. M. van der Ploeg and A. S. van der Woude, *Le Targum de Job*, 1971, pp. 64f.) If the 11Q Targum be interpreted correctly, it too may have read "holy ones," understanding them as death-bringing angels, for which see Prov. 16:14; Isa. 37:36 and the Rabbinic "angel of death." Admittedly, the present restoration is tenuous; for, even if the right meaning is conjectured for the lacuna, the precise terminology is uncertain.

"[Who attac]ked him." This part of the restoration of Dupont-Sommer is good. For the use of the preposition *Bêt* with the object of the verb, עלל in the *hitpaᶜēl*, cf. Ex. 10:2; I Sam. 6:6; Num. 22:29; Jud. 19:25. The verb is associated with pain in Lam. 1:12 and 3:51. The word is more suitable, in

context, than Delcor's suggestion of reading *qillĕlû vô* ("ils le maudirent")—
which should mean "curse *by* him."

viii,17-ix,1. ל[מֵעַ]ל נגועו [מֵעַ]ל "in [order to] plague him." The latter word could be
the noun "plague" or "blow" which in the Scrolls is often spelled נגיע or נגוע,
rather than נגע. Yet, cf. ix,11. As a noun, it could be of the *qiṭṭûl* formation;
(see van der Woude, *Die Messianischen Vorstellungen*, pp. 37f.; B.
Jongeling in *RQ*, 4 pp. 483-494.) Reading the noun would suggest that the
Lāmed at the end of the preceding column introduced an infinitive, as Vermès
seems to read. However, one would expect this to be complemented with a
prepositional phrase (*ᶜālâw* or *bô*), as in Ex. 15:26; 20:5; Deut. 7:15; 28:60;
Amos 3:2.

ix.1f. "in recompense for (his) wicked laws and abominable acts." Martin
(§33) thinks the preposition *B* was inserted by "Hand B," "Hand A" having
mistakenly read a series of constructs: נגיעי משפטי רשעה. Alternative
constructions of li. 1 are the following: (1) "to plague him *for* (his) judgments
of wickedness, etc."(2) "to plague him *with* the judgments due for wickedness,
etc." The former gives essentially the same meaning as the translation adopted
here and is the construction of Reicke, except that he terminated the sentence
at "wickedness." The latter syntax (Molin's) introduces the instrumental *B*
after the verb *NGᶜ*, for which I have found no attestation. *Mišpāṭîm* is taken
in different senses in these constructions. In the former, it refers either to
"unjust legal decisions" or to "wicked laws"; in the latter, it refers to penalties
inflicted by the "tormentors." All three senses of *mišpāṭîm* (laws, legal
decisions and punishments) are abundantly attested both in the Old
Testament and in the literature of the Scrolls. However, the statement of
viii,17 that the priest had "abrogated the ordinances *of God*" favors here a
reference to the "laws *of wickedness*" which he had put in their place. Contrast
the *mišpāṭê ᵓēl* of 1Q S iii,5, as also the *mišpāṭê ṣedeq* (righteous laws) of Ps.
119:7, 62, 106, 160, 164; 1Q S iii,1; iv,4. For the substitution of bad laws for
good, see 1Q H iv,10f.: "They have plotted vileness against me, in order to
replace Thy Torah which Thou hast drilled into my heart with smooth things
for (teaching) Thy people."

My first rendering of ix,1 was: "his smiting with the judgments of
wickedness; and the horrors of evil diseases they inflicted upon him . . ."—
"his smiting" rendering either an infinitive or a noun. This construing of *wĕ-
šaᶜᵃrûrîyôt* in construct relationship with *maḥᵃlîm rāᶜîm* was followed by van
der Ploeg, *Bi. Or.* VIII, p. 8; Lambert; and Vermès, *NRTh*, April, 1951, p. 394.
Michel (p. 14) translated with an appositional relationship, "et des choses
horribles, [c'est-à-dire] des maladies pernicieuses." Bardtke, p. 129 (followed
by Carmignac, *Textes*, p. 108), interpreted *šaᶜᵃrûrîyôt* as the object of the
verb: "and severe diseases wrought horrors upon him and acts of vengeance
upon his body of flesh." The Hebrew word order does not favor this
construction; and the noun *šaᶜᵃrûrîyāh* is used only to refer to the sin of
idolatry under the figure of adultery (Hosea 6:10; Jer. 18:13); and the related

term *ša^c^arûrāh* is used for a number of ethical offences (Jer. 5:30; 23:14). There is no evidence that these words can be used to depict the horrors of torment. The ethical sense of *ša^c^arûrîyôt* requires that this word be linked with the preceding. The plural, which is unattested in the Old Testament, is perhaps due to the word being conjoined with the preceding plural (*mišpāṭîm*). Or it may serve to indicate that the Wicked Priest was guilty of several of the offences of Jer. 5:31; 23:14.

The construction of ix,1f. which is adopted here is largely indebted to R. de Vaux (*RB*, 1951, p. 441): "En retour de jugements d'iniquité et d'horreur, des maladies malignes s'exercerent contre lui." In modification of de Vaux, one should not take *ša^c^arûrîyôt* as a second genitive of *mišpāṭê*, but as a second type of sin. In favor of this understanding is the fact that the second offense, like the first, is in the plural. De Vaux probably understood the *mišpāṭê riš^c^āh* as unjust judgment rather than iniquitous legislation.

"They inflicted evil diseases." The plural verb might be translated as a third plural indifinite: "serious diseases were inflicted upon him." So de Vaux translated. However, it is unlikely that the "tormentors" of the Biblical text went unidentified; and disease is attributed in Qumrân thought to "pain-inflicting angels," which were probably mentioned in viii,17. Gaster's facile rendering, "The horrors of evil diseases acted upon him," would seem to personify the diseases. All efforts to identify the "tormentors" with human enemies, whether they be of the Wicked Priest or of the Righteous Teacher (cf. the restorations of viii,17), must find difficulty with the phrase "serious diseases" (*maḥ^a^lîm rā^c^îm*). Dupont-Sommer (*RHR*, pp. 146f., 164, now in *Essene Writings*, p. 264) tried to find in the word a designation of the Teacher's executioners, suggesting the *hif^c^îl* participle of either *ḤLL* I or *ḤLL* III (or II), the former meaning "piercers," and the latter "profaners." For such a meaning, however, one would expect the *pi^c^ēl* in both cases (necessitating two *Lāmed*s). The *hif^c^îl* is unattested for the former root; and the *hif^c^îl* of the latter usually means "to begin," rather than "to profane." The only two exceptions with regard to *ḤLL* III (or II) concern the breaking of one's word (Numbers 30:3 [Heb.; otherwise 30:2]) and the profaning of God's name (Ezek. 39:7). The word is never employed for maltreating others. Dupont-Sommer proposed the alternative meaning "piercers," since this would allow comparison with Isa. 53:5 and Isa. 53:10 in 1Q Isa. Cf. also Ps. 22:17 (Heb.; otherwise 22:16). He overlooked a more defensible derivation from *ḤLH* I, which either in the *pi^c^ēl* (as Deut. 29:21) or in the *hif^c^îl* (Mic. 6:13) means "make sick." In the MT of Isa. 53:10, the latter is used; and, as in II Kings 8:29; Mic. 6:13, and Nah. 3:19 (here the *nif^c^al*), the root *ḥālāh* is associated with wounds. The possible derivation from *ḤLH* does not tempt one, however, to posit a designation "sickener" for the "pain-inflicting angels"; for there is really no difficulty in reading *maḥ^a^lîm* (diseases). Although the noun *MHLH* is employed in the Old Testament only in the singular and in contexts where one cannot determine the gender, twice the Massoretes have vocalized the word as a masculine (Prov. 18:14 and II Chron. 21:15), as Yalon, *KS*, 1951, p. 174*a*, has noted. In the other occurrences the Massoretes have vocalized the noun as a feminine, perhaps erroneously. The association of the adjective *rāᶜ* with a variety of terms for disease in the Old Testament suits the use of the term here (Deut. 7:15; 28:59; Eccles. 6:2; II Chron. 21:19). Note that in Deut. 28:59, *rāᶜ* is parallel with *gādōl* which indicates the nuance of "evil" in connection with disease. *Maḥᵃlāh* is paralleled by *negaᶜ* in I Kings 8:37 and II Chron. 6:28. Now we also have the expression מחלים רעים בבשר in 4Q 181 i,1f., which should remove all doubt as to the reading "evil diseases."

ix,2. "Vengeful acts on his body of flesh." These are probably synonymous with the "evil diseases." The expression "body of flesh" serves to indicate that the rebellious priest, despite his insolence in substituting his own laws for those of God, was *only* human. A. Dupont-Sommer (*RHR*, p. 164) saw in this a reference to the Teacher as divine, but with a human body. For this interpretation he appealed to Col. 1:22. Cf. Rom. 1:3f. Thus he found an indication of a pre-Christian doctrine of the Incarnation! In the controversy which ensued in the French press, Dupont-Sommer (in *Figaro Littéraire*, Feb. 24, 1951) challenged Bonsirven to find the expression "body of flesh" a single time in the Old Testament when it signifies simply the material side of the human person. Forthwith, R. de Vaux (cited by Bonsirven in *Études*, Feb., 1951, p. 217) found the expression in the Wisdom of Sirach 23:17 (=23:16): ἄνθρωπος πόρνος ἐν σώματι σαρκὸς αὐτοῦ ("a man who is a fornicator in his body of flesh"). He also pointed out that the same expression occurs with reference to the Christian in Col. 2:11, where it designates the seat of sin. Marc Philonenko, "Sur l'expression 'corps de chair' dans le commentaire d'Habacuc," *Semitica*, V, 1955, pp. 39f., found still another reference in I En. 102:5, where the Greek version preserves the expression fully, but the Ethiopic reads "your body." Cf. also 4Q p Nah. ii,6: "Indeed, they will stumble over their own body of flesh through their guilty counsel." An equivalent expression appears in I En. 16:1, which speaks of the deceased giants ἀφ᾽ ὧν τὰ πνεύματα ἐκπορευόμενα ἐκ τῆς ψυχῆς τῆς σαρκὸς αὐτῶν ("whose spirits had departed from their body of flesh"). Obviously this use of ψυχή derives from the Aramaic *min nafšāʾ dĕ-visrĕhôn* (or approximately), in agreement with the Hebrew usage of *nefeš* with the meaning "body/corpse." Cf. Lev. 21:1; 22:4; Num. 5:2; 6:11; 9:6f., 10; 19:11, 13; Hag. 2:13. Num. 6:6 and Lev. 21:11 even speak of a "dead *nefeš*," which may be contrasted with the "living *nefeš*" of Gen. 2:7. For further discussion see Delcor, *Midrash*, pp. 33f.; van der Woude, *Die Messianischen Vorstellungen*, pp. 160f.; and J. Carmignac, *Christ and the Teacher of Righteousness*, pp. 17f.

ix,3. Hab. 2:8*a* is quoted anew, having been used previously indirectly in the interpretation of 2:7 for establishing the principle of exact retribution, esp., in ix,1f.: "In recompense for his *wicked laws* and *abominable acts*, they inflicted *evil diseases* upon him and *vengeful acts*." The two offences were matched by an appropriate pair of punishments.

ix,5. "The *last* priests of Jerusalem." Curiously, Michel, pp. 14f., rendered "les prêtres autres" (the *other* priests). These belong to the "*last* generation" (ii,7; vii,2) and to the "*last* days" (ii,5f.) which are always referred to in the imperfect mood, as though future (or present). Thus there is a separation in time between the priest who in the past (perfect tense) met his doom through terrible diseases and these "last priests." The latter will surrender their wealth to the Kittim. With the Kittim identified as the Romans, one is reminded that this was a time of rival priests, Hyrcanus II and Aristobulus II. As at viii,16, the term "priest", without the attribute "wicked", means "chief priest," so also, here, the plural means "chief priests." A reference to the contemporary priests seems to be likely.

ix,5. "By plundering the peoples." Literally, "from the plunder of the peoples," but the ambiguity of the latter has been avoided in translation. The genitive is objective, not subjective.

ix,7. "For they are the remaining peoples." Why there is a space before these words is uncertain. Was the manuscript too rough to receive the ink properly? Did the scribe who copied this text mistakenly suppose that this began a new section? Or was this space left for emphasis? Cf. the use of the dash at this point in the English translation.

Yeter hā-ᶜammîm might conceivably have been understood as "the remnant of the peoples" and have been applied to those surviving the attacks of the Kittim. Cf. the use of *yeter* in connection with God's own people in Zeph. 2:9, as also in the expression "the remnant of the nations" (Josh. 23:12). In spite of its translation "all that remains of the peoples," The Jerusalem Bible interprets Hab. 2:8 as meaning: "Not 'of the oppressed peoples' nor 'of the peoples who have escaped oppression' but of every race, other than the Chaldaeans, whether oppressed or not." The same sweeping interpretation is found in The New English Bible, "all the rest of the world." Most probably *yeter* in 1Q p Hab was given an eschatological meaning—the ancient commentator having in mind a theory of successive world powers like the four kingdoms in Daniel. The final world power will be the Kittim, "for they are the ones *remaining to come.*" The perspective of the commentary, whatever its date, is prior to the coming of the Kittim. An alternative would be that *yeter*, after the analogy of *ᵓahᵃrît*, may be given a temporal meaning, "for they are the last of the peoples." Van der Ploeg, *Bi. Or.*, VIII, p. 8, translated the word as "l'élite"; and he was followed by Silberman, "Riddle," p. 350, who rendered the clause: "for they are the greatest of the peoples." Outside the theoretical root meaning, there is no evidence of this sense.

THE MIDRASH PESHER OF HABAKKUK

¶27 (ix,8-12)

יוֹשְׁבֵי
מִדְּמֵי אָדָם וַחֲמַס אֶרֶץ קִרְיָה וְכֹ[ו]ל בָּהּ   8
פִּשְׁרוֹ עַל הַכּוֹהֵן הָ[רָ]שָׁע אֲשֶׁר בַּעֲווֹן מוֹרֵה   9
הַצֶּדֶק וְאַנְשֵׁי עֲצָתוֹ נְתָנוֹ אֶל בְּיַד אוֹיְבָיו לְעַנְּתוֹ   10
בְּנֶגַע לְכַלֵּה בִּמְרִירֵי נֶפֶשׁ בַּעֲבוּר אֲשֶׁר הִרְשִׁיעַ   11
עַל בְּחִירוֹ   12

8 (2:8b) Because of man's shed blood,

     there will be hostility from the land,

     from the city and all who dwell in it. /

9   Its prophetic meaning concerns the [Wi]cked Priest, whom (for an

10 offense against the / Righteous Teacher and the men of his council) God

11 gave into the power of his enemies to afflict / with blows and to waste

away with the festering wounds of the soul, because he had done evil /

12 against His elect.

¶27 *Exposition*

ix,8. For the variants of 2:8*b*, see *Text*, §§95f.

"Hostility *from*" interprets the genitives following *ḥāmās* as subjective genitives—as against previous translations. This interpretation is just the opposite of *ḥᵃmas hal-lĕvānôn* of Hab. 2:17*a* (¶33). It differs even from the identical text of Hab. 2:17*b*, not only as to the genitive (which is objective), but also as to the significance of *ḥāmās* (where it means "pillage"). For the meaning "hostility," note the following expressions: *ᶜēd ḥāmās* ("malicious witness") in Ex. 23:1; Deut. 19:16; *ᵓîš ḥāmās* in Psalm 18:49 (otherwise, 18:48=II Sam. 22:49) where it parallels "my enemies" and "my adversaries." *Ḥāmās* is used by itself in association with enemies in II Sam. 22:3f., where *mē-ḥāmās tōšîᶜēnî* receives as its parallel *ū-mē-ᵓōyĕvāi ᵓiwwāšēaᶜ*. Cf. also Ps. 25:19; 27:12; Prov. 10:6, 11. Thus it appears that *ḥāmās* means not only "violence," but also "enmity." For the subjective genitive, see Ezek. 12:19.

ix,9. "For an offense against." This was first read as לעיין and was translated "in the sight of." Molin (p. 15) followed suit. However, one would expect in that case לעיני. Yalon (*KS*, XXVII, p. 174a), followed by Baer (p. 21), has wrongly supposed that a corrector altered *ᶜAyin* to *ᵓĀlef*, in order to read אוין, an expression for sighing. He mistook the stained edge of a crack in the manuscript for a corrector's mark. (Here the earlier black and white photograph preserves the manuscript more fully than the colored photograph, taken at a later date when a small piece had fallen out.) Back of these misunderstandings lies the assumption that the word *ᶜāwôn* must always have the subjective genitive and never have the objective. Yet there are two possible occurrences in the MT of the objective genitive. The first is the *kĕtîv* of II Sam. 16:12: "It may be that the LORD will look *upon this offense against me* (בעוני)." The second is Ps. 31:11 (=31:10): "My strength fails *because of the wrong done me* . . ." In the former instance the *qĕrê* would alter the text to read ("upon my eye")—meaning thereby that the Lord will see the sorrow in David's eyes. This reading was intended to prevent the understanding that David was suffering for his sins ("look upon *my iniquity*"). In the latter instance the RSV has followed the reading of Symmachus *bĕᶜonyî* ("because of my misery"). The RSV adopted the same emendation in II Sam. 16:12 (a reading which is supported by the Greek, Syriac, and Vulgate versions): "It may be that the Lord will look *upon my affliction*." S. R. Driver (in *Notes on the Hebrew Text of the Books of Samuel*, 1890, p. 247) argued that for the objective genitive one should have had *ḥᵃmāsî* (as in Gen. 16:5) and that *ᶜāwôn* cannot be used in the sense of "injury, offense." For the latter meaning, however, he did cite the case of the Medieval work "Rule of Asher ben Jehiel" which states יש לי עון ממנו ("There is injury to me from him" = "I am the injured party"). It is particularly interesting that Driver insisted that *ḥāmās* is the word that should be used rather than *ᶜāwôn*; for the former word does appear in the text of Habakkuk, where if read with the objective genitive it affords a precise parallel with $^c\bar{a}w\hat{o}n$. Even though the primary interpretation of the verse calls for the subjective genitive for the word *ḥāmās* in Hab. 2:8*b*, this suggests the secondary interpretation of the verse as containing the objective genitive also:

> Because of man's shed blood,
> and a crime against the land,
> against the city and all who dwell in it.

In that case the "land," "the city," and "all who dwell in it" would be interpreted as "the Righteous Teacher and the men of his council." One could reinforce this interpretation by appealing to ¶33, where "Lebanon" is interpreted as the "Council of the Community" and "the land" is equated with 'the cities of Judah where he robbed the wealth of the Poor."

The nature of the "offense" against the Teacher and the members of his party is not specified. Yet the natural inference (contra Carmignac, *Textes*, p. 109, n. 9) is that this refers to a bloodletting. It is probably not the same crime as that referred to in ¶33, where the shedding of blood is limited to Jerusalem and is not explicitly applied to the sectaries of the Scrolls. In the present passage we naturally suppose that the victims of the bloodletting are "the Righteous Teacher and the men of his council." This need not mean that the Teacher was himself killed; but it naturally suggests that some of those associated with him were killed and that he himself may have suffered wounds, if not death, as a result of this bloodletting. Silberman ("Riddle," pp. 350 f.) has denied all bloodshed, "by taking מדמי as being derived from דמים, meaning 'equivalent, compensation'"—a Rabbinic term related to דמי or דמה. Yet, the author of the Hymns (often identified with the Teacher) could write of those who sought to spill his blood (either with or without success):

> Thou hast redeemed the soul of this poor man
> whom they planned to destroy
> by spilling his blood because he served Thee.
> (1Q H ii, 32f.)

The author of the Damascus Covenant was able to look back upon the Teacher's death simply as a "gathering-in," without making any special point of the manner of his death (CDC xix,35; xx,14 [=9:29-30]). Still his possible martyrdom is a subject on which one must maintain an open mind, as he awaits further evidence.

ix,9f. "The Righteous Teacher and the Men of his council." Should $^c\bar{e}ṣ\bar{a}h$ be rendered "counsel?" In the present passage, either translation is equivalent to the other, for what is a "council" but "men of counsel?" See further at xii,4 (¶33). In v,10, "the house of Absalom" have "the men of their council [or counsel]." In both cases probably (and certainly in the former case) one has in mind a clearly defined and organized group. At Qumrân the Council received counsel from its members (1Q S vi,3, 22f.). For this reason one should not soften the expression into "ses partisans"(Dupont-Sommer, *RHR*, p. 137), or "son parti" (van der Ploeg, *Bi. Or.*, VIII, p. 8), or "les hommes de son association"(Carmignac, pp. 109f.) or "the men associated with him"(Gaster, p. 254).

ix,10. "God gave him into the power of his enemies." In view of the subjective genitives in Hab. 2:8*b*, the "enemies" are identified with "the land, the city, and all who dwell in it." These are internal enemies, the Priest's own fellow countrymen. Whether the enemies are to be interpreted as members of the Teacher's party and/or others in society is not clear. It is not certain whether "into the power of his enemies" means that the priest was actually taken captive, or was simply placed in jeopardy and suffered injury.

ix,10f. "To afflict him with blows." It is not clear how these "blows" were administered; but see the translation of Gaster, p. 254: "that they might torture him with scourging." The Hebrew words are sufficiently indefinite to allow for other interpretations also. Note that in Jer. 6:7 "sickness and *wounds*" are associated with *ḥāmās*. Michel, p. 15, rendered: "pour l' humilier par une plaie [allant] jusqu' à l'extermination." The meaning "plague" for *nega*ᶜ is excluded by reference to human foes. Assuming that *plaie* here means "wound," this is possible; but *humilier* appears too weak. F. M. Cross (*Canaanite Myth*, p. 340) translates: "to bring him low with a mortal blow." This is better, but it is not clear that the "blow" was "mortal."

ix,11. "And to waste (him) away with the festering wounds of the soul." The manuscript reads clearly *BLH* (not *KLH*, as in *DSS*, I), literally "to wear (him) out." *Lĕ-ballēh* (rather than *lĕ-ballōt*) indicates either the use of the infinitive absolute, or the derivation of the verb from *BL*ᵓ. The interchange of *Hē* and *ᵓĀlef* is common in the Scrolls. Yalon first insisted upon this reading and he has been followed by Habermann and Baer, p. 21. Yalon calls attention to the substitution of *lĕ-ballōtô* for *lĕ*ᶜ*annōtô* in the revision of II Sam. 7:10 in I Chron. 17:9. These same infinitives are used as parallel terms here. The use of the root *BL*ᵓ for persecution is attested in the Aramaic of Dan. 7:25, where it is declared that the "little horn" "will wear out [*yĕballē*ᵓ] the saints." In the present passage, it is the persecutor who is to be worn out by affliction. Although perhaps the priest's death is thus described, it is likewise possible that no reference to mortal suffering is intended. Thus, see Lam. 3:4: "He has made my flesh and my skin waste away," and Isa. 3:15 (Targum): "The faces of the poor do you waste away." Martin Noth has argued that, since in Dan. 7:25 the "Saints of the Most High" are angels, the verb בלא can mean nothing stronger than *kränken* (vex, grieve, insult, offend). (See his *Gesammelte Studien zum Alten Testament*, pp. 285ff.) Contrarywise, see C. H. W. Brekelmans in *OS*, XIV, 1965, pp. 305, 329. Even if one were to read here *LKLH*, this would not necessarily mean a quick death. Cf. 1Q H viii,32.

"With the festering wounds of the soul." Perhaps, rather, "with bitter things of the soul"; for one may read either מרורי or מרירי. The former appears in 1Q H viii,28,37; xi,19. The latter is the Rabbinic spelling. Yalon, followed by Habermann (ᶜ*Edah*, p. 52; *Megilloth*, p. 47) and Baer, has produced evidence to prove that the Rabbinic term means "wounds which flow with discharge, or puss." Thus *bimrîrê nefeš* is in strict parallelism with *bĕ-negaᶜ* ("with blows"). (Yet compare 1Q H viii,27f., נ.[גי]עי למרורים). Perhaps both terms have similar meanings. C. C. Torrey (*The Second Isaiah*, p. 422) argued that the ᶜᵃ*mal nafšô* of the Lord's Servant (Isa. 53:11) "means a struggle in which the very life is at stake." In that case, one might surmise that "the festering wounds of the soul" refer to "mortal wounds." In any case, "festering [or, bitter] wounds" do not suggest immediate death; and the whole expression may mean rather emotional suffering, the blows to the body being accompanied by mental anguish. Certainly one should not see here purely spiritual sickness, as Philo, *On the Migration of Abraham*, §124, where he speaks of "soul wounds which were left gaping by the sword-edge of follies and injustices and all the rest of the horde of vices."

ix,12. "His elect" may refer to the Teacher as Fitzmyer (*Essays*, p. 152) asserts. Yet this is not unambiguously so, since the word "elect" could also include "the men of his council." Either *BḤYRW* should be vocalized as a defective plural *bĕḥîrāw*, or as a singular *bĕḥîrô*. Cf. the discussion of v,4 in ¶16.

Nevertheless, it seems probable that in 4Q p Pssᵃ the Teacher is spoken of as God's elect. At iii,15f., one may restore: "the priest, the [Righteous] Teacher [whom] God [ch]ose to take office [and whom] He ordained to build for Him the congregation of the [poor]." Yet where I restore בֹֹ[ה]ר, Allegro restores [ד]בֹר (DJD, V, p. 44). Also at iv,11f. I restore: "[Its prophetic meaning concerns the Congregation of the Poor] who will look upon the damnation of the wicked society and rejoice with His elect (one) in the heritage of [mankind]." One reads also of "the congregation of His elect (one)" (ii,5).

THE MIDRASH PESHER OF HABAKKUK

¶28 (ix, 12—x, 5)

הוֹי הַבּוֹצֵעַ בֶּצַע רָע לְבֵיתוֹ לָשׂוּם 12

בַּמָּרוֹם קִנּוֹ לְנָצֵל מִכַּף רָע יַעֲצְתָּה בֹּשֶׁת 13

לְבֵיתְכָה קְצוֹות עַמִּים רַבִּים וְחוֹטֵ֤א [נַפְ]שָׁכָה כִּיא 14

אֶבֶ֤ן מִ[קִּיר תִּזְעָק [וְ]כָפִיס מֵעֵץ יַעֲ[נֶ֤]גֶּ֤ה] 15

[פֵּשֶׁר הַדָּבָ]ר֤ עַל הַכֹּ[והֵ]ן אֲשֶׁר בֹּ] ר֤ [16

[ ] 17

לִהְיוֹת אַבְנֶיהָ בְּעֹשֶׁק וּכְפִיס עֵצָה בְּגָזֵל וַאֲשֶׁר x,1

אָמַר קְצוֹת עַמִּים רַבִּים וְחוֹטֵי נַפְשֶׁכָה 2

פִּשְׁרוֹ הוּא בֵית הַמִּשְׁפָּט אֲשֶׁר יִתֵּן אֵל אֶת 3

מִשְׁפָּטוֹ בְּתוֹךְ עַמִּים רַבִּים וּמִשָּׁם יַעֲלֶנּוּ לַמִּשְׁפָּט 4

וּבְתוֹכָם יַרְשִׁיעֶנּוּ וּבְאֵשׁ גָּוּפְרִית יִשְׁפָּטֶנּוּ 5

12 (2:9) Alas!
        for the grasper of evil gain for his house
13   that he may put / his nest up high
        to be safe from the reach of harm!
14 (2:10) Thou hast planned shame / as thy house:
        the confines of many nations
        and the bonds [of] thine own [sou]l!
15 (2:11) For / the s[tone] shall make outcry [from] the wall
        and the rafter from the woodwork shall e[cho it].
16   [The prophetic meaning of the passag]e concerns the [Pries]t who
17-x,1   . . . / . . . / that its stones should suffer pillage and its rafter of wood
2   endure robbery; and as for that which/ He said, "the confines of many
3   nations and the bonds of thine own soul," / its prophetic meaning is:
4   This is the House of Damnation where, / in the midst of many peoples,
        God will put His judgment; and from there He will raise him up for the
5   Judgment. / Then in their midst He will pronounce him guilty and
        damn him with the fire of brimstone.

¶28 *Exposition*

ix,12-14. For the variants of Hab. 2:9-11, see *Text*, §§ 97-104. Curiously, Lohse still gives the text of ix,10 as הישע instead of הביצע.

ix,14. "Shame for thy house"—or, "that shame be thy house." The nature of the "house" is defined in the subsequent phrases. For the association of "shame" with future punishment, cf. 1Q S iv,12,23.

The *plene* spelling *QSWWT* indicates that in this text we do not have an infinitive "to cut off," but the plural of the theoretical absolute singular feminine noun *qĕṣāt* (as in *BDB*, p. 892b) or *qaṣwāh* (as in Alexander Harkavy, *Hebrew and Chaldee Dictionary to the Old Testament*, p. 673b). *Qĕṣāwôt*, the plural absolute appears in the MT of Ex. 38:5 and Ps. 65:9. The *kĕtîv QSWWTYW* at Ex. 37:8 and 39:4 receives the *qĕrê* vocalization *qĕṣôtāw*. Accroding to Harkavy, the *ketîv* should be *qaṣwôtāw*. Köhler-Baumgartner, p. 847a, employ the theoretical $\sqrt{qāṣû}$ to account for the masculine plural construct forms *qaṣwê* (Isa. 26:15; Pss. 48:11; 65:6). Other cognate noun forms are *qāṣeh* (masculine) and *qāṣāh* (feminine). The latter accounts for the plural construct *qĕṣôt* and for the *qĕrê* readings of Ex. 37:8; 39:4. Two of three occurrences of *QSWT* (*qĕṣôt*) in Isaiah are spelled *QSWWT* in 1Q Isaᵃ (40:28; 41:9). The third is spelled *QSᵓWWT* (41:5), indicating the pronunciation *qĕṣâwôt* even in the construct. Unless this is a scribal error, the ᵓ*Ālef* represents an irreducible *qāmeṣ*, most likely from a singular *qĕṣāt* with the plural absolute *qĕṣāwōt*. Cf. the vocalizations in Neh. 7:69 and Dan. 1:5. The plural absolute naturally retains the long vowel (Ex. 38:5; Ps. 65:9). It is only the plural construct which comes into question. Gesenius (as translated by Edward Robinson, 1871, p. 936b) vocalized the suffixed plural of the *Kĕtîv* reading *QSWWTW* (Ex. 37:8; 39:4) as *qĕṣāwōtāw*. The word may be an Aramaizing form preferred by Qumrân usage. Cf. the construct *qĕṣāt* of Dan. 2:42; 4:26,31.

The *qĕṣāwôt* of Hab. 2:10 appears to be interpreted as "bounds, confines." One may compare here Num. 20:16 *qĕṣēh gĕvûlekhā* which was rendered recently by the Jewish Publication Society as "on the *border* of your territory." Van der Woude (*Bijbelcommentaren*, pp. 36f) translated correctly "in het gebied van vele Volken" ("in the territory of many peoples"), with the caveat (p. 44, note 4): "This translation is not certain, but very probable." Similarly, note Num. 22:36. See, below, the discussion on *bĕtôkh* at x,5.

The word *qĕṣāwôt* appears to be taken in more than one sense, but first of all as "boundaries, or confines," which ingeniously are interpreted as designating the place of punishment in Sheol. Dupont-Sommer (*Essene Writings*, p. 265) rendered the text as "Many peoples are in *extremities* and the sinner is thyself." For this metaphorical usage there appears to be no support. Yet he is right in trying to relate this word of the text to the punishment in the *pēšer.* Del Medico (*Riddle*, pp. 255ff.) renders the word "cuttings-off," not in the sense of destruction, but in the sense of refuse, "scum of many nations."

One might also read *ḥôtê = ḥôṭēʾ* in conformity with the MT.; but the corruption of *ḥôṭēʾ* ("[thou art] forfeiting") into *ḥûṭê* ("cords, ropes, bonds") facilitated the allusion to Sheol in Hab. 2:10. Cf. the ropes with which Delilah bound Samson in Jud. 16:12. As bonds and imprisonment were often associated, so here the "bonds" parallel "confines" as indicating the nature of the "house" of "shame" which the guilty priest had "schemed" for himself. Cf. the "chains" of Sheol in I En. 103:8; Jude 6.

ix,16f. Though at li. 16, the adjective "wicked" has been omitted, "the priest" is so nevertheless. The missing text was concerned with his building operations and how he obtained his "evil gain." Gaster, p. 254, freely supplied "Who planned to build himself a mansion in such a way that its very stones would be furnished through oppression." Though this may be a correct guess as to the nature of the missing contents, we have no parallel passage to suggest any of the wording. One might even think of an elaborate tomb; but, most likely, the priest's "nest on high" was a fortress or a palace, which contrasts with his later house in Sheol. One may recall the tower built by John Hyrcanus near the temple, where he normally dwelled and kept the priestly vestments. Herod rebuilt it and named it Antonia. (See Josephus, *JA*, XVIII, iv,3 [§§ 91-2]). One may likewise recall Alexandreion built by Jannaeus (*JA*, I, vi,5 [§ 134]; *JA*, XIV, iii,4 [§ 49]; XVI, xi,7 [§ 394]), also Masada. Though Josephus says that this last was first built by Jonathan (*JW*, VII, viii,3 [§§ 280-94]), Yadin (*Masada*, New York: Random House, 1966, p. 205) interprets the archaeological data as favoring his identification with Jannaeus. No actual ruins are earlier than Herod. One may also recall the fortress Dok where Simon met his end; but this is said to have been built by Ptolemy, the high priest's son-in-law (I. Macc. 16:11-17).

x,i. "Suffer violence . . . robbery." Literally: "to be *in* violence . . . *in* robbery." Cf. the Targum of Jonathan: *ʾarê ʾavnāʾ mikkûtělāʾ ṣāwěḥāʾ ʿal děʾānês* ("For the stone cries out from the wall against him *who does violence to it.*") "This interpretation," wrote Lehmann (*PEQ*, Jan., 1951, p. 36) "seems to have been familiar to the writer." According to Habakkuk the natural objects of wood and stone are not willing accomplices of men who use them for evil. Therefore, they "make outcry," as truly as the persons who have been wronged (cf. Jer. 22:13). The ancient commentator interprets the cries of the stone and wood as merely poetic expressions for their having undergone violence and robbery.

"*Its* rafter of wood." Read *ʿēṣāh* (*ʿēṣ* + pron. suf.), not *ʿēṣāh* (counsel/council). Cf. *ʾavānehā* (*its* stones). Lehman (*loc. cit.*) has argued that the supralinear *Yôd* was intended to suggest *ʿēṣāh* (counsel) as a double meaning; but it may stand for *Ṣērê*, which goes equally well with *ʿēṣ* wood). Delcor, p. 34, said that the feminine antecedent of the pronominal suffix was probably a city. However, one may equally think of *binyah* (building) or *mesûdah* (fortress).

x,2. The word *qĕṣāwôt* is spelled defectively; but it was unnecessary to repeat the *plene* spelling after ix,14.

x,3. "Its prophetic meaning is: This is the House of Damnation . . ." An interesting effort to relate the *qĕṣāwôt* to the *bêt ham-mišpāṭ* is that of P. R. Weis, in *JQR*, xli, 1950, p. 139, where he sees in "the house of judgment" an interpretation of קצות. He proposed a relating of *QṢWT* to the Arabic verb *QḌY*, "to judge," which for him was a sign of a very late date for the composition of 1Q p Hab. However, Silberman, "Riddle," p. 352, has called attention to James A. Montgomery's comment on the use of the noun *qāṣîn* in Dan. 11:18 (*A Critical and Exegetical Commentary on the Book of Daniel*, ICC, p. 443): "A somewhat rare word has been nicely selected to denote the Roman Consul, *ḳaṣîn* 'judge.' (our Arabic 'Cadi'), parallel in meaning to שפט, 'judge.'"

"This is the House of Damnation *where*." So understand Michel, p. 15; Theodor Gaster, p. 254. My translation "whose," held to as late as *BASOR*, 126 (April, 1952), p. 14, has been followed by Burrows, p. 369 ("of which") and by G. Vermès, *DSSE*, p. 241. However, Dupont-Sommer (*RHR*, p. 137), Bardtke, p. 129, van der Woude, Carmignac (*Textes*, p. 110), Elliger and Lohse treat ᵃšer as the causal conjunction "for." However, without the understanding of *bêt ham-mišpāṭ* as a place, all interpreters encounter difficulty in interpreting the later *miš-šām*. To have been completely unambiguous, ᵃšer should have been followed by *šām*, to be inserted before *bĕtôkh*; but, since this latter word introduces a place designation, the insertion of *šām* may have been regarded as redundant, especially since the phrase itself is followed by *ū-miš-šām* ("and from there"). For another example of ᵃšer as "where," see xii,9 (¶ 33).

The following scholars interpret the *bêt ham-mišpāṭ* as a tribunal or courtroom (some of them citing the Rabbinic *bêt dîn*): Solomon Zeitlin, in *JQR*, xxxix, 1949, pp. 350f.; *JQR*, 1950, p. 38; G. R. Driver, *Hebrew Scrolls*, p. 42; Michel, p. 256; Elliger, p. 208; Carmignac, p. 111, and Silberman, "Riddle," p. 352.

Dupont-Sommer in *RHR*, p. 145 (cf. also pp. 162, 167) interpreted the "house of judgment" as "la Maison d'Israel coupable et damnée;" but in *Essene Writings*, p. 263, he interprets it as "the tribunal before which mankind will be judged at the end of time." This view does not accord with "from there"; for, if it is from the "house of judgment" that one is "brought up to judgment," then this cannot be the place of final judgment. Silberman would relieve this problem by explaining that the commentary "seems to indicate a distinction between the place of sentencing and the place of execution." This then would run afoul the following statement, in which the verb *yaršîᶜennû* ("He will pronounce him guilty") occurs only after the Priest has been brought up from the House of Judgment. Sensing this problem, Silberman explains (p. 353): "The comment is made up of parallel bi-cola, the second repeating the first."

The abrupt $h\hat{u}^{\circ}$ ("this") refers to Hab. 2:10b-c which has been singled out for requotation in order to explain the house of shame mentioned in Hab. 2:10a. The intention is to interpret these phrases as a description of "the House of Judgment [or Damnation]." This is the prison of the wicked in the netherworld. In BASOR, 112, p. 18. n. 67, I wrote:

> This passage employs deeply eschatological language. 'The house of judgment' may be a body of men confined in a certain section of Sheol (or Hades) until they are raised 'from there' and made subject to a final judgment of sulfurous fire (Cf. Revelation 20:13-14).

The "body of men" was later explained as "the partisans of Jannaeus," the term perhaps alluding to the bêt dîn, the Sadducean Sanhedrin, but "given an adverse meaning . . . 'house of damnation,' i.e., 'doomed house.'" This doom was interpreted as two-fold, first as defeat in battle and second as resurrection for the final judgment. (So in BASOR, 126). This attempt to deal with the text historically was probably a mistake.

The view that the "house of judgment" is a place of infernal punishment was early held by Lambert, p. 295, n. 125. It has been ably set forth by Habermann, ^{c}Edah, pp. 52f. and by Widengren, Tradition and Literature in Early Judaism and the Early Church, 1963, p. 54. Both scholars cite the expression "place of condemnation" in Jub. 10:9, as translated by R. H. Charles from the Ethiopic makâna dain; for the Hebrew Book of Noah (published in Jellinek's Bet ha-Midrasch, 1856, iii, pp. 155-156 and extensively quoted by R. H. Charles, The Ethiopic Version of the Hebrew Book of Jubilees, 1895, Appendix I, p. 179) contains numerous parallels to Jub. 10:1-15, the equivalent to 10:9 reading: ויעש המלאך כן ויכלאם אל בית המשפט אך אחד מעשרה הניח להתהלך בארץ לפני שר המשטמה, namely: "And the angel did so: he imprisoned them at the house of judgment. Only one tenth [of the demons] did he allow to walk to and fro in the earth, (serving) before the Prince of Hostility." Already, Jellinek had noted in his Einleitung, pp. xxx ff., the parallelism with Jubilees, and he attributed both works to the Essenes. The question is whether this Book of Noah used Jubilees as a source (so Jellinek and Charles), or whether it is one of the sources of the Book of Jubilees (so Widengren). In either case, the Ethiopic phrase makâna dain translates the original Hebrew expression bêt ham-mišpāṭ. This expression occurs also in Jub. 10:5, which is a place of confinement of the evil spirits. In Jub. 22:22, however, idolatrous men are also consigned there:

> And as for all the worshippers of idols and the profane,
>   there will be no hope for them in the land of the living;
> for they will descend into Sheol,
>   and into the place of condemnation will they go,
>   that there may be no remembrance of them on earth.

Notice that Hab. 2:10b-c is the middle portion of the passage cited at ix, 12-15, and that all the surrounding text has already been interpreted with regard to the unjust priest. This central portion is now requoted, not to apply it to a new party, but to indicate that the palatial residence of this evil man will soon be followed by a shameful abode in Sheol. It is his own wicked scheming on earth which will bring him to this other house. Cf. the use of "house" for Sheol in Job 17:13. From his "nest" where he perched "on high," he is to be thrust down to the netherworld, as Babylon in Isa. 14:12ff. Cf. esp., Ob. 3-4; Jer. 49:16. Similarly in I Enoch 63:10, the "kings and mighty who possess the earth" (vs. 1) declare: "Our souls are full of unrighteous gain, but it does not prevent us from descending from the midst thereof into the *fortress* of Sheol." (The Ethiopic reads "burden of Sheol," but R. H. Charles, *Apocrypha and Pseudepigrapha*, Vol. II, p. 230, suggests a misreading of the underlying Greek version, a confusion of Βάριν with Βάρος).

x,4f. "Where, in the midst of many peoples, God will put His judgment." The most relevant parallels seem to be Num. 31:3, *lātēt niqmat YHWH bĕmidyān* ("to put Yahweh's vengeance upon Midian") and Zeph. 3:5, *mišpāṭô yittēn* (He will dispense His justice"). Since this is verbally very close to the text of our *pēšer*, I favor the subjective genitive, "His judgment," instead of the objective genitive "his judgment." Scholars favoring the subjective genitive are: Dupont-Sommer; van der Ploeg, *Bi. Or.*, VIII, p. 8; Molin, p. 15; Gaster; and Carmignac; but those taking this as the objective genitive are: Lambert; Bardtke; Del Medico; Elliger; Maier, I, p. 154; Vermès, and Lohse. There may even be a double-entendre here, "where God will place the Priest's damnation," and not simply "His own judgment." The use of the imperfect form of the verb, *yittēn* would suggest the following possibilities: (1) that the Wicked Priest was still alive at the time of the composition of this midrash; (2) that he was dead, but that the imperfect was employed to indicate that this judgment is a continuous work of God; and (3) that he was dead, but that the wording of this particular pericope was received by tradition from an earlier time, when the Wicked Priest was yet living.

Judgment (i.e., punishment) begins in the intermediate state and does not wait for the Day of Judgment. When one recalls the ancient practice of torture in prison, even while the prisoner was awaiting trial, the attribution of punishment to Sheol does not seem surprising. For punishment in Sheol, see I En. 63:10; 99:11; 103:7f.; Luke 16:22ff.; esp. II Pet. 2:9: "The Lord knows how to rescue the godly from trial, and to keep the unrighteous *under punishment* until the day of judgment" (RSV).

x,5. "In the midst of many peoples." The word *qĕṣāwôt*, which was previously interpreted as the bounds of the House of Damnation is here interpreted as also meaning "in the midst." Just as מקצות in the O. T. often means מתוך, so קצות is interpreted here as בתוך. E. L. Sukenik was the first to note this equation, *Mĕgillot Gĕnuzot*, II, p. ṣ.

That the priest's "damnation" should be located "in the midst of many [or, great] peoples" accords with the Old Testament. Cf. Babylon's descent into Sheol, where other great nations had preceded her (Isa. 14:9f.); also the descent of Egypt (Ezek. 32:18-32), where she joined Assyria (v. 22), Elam (v. 24f.), Meshech and Tubal (v. 26ff.), Edom (v. 29), and Phoenicia (v. 30). In this passage, moreover, *bětôkh* and its synonym *ᵓet* are oft repeated words. The descent of Jewish leaders into such a realm was presaged by Isa. 5:14. Cf. Ps. 9:18(=9:17): "The wicked will turn away to Sheol, all nations who forget God." See also II Baruch 85:9—"And that we may rest with our fathers, and not be tormented with our enemies."

x,5. "And from there He will raise him up for the Judgment." The word *û-miš-šām* taken in any other sense than "and from there" represents a misunderstanding not only of this word, but also of the preceding sentence. Assuming that the passage has spoken of a doomed party which has fallen in battle among foreign troops, any eschatological judgment of the priest would follow this, and hence "afterward" (so Dupont-Sommer, *RHR*, p. 145; Bardtke, p. 130) would be a suitable meaning. Gesenius, p. 1080a, lists this meaning for Hos. 2:17 (=2:15). Bo Reicke, *Handskrifterna*, p. 37, interprets *miš-šām* as equivalent to *šām*; and this is the interpretation of the RSV at Hos. 2:15. Even if this meaning be granted for Hosea, it would shed no light on 1Qp Hab, for the verb of motion which follows would in that case require *šāmmāh*, "thither." The full pair of words, *ᵓašer . . . û-miš-šām* is rendered "where . . . and from there" by J. van der Ploeg, *Bi. Or.*, VIII, p. 8; Lambert, p. 295; Edelkoort, p. 60; Molin, p. 15; Michel, p. 15; Del Medico, *Riddle*, p. 254; Maier.

"Raise him up" (*yaᶜᵃlennû*). Cf. 1Q M i,3 (*miššām yaᶜᵃlû*). The energetic pronominal suffix of 1Q p Hab is the 3rd per. masc. sing., as with the following verbs. It probably does not refer to the "House of Damnation" (although *bayit* is masc.), but to the Wicked Priest, as Delcor, p. 34, also interprets. For the use of the *hifᶜîl* of ᶜ*LH* for raising up from Sheol, one may note Pss. 30:4; 40:3, and especially I Sam. 2:6: "The Lord kills and brings to life; he brings down to Sheol and *raises up*." The Targum interprets this with respect to the final resurrection "in eternal life." See J. F. A. Sawyer, "Hebrew Words for the Resurrection of the Dead," *VT*, XXIII, 1973, pp. 218-34, esp. pp. 224f. According to the Babylonian Talmud, Sanhedrin 92*b*, I Sam. 2:6 was sung by the resurrected warriors in Ezekiel's vision. The present passage differs from these in appropriating the same verb for the resurrection of the wicked. However, an eschatological interpretation of Joel 4:9, 12 could yield the meaning that the nations gathered and judged in the Valley Jehoshaphat will be raised up for this purpose. Note esp., vs. 12, which in *pēšer* exegesis could be interpreted: "Let the nations *awaken* [from the sleep of death] and *come up* [from Sheol] to the Valley of Jehoshaphat." On belief in immortality by the Essenes, see: van der Ploeg, in *VT*, II, 1952, pp. 171-75; *Bi. Or.*, XVII, 1961, pp. 118-124; Delcor in *NRTh*, LXXVII, 1955, pp. 614-630; Burrows, *More Light*, pp. 344-47; R. B. Laurin in *JSS*, III, 1958, pp. 344-55; Mansoor,

The Thanksgiving Hymns, pp. 54, 84-89; Matthew Black, "The Account of the Essenes in Hippolytus and Josephus"; Brownlee, "Anthropology and Soteriology," p. 235, n. 51.

"For *the* Judgment." Vocalize: *lam-mišpāṭ*, for "the Day of Judgment" (xiii,4f.). Sheol is a prison where one awaits the final judgment. Cf. Isa. 24:22; II Pet. 2:9. Resurrection precedes judgment, as in Dan. 12:2; John 5:28f.; Acts 24:15; and Rev. 20:13.

x,5. "In their midst He will pronounce him guilty." The wicked are to be judged twice, each time "in the midst of many peoples." Hence it is possible that the *qěṣāwôt* were taken as "ends, dooms, judgments"—the plural justifying the application here. The gathering of the nations for the grand assize is indicated in Matth. 25:32, an idea perhaps derived from Joel 4:9, 12; Zeph. 3:8.

"And damn him with the fire of brimstone." O. H. Lehmann (*PEQ*, 83rd year, 1951, pp. 37f.) has made the interesting speculation that the *ḥûṭê nafšô* of x,2 were streams of fire, and that this presupposes a knowledge of the tradition of a Baraita found in the Babylonian Talmud, Sanhedrin 52a f. and in the Midrash Sifra to Leviticus that declares how "threads of fire" (*ḥûṭîm*) went forth from the sanctuary in order to kill the souls of Dathan and Abiram without consuming their clothes. This sort of interpretation is favored also by Elliger, p. 207. Judgment by fire was a common idea in the prophets. Cf. Amos 7:4; Zeph. 3:8; Dan. 7:9-11, etc. According to Jer. 49:16-18, the doom of one who "sets his nest on high" is to be hurled down to a judgment "like Sodom and Gomorrah"—the very places once destroyed by fire and brimstone (Gen. 19:24; Luke 17:29). Note similarly the judgment of Gog (Ezek. 38:19, 22) and of the wicked (Ps. 11:6). See likewise Job 18:15 and 20:23 as amended by M. Dahood, *Biblica*, XXXVIII, 1957, pp. 314f. (Marvin Pope adopts Dahood's restoration in *Anchor Bible, Job*, p. 126). Gehenna was frequently referred to as a place of fire and the Apocalypse adds brimstone as well (Rev. 9:17f.; 14:10; 19:20; 20:10; 21:8). Note also 1QS iv, 13f. which describes the miserable lot of the backslider:

> in everlasting terror and perpetual disgrace, together with the shame of destruction *in the fire of the dark regions*; and all their times in their generations will be in grievous mourning and bitter misfortune amid the calamities of darkness *until their destruction*, without remnant or survival of them.

Unlike 1Q p Hab, this passage does not clearly distinguish between the punishment of the intermediate state and that of the Last Judgment. Still it is possible that this latter is alluded to in the words "*until* their destruction." Perhaps the suffering of the netherworld was conceived of as a temporary condition ending in annihilation at the Day of Judgment. It may be the function of the "fire of brimstone" to destroy and not merely torment. Hippolytus, *Adv. haer.*, (as noted by K. Schubert, *ZKTh*, 1952, p. 36) ascribes to the Essenes the doctrine that the world will be destroyed by fire and that the

wicked will be punished for ever. Cf. the fiery torrents of Sheol in 1Q H iii,28-
32. On Hippolytus, see Matthew Black.

THE MIDRASH PESHER OF HABAKKUK

¶ 29 (x, 5-13)

הוֹי 5

בּוֹנֶה עִיר בְּדָמִים וְיכוֹנֵן קִרְיָה בְּעַוְלָה הֲלוֹא 6

הִנֵּה מֵעִם יהוה צְבָאוֹת יָגְעוּ עַמִּים בְּדֵי אֵשׁ 7

וּלְאֻמִּים בְּדֵי רִיק וְיָעֵפוּ 8

פֵּשֶׁר הַדָּבָר עַל מַטִּיף הַכָּזָב אֲשֶׁר הִתְעָה רַבִּים 9

לִבְנוֹת עִיר שָׁוְא בְּדָמִים וְלָקִים עֵדָה בְּשֶׁקֶר 10

בַּעֲבוּר כְּבוֹדָהּ לוֹגִיעַ רַבִּים בַּעֲבוֹדַת שָׁוְא וּלְהַרְוֹתָם 11

בְּ[מַעֲ]שֵׂי שֶׁקֶר לִהְיוֹת עֲמָלָם לָרִיק בַּעֲבוּר יָבוֹאוּ 12

לְמִשְׁפְּטֵי אֵשׁ אֲשֶׁר גִּדְּפוּ וַיְחָרְפוּ אֶת בְּחִירֵי אֵל 13

5   (2:12) Alas, /

6   for him who builds a city through bloodshed
            and sets up an assembly through deceit! /

7   (2:13)   Is is not, / indeed, from YHWH of Hosts
            that peoples have toiled only for fire, /

8   and folks to no avail, and grow weary? /

9   The prophetic meaning of the passage concerns the Prophet of Lies,

10 who beguiled many / into building through bloodshed his city of vanity

11 and into erecting through falsehood a congregation / for enhancing its

glory. He thereby forced many into tiresome toil at his labor of vanity and

12 sated them / with [wor]ks of falsehood, so that their travail should be to

13 no avail—with the result that they should enter / the judgments of fire,

since they have reviled and insulted the elect of God.

¶29 *Exposition*

x,5-8. For the textual variants of Hab. 2:12f., see *Text*, §§ 105-109.

x,6. The noun *qiryāh* in parallelism with ʿîr should mean "town." However, 1Q p Hab interprets the noun as ʿēdāh at x,10. Thus *qiryāh* was interpreted as "congregation," and this accords with the discussion of *BDB* which derives the word from the √*QRH* and ascribes to it the etymological sense of "meeting-place of men." The ancient commentator, however, may have associated the term *qiryāh* with *miqrāʾ* and thereby with *lĕ-miqrāʾ hā-ʿēdāh* in Num. 10:2, "for summoning the congregation."

x,7. The text and translation are here treated as harmonistic accommodations to Jer. 51:58, in line with Segert's suggestion discussed in *Text*, §§ 108, 110. The words *hᵃlôʾ hinnēh* are interpreted by The Jerusalem Bible, in the light of II Chron. 25:26, as "a formula prefacing a quotation . . . here introducing a word of Yahweh in the two following lines." If the ancient commentator had this understanding of the idiom, it may have served as a hint for his application of the passage to the Prophet of Lies. As he interpreted it, the passage would mean: "It cannot be, can it, that such and such activity is according to an oracle from YHWH of Hosts, as the False Prophet alleges?" This, however, would not exhaust the meaning; for in a sense the passage requires a positive answer: "It is from YHWH that such evil activity leads only to judgments of fire." *Hᵃlôʾ*, to be sure, always invites an affirmative answer; but it could, perhaps, have been pressed into the opposite meaning by being construed as irony.

x,9. "The Prophet of Lies" (*maṭṭîf hak-kāzāv*), literally, "the Dripper of Lie[s]." He is probably the same as the *ʾîš hak-kāzāv* of ii,1f. (¶ 7); v,11f. (¶ 17), x,17-xi,1 (¶ 30), who is also referred to as the *ʾîš hal-lāṣôn* of CDC i,14f. (= 1:10):

> When there arose the Man of Scorn,
> who dripped to Israel water of lies,
> and led them astray into pathless chaos.

The *hifʿîl* of *NṬP* is used in the Old Testament for both true prophecy (Am. 7:16; Ezek. 21:2, 7[=20:46; 21:2) and false prophecy (Mic. 2:6, 11). F. M. Cross (*Ancient Library*, pp. 154f.) notes: "The title is taken from Micah 2:11 and is regularly combined in sectarian exposition with Ezekiel 13: 8-12." This language of precipitation makes it antithetical to *môreh haṣ-ṣedeq*, "the one who showers righteousness [or, truth]." See *NTS*, III, 1956-57, p. 13.

"Who beguiled many" (or, "who led many astray"). Cf. the above citation of CDC i,14f., also xx,10ff. (=9:36f.):

> With a judgment like that of their fellows who turned away with *the men of scorn* shall they be judged, for they spoke out for *straying* contrary to the ordinances of righteousness and they rejected the covenant and pledge of faith which they had confirmed in the Land of Damascus; and this is the New Covenant.

These "men of scorn" (cf. Isa. 28:14), like the "Man of Scorn," are characterized by leading others astray. In 4Q p Nah iii,8 (¶ 8), the same charge of beguiling, or misleading, is laid to the false teachers of Ephraim (apparently the Pharisees). In 4Q p Pss i, 26f. (¶ 7), it is "the Man of Lies who beguiled many with words of falsehood." From all these passages, it seems clear that the Prophet of Lies (alias, Man of Lies, or Man of Scorn) must be a man of religious authority among the Jews. Hence, he cannot be Antiochus Epiphanes as H. H. Rowley proposed in *The Zadokite Fragments*, p. 70.

x,10. The word *lāqîm* = *lĕ-hāqîm*, is a characteristic syncope of Qumrân literature. Cf. *lôqîaᶜ* of li. 11. The first printing of *DDS*, I, read לקום. In contrast with the "city," which is simply repeated in the interpretation, the noun *qiryāh* is explained as *ᶜēdāh* ("congregation"). This interpretive equation, as also its parallelism with *ᶜîr*, militates against interpreting *ᶜēdāh* as "testimony," or "memorial" (as in Gen. 21:30; 31:52; Josh. 24:27), as translated by Dupont-Sommer (*RHR*, p. 138, but not in *Essene Writings*), Bardtke (p. 130), Del Medico (*Riddle*, p. 255). Just as a city contains a congregation (or community), so it might be thought of as being the location of a *court* (as in the translation of *BASOR*, 112, p. 14), a Rabbinic meaning of *ᶜēdāh*; but "congregation" is better. The sect of the Scrolls is the "congregation of God" (1Q M iv,9), the "congregation of holiness" (1Q Sa i,12f.), as also "the congregation of the men of perfection of holiness" (CDC xx,2 [9:30]); but apostate Israel constitutes the "congregation of Belial" (1Q H ii,22), "of vanity" (vii,34), "of traitors" (CDC i,12 [1:8]), and "of wickedness" (1Q M xv,9).

The "city" probably refers to Jerusalem (as in Mic. 3:10); whereas the "congregation" refers to "the congregation of the expounders of smooth things which is in Jerusalem" (4Q p Isaᶜ ii,10f.; cf. 1Q H ii,32). "*His* city of vanity" interprets *ŠWW* as *šāwô*, the quiescent *ᵓĀlef* being omitted before the pronominal suffix. Cf. the single *Wāw* (*ŠW*) at Isa. 59:4(1Q Isaᵃ); 1Q H vii,34. The *ᵓĀlef* of *Šāwᵓ* was probably unpronounced, even in MT, and hence it is omitted in the *kĕtîv* spelling of Job 15:31. The meaning of the word is not simply "emptiness" or "futility," though that is part of the meaning, but as a synonym of *šeqer* and as a qualification of the *maṭṭîf hak-kāzāv* it designates that which is false. On the use of *šāwᵓ* with false prophets, see Zech. 10:2; Ezek. 13:6f., 9, 23; 21:34; 22:28.

It has been a matter of dispute whether this building activity is literal or metaphorical. It seems probable that the two infinitive clauses are complementary; the first concerns the building of a "city," and the second concerns the nature of the "congregation" within it. This becomes particularly clear in the discussion of li. 11; but already one notes that the physical character of the "city" is matched by the shedding of physical "blood," whereas the "erecting of a congregation" is "through falsehood," a spiritual matter. Through war one may capture a city which one undertakes to rebuild, or "through bloodshed" he may conquer people who are compelled to participate in the building operations. False teaching, however, is the basis of establishing an apostate congregation. No telling point can be made of the fact that *bānāh* is used of the "city" and *hēqîm* of the "congregation." Not only is the former verb often used metaphorically in the Old Testament, it is even used of the true ʿēdāh in 4Q p Pss iii,16 (¶ 21), as built by the Righteous Teacher. Likewise, the *hifʿîl* of *qûm* can be used as a simple synonym for *bānāh*, as in the erection of an altar (II Sam. 24:18, cf. 25). Consequently, one should not take *lāqîm* in a purely general sense appropriate to establishing a people (as in Deut. 28:9; 29:12), but as a building term, "erecting," employed metaphorically.

x,11. "For enhancing its glory," i.e., "for the sake of the city's glory." The feminine suffix of *kĕvôdāh* should not be taken as an error for *kĕvôdô* ("his glory") as in *BASOR*, 112, p. 14, and followed by: Vermès, *Discovery*, p. 130; Bardtke, p. 130; Elliger; Sutcliffe, *Monks*, p. 176; and Dupont-Sommer, *Essene Writings* (p. 265). Earlier, Dupont-Sommer read the feminine suffix, as also does the later translation of Vermès, *DSSE*, p. 241. No one has discussed the syntax, but translations generally connect it with what precedes, in contrast with my first translation which was followed here by Vermès, *Discovery*, and by Sutcliffe. Once the pronominal antecedent is recognized as the "city," all ambiguity is removed. The "congregation" was raised up to enhance the city's glory. By making it a center of religion and culture, the Prophet of Lies sought to glorify the "city." Hence, this phrase reinforces the distinction between the "city" and the "congregation." One therefore agrees with Paul Winter that the present passage is non-allegorical. See *PEQ*, 1959, pp. 39-42. Cf. "the builders of the wall" in CDC iv,19 (= 7:1); viii, 12f., 18; xix,24-26, 31 (= 9:21, 26), a phrase borrowed from Ezek. 13:10. From the fact that *maṭṭîf hak-kāzāv* figures in viii,13 and xix,24f., as also the verb in iv,19, it is clear that the same person is involved there as in 1Q p Hab. Since his building efforts were both material and spiritual, one cannot be certain that CDC is concerned solely with the latter.

x,llf. "He thereby forced many into tiresome toil . . . and sated them." This is virtually an independent sentence; and yet, since the text uses infinitives instead of the finite forms of the verbs, some sort of connection with that which precedes was intended. The loose connection is indicated in translation by the retrospective adverb "thereby." The break is indicated grammatically by the fact that these infinitives, unlike the preceding ones, are not governed by the verb *hitʿāh* of li. 9; nor is *rabbîm* ("many") any longer the subject of the infinitives, but the "Prophet of Lies."

The *hifʿîl* infinitive *lĕ-hôqîaʿ* is here contracted to *lôqîaʿ*, the *Hē* being elided. The meaning of the verb is twofold: "to cause to labor" and "to weary," hence "tiresome toil." *Rabbîm*, which has now become the object of the verb, does not refer to members of the sect, as frequently in 1Q S. It interprets rather ʿammîm and lĕʾummîm of Hab. 2:13. Though in Isa. 51:4 both terms appear in the singular as a designation of the Jews, the plural should refer to nations other than Israel—or, at most, to nations among whom the Jews are included (Gen. 25:23). Under John Hyrcanus (whom some have regarded as the "False Prophet"), Idumeans were forcibly proselytized to Judaism and similar pressure was brought to bear upon the Samaritans. Whether labor battalions were organized from such people for building up Jerusalem is unknown. An underlying allusion to Samaritans, Idumeans, and Jews would make sense out of the "peoples;" but the thought could be that the Jews themselves were so unorthodox that they are no better than ^{c}*ammîm*.

"Sated them" (*lĕ-harwôtām*), the *hifᶜîl* infinitive of *rāwāh*. This has been read hitherto only by Vermès, *Discovery*, p. 130, who rendered "making them drunk with works of falsehood," but vocalized it as *harôthām*. Cf. *hā-rĕwāyāh* at xi,14. The first reading was *lĕ-hōrôtām*, "to instruct them" (*BASOR*, 112, p. 14). This has been followed by: van der Ploeg (*Bi. Or.*, VIII, p. 8), Edelkoort (p. 61), Habermann (ᶜ*Edah*, p. 54; *Megilloth*, p. 47), Molin (p. 15), Gaster (p. 255), van der Woude (*Bijbelcommentaren*, p. 37), Maier, I, p. 155), Sutcliffe (*Monks*, p. 177).

Another popular reading is *lĕ-hārôtām*, "that they might conceive." This reading proposed by Dupont-Sommer (*RHR*, pp. 138, 148) has been followed by Delcor (p. 27), Reicke (*Handskrifterna*, p. 37), Bardtke (p. 130), Elliger, Michel (p. 16), Burrows (p. 369), Vermès (*DSSE*), Carmignac (*Textes*, p. 112), and Lohse. It has an advantage over the previous two in that one need not suppose defective spelling. However, *Ḥôlem* is not always represented by a *Wāw*. Note: *WRZNYM* (iv,1), *LMŠL* (v,13), *ZBḤYM* (vi,4), *QṢWT* (x,2 = *QṢWWT* of ix,14), and *LRB* (xi,2). The crowding of this word at the end of the line would be a special inducement for omitting *Wāw* where it is not a consonant.

Yalon (*KS*, p. 175a) declares that it is impossible to explain this infinitive as from *hôrāh* ("teach"), in view of its parallel *lôqîaᶜ* (=*lĕ-hôqîaᶜ*). In his view it should be explained from the √*HR, HRHR* which occurs in Syriac. The cognate noun *hertā*⁾ occurs in the Syriac of Ezra 4:22 as a translation of the Aramaic *ḥᵃvālā* ("damage"). The verbal root in Syriac, however, is only *HR* (the ⁾*afᶜ ēl* being required for "cause harm"). *HRHR* is a Rabbinic term meaning "to conceive in mind" or "to heat, make sick with fever" (Jastrow, *Dictionary*, p. 366b). Neither of these can account for the spelling in 1Q p Hab. Yet this derivation would seem to be necessary to account for the translation of Del Medico (*Riddle*, p. 255): "and brought about their destruction by works of imposture."

The reading "conceive" (or "be pregnant") would require a sudden shift of subject from the Prophet of Lies to the people. Moreover, the preposition *B* is not normally employed with this verb. The fact that this is the preposition of subject matter in Qumrân usage does favor the meaning "instruct, or teach." As for verbs of knowing or understanding, see not only the √ *BYN* (with which the preposition *B* would be expected), but also *YDᶜ* (1Q H ix,9f.; xiii,18f.; xiv,17; 1QS viii,18), *NBṬ* (1Q S xi,19), and *ŚKL* (1Q S xi,18f.; 1Q H xi,14). As for verbs of teaching, see not only the √BYN, but also YD^c (1Q H iv,27f.; vii,27; x,4; xi,4), $\acute{S}KL$ (1Q H vii,26; x,4; xi,4; 1Q S ix,18), and LMD (1Q Sa i,7; 1Q S iii,13f.). The absence of the $hif^c\hat{\imath}l$ of YRH is conspicuous, the verb being evidently avoided except with respect to the Righteous Teacher. It is also the honored root for the noun *Torah*. Consequently, its use for teaching by the Prophet of Lies would be surprising. Nevertheless, we should probably see in the present verb a sarcastic and punning surrogate for the verb *lĕ-hôrôt*, and the reading of *lĕ-harwōtām* seems best for the following reasons: (1) The sect liked the symbolism of verbs of precipitation for different kinds of teaching. See the comments at li.9. *Rāwāh* means "to drench, to saturate, to water abundantly." It is thereby an apt figure of speech for instruction by the "Dripper of Lies." Cf. Isa. 55:10f. for the figurative use of this verb. (2) The preposition B is still appropriate as indicating subject matter after a verb of instruction. (3) The meaning "sate" is an apt complement to the previous verb "to weary." It is this which makes it more suitable to the context than simply "teach." To be sure, *rāwāh* in its various forms may be used in a good sense to "satisfy;" yet in Rabbinic Hebrew it is often employed of intoxication, as also its cognate noun in 1Q p Hab xi,14. Likewise, when used of an undesirable means of satisfaction ("works of falsehood"), its import is adverse, as in Lam. 3:15. (4) The subject of the verb remains unchanged from that of the previous infinitive.

The parallelism is still a matter of the physical and spiritual sides of the "city"/"congregation." "To force many into tiresome toil at his labor of vanity" is physical and "to sate them with works of falsehood" is spiritual, since the latter refers to erroneous teaching and practice. "His labor of vanity" harks back to "his city of vanity," and the "works of falsehood" are those of the "congregation" which was established "through falsehood"—an expression which interprets *bĕ-^{c}awlāh* of the Biblical text. The "angel of darkness," who is the enemy of "truth," is variously called by the Society Manual as the *rûaḥ ^{c}āwel* (1Q S ii,18f.) and the *rûaḥ ^{c}awlāh* (iv,9). The whole gamut of vices into which this spirit seduces (iv,9-11) emphasizes strongly the practical and moral character of "falsehood" and "error." The phrase "with works of falsehood" refers to false interpretations of the Law, falacious *h^{a}lākhot*. Contrast the *ma^c^{a}śē $^{\gamma e}$met* ("works of truth") of 1Q S i,19; 1Q H i,31; 1Q M xiii,1f., 8.

x,12f. "So that their travail should be to no avail—with the result that they should enter the judgments of fire." The second purposive clause is epexegetical to the first, and its introductory conjunction *ba^c^{a}vûr* is emphatic. Note that in the interpretation the order of the words "to no avail" and "fire" is that of the parallel passage of Jer. 51:58, not that of Hab. 2:13. The "travail" of the people leads to "judgments of fire," whereas that of those faithful to the Righteous Teacher delivers them from the "House of Damnation" (viii,2f.).

"*Enter* the judgments of fire" suggests that $YG^c W$ (Hab. 2:13) be read not only as *yāgĕʿû* (from *YGᶜ*), but also as *yiggĕʿû* (from *NGᶜ*): "that peoples may *reach* the flames [(] of fire." See Finkel, p. 369.

x,13. "Since they have reviled and insulted the elect of God." "Since" interprets *ᵃšer* as a causal conjunction. However, it would also be possible to translate: "that they may enter the judgments of fire, *they who* have reviled . . ."—the subject being supplied at the end as a climactic accusation. This is exactly the construction of van der Woude, *Bijbelcommentaren*, p. 37 and F. M. Cross (p. 155). For the two verbs, but in reverse order, see II Kings 19:22 (= Isa. 37:23) and Ps. 44:17 (Heb.; otherwise, 44:16). The phrase "elect of God" (*bĕḥîrê ʾēl*) is in this case clearly plural. Contrast *bĕḥîrô* (= *ᶜammô*) in v,4 (¶ 16). A fundamental question with respect to this clause is whether the verbs *GDP* and *ḤRP* were in any way inferred from the Biblical text. Any connection would need to be by inference from the nature of the punishment, "fire." Korah's rebellion, which took the form of reviling Moses, was punished by fire (Num. 16). In I En. 91:7-9, "blasphemy" is one of several sins to be punished on the Day of Judgment with fire. According to CDC v. 11-13 (= 7:12-14) those who possess "a tongue of blasphemies" (*lĕšôn giddûfîm*) are the "kindlers of fire and setters aflame of firebrands" (Isa. 50:11).

THE MIDRASH PESHER OF HABAKKUK

¶30 (x, 14–xi, 2)

14 כִּי תִמָּלֵא הָאָרֶץ לָדַעַת אֶת כְּבוֹד יהוה כַּמַּיִם

15 יְכַסּוּ עַל הַיָּם   פֵּשֶׁר הַדָּבָר [אֲשֶׁר]

16 בְּשׁוּבָם מִ[נְּתִיבוֹת צֶדֶק יֶחֱרֶה אַף אֵ]ל [בָּהֶם כִּיא]

17 [בְּהוֹפַע כְּבוֹדוֹ לְיִשְׂרָאֵל יִכָּרְתוּ הַשָּׁבִים עִם אִישׁ]

xi, 1 הַכָּזָב וְאַחַר תִּגָּלֶה לָהֶם הַדַּעַת כְּמֵי

2 הַיָּם לָרֹב

14 (2:14) For the land will be filled with knowledge,
along with the LORD's glory,

15   as water / swells the sea.

16   The prophetic meaning of the passage is [that] / when they turn aside [[from the paths of righteousness, the wrath of Go]]d [[will be kindled

17 against them; for / when His glory shines out to Israel, they who turned

xi,1 aside with the Man of]] / Lies *[[will be cut off]].* Then, afterward, the

2 knowledge will be revealed to them, as the water of / the sea for abundance.

174

¶30 *Exposition*

x,14f. For the variants of Hab. 2:14, see *Text*, §§ 111-112.

x,14. "The *land*," or "earth." In Habakkuk the meaning is probably universal, hence "earth." Yet the Jerusalem Bible renders "the country," as at Isa. 11:9, where the parallelism with "all my holy mountain" favors the more restricted application to the land of Israel. The present commentary seems not to give a universal application.

"Filled with knowledge, along with the LORD's glory"—or, "filled with knowing the LORD's glory." The former construes da^cat as a noun followed by the preposition $^{\jmath}et$; but the latter takes it as the infinitive followed by the sign of the accusative. The latter is certainly the more probable meaning for Habakkuk, but not for the scroll.

x,15. For the restoration of $^{\jmath a}\check{s}er$ after $p\bar{e}\check{s}er\ had-d\bar{a}v\bar{a}r$, cf. $pi\check{s}r\hat{o}\ ^{\jmath a}\check{s}er$ at vii,7, 15 (primary quotations), v,7; vi,3 (secondary quotations). There is no room for the more usual ^cal followed by the mention of the person or party involved. The full expression is now attested at 4Q p Isa^b i,2, 4Q Catena^a, fragments 1-4, li. 6.

x,16. "When they turn aside [from the paths of righteousness]." For the restoration, cf. CDC i,15f. (=1:10). Another possibility might be "from the ways of truth." Cf. 1Q S iv,17, CDC iii,15 (=5:2). Apostasy at Qumrân meant a departure from the way of righteousness taught by the True Teacher. For the indefinite subject of the verb, cf. vii,15f. The meaning of the verb $\check{s}\hat{u}v$ is determined by the preposition used with it: (1) "turn aside [with]," (2) "return [to]," (3) "turn, return, or repent [from]." A free translation such as "at their conversion," or "when they are converted" covers both the second and third alternatives. Thus have rendered Dupont-Sommer, *RHR*, p. 138; Lambert, p. 295; Delcor, p. 27; Vermès, *Discovery*, p. 139 (but in *DSSE*, p. 241, "when they return"); van der Woude, *Bijbelcommentaren*, p. 37. My first translation (*BASOR*, 112, p. 15) opted for no. 3 "when they re(pe)nt from." Burrows, p. 369, also renders "when they repent." Habermann in *Megilloth*, p. 47, restores בשובם [אל א]ל "when they return to God"). Gaster, p. 255, translates "when God restores them to their former glory." This would require בהשיבם א[ל] (which is impossible). Both Habermann and Gaster seem to suggest that the preserved traces of the first letter are an $^{\jmath}\bar{A}lef$. I first supposed that I could see the two upper points of the *Mêm*. Later, I came to doubt the presence of the upper left trace and suggested restoring [עם א]יש שׁ הכזב in agreement with CDC xx,14f. (=9:30). See the restoration in "Anthropology and Soteriology," p. 239, n. 60: "When they turn aside [with the Man of Lies, the wrath of Go]d [will be kindled against them . . .]" Now, however, Trever's colored photographs seem once more to assure the reading *Mêm*.

The basic contents of the restoration, as pointed out in my article "The Composition of Habakkuk," p. 270, n. 2, are based upon CDC xx,10, 14ff., 25f. (=9:36, 39, 49):

With a judgment like that of their fellows, who turned aside with the scornful men, will they be judged . . . And from the day when there was gathered in the Teacher of the Community until the destruction of all the men of war who turned aside with the Man of Lies, about forty years, at that time the wrath of God will be kindled against Israel. . . . And for all those who have broken down the landmark of the Law amongst those who entered into the covenant, when there shall shine forth the glory of God to Israel, they shall be cut off from the midst of the camp, with all those who do wickedly in the days of its testing.

In view of the length of the restoration, the materials are double bracketed. Although the precise wording is uncertain, the general nature of the lost contents seems probable, as the following observations show: (1) A reference to either ʾîš hak-kāzāv or maṭṭîf hak-kāzāv seems probable for x,17f., in view of the fact that the second word is preserved at xi,1. The use of the article occurs only in connection with these synonymous expressions (1Q p Hab ii,1f.; v,11; x,9; CDC xx,15). Those who restore "Man of Lies" include: Brownlee; Maier, I, p. 155; Elliger; van der Woude, Bijbelcommentaren, p. 38. Molin, p. 15, restores "Prophet of Lies." Habermann's restoration [mêmê] hak-kāzāv ("water of falsehood") employs an expression from CDC i,15 (=1:10), which is used of the "Man of Scorn"(=Man of Lies), but which lacks the article. Unimpressive is the restoration of Lambert, p. 295, based on 1Q S iv, 21: "[Dieu répandra sur eux l'esprit de vérité pour les laver de toutes les abominations du] mensonge." The parallel in 1Q S would call for šeqer, not hak-kāzāv. (2) The word bĕ-šûvām recalls the use of the same verb in connection with apostasy with the Man of Lies in CDC xx,10, 14. In CDC i,13, 15f., the verb employed is sûr, but with the same meaning: "those who turned aside from the way" and "to turn aside from the paths of righteousness." (3) "The knowledge" is considered alone in xi,1f. Hence, the interpretation of "the LORD's glory" must have preceded. According to CDC xx,25f., this revelation of "glory" is to be made "to Israel" as an act of judgment. In "The Composition of Habakkuk," p. 270, I argue that kāvôd was interpolated into Isa. 11:9 as quoted at Hab. 2:14 in order to indicate a theophany of judgment. Thus, 1Q p Hab gives a correct interpretation at this point. For the manifestation of God's glory in judgment, cf. Isa. 59:15b-21, also the theme of Yahweh's coming in judgment in Isa. 35:4; 40:10; 42:13; 63:1-6; 63:19b; 66:15f.; Zech. 14:3-5. The eschatological theophany appears also in 1Q M i,8-14; xviii, 1,9f.; 1Q H xii, 22; 4Q p Nah, fragments 1-2. (4) The same theme of judgment may be expressed also by a reference to the "wrath of God" (as restored in li. 16). (5) The statement of xi,1 that "the knowledge will be revealed to them" requires an antecedent; and this is provided by lĕ-yiśrāʾēl in the restoration of li. 17, once more according to CDC xx,26.

xi,1. "Then, afterward, the knowledge will be revealed to them." The restriction of this revelation to Israel (in contrast with Isa. 40:5) suggests that hā-ʾāreṣ (li. 14) is to be taken here as meaning "the land" rather than "the earth." "Israel" is often limited in the Scrolls to members of the sect, esp. in 4Q p Nahum iii,5, where other Jews "join Israel." Here, however, there is a judgment upon apostate Jews, so that "Israel" must include "all the wicked of His people" (v,5).

The fact that "the knowledge" is separated from the "glory" in the interpretation implies the meaning "filled with knowledge, *along with the LORD's glory*, as water swells the sea." The middle portion is treated as parenthetical, the analogy with "the sea" relates to "knowledge" and not to the "glory." Delcor, p. 35, deduces: "Nous sommes dans un langage de gnose et d'apocalypse." With this idea one may compare the "mysteries of knowledge" (1Q S iv,6) and the role of the psalmist in 1QH: "an interpreter of knowledge regarding marvellous mysteries" (ii,13), "to open the fountain of knowledge to all the perceptive" (ii,18). On the other hand, the psalmist's opponents, as. Delcor notes, "withhold the drink of knowledge from the thirsty" (1Q H iv,11). The Righteous Teacher is referred to as "the interpreter [or spokesman] of knowledge" at the end of col. i of 4Q p Psalms[a]. In the present passage, however, there is no hint that this revelation of "knowledge" comes from the Teacher. On the importance of "knowledge" in Qumrân thought see W. D. Davies in *HTR*, XLVI, 1953, pp. 113-139; Friedrich Nötscher, *Zur theologischen Terminologie der Qumran-Texte*, pp. 38-52; Helmer Ringgren, *The Faith of Qumran, Theology of the Dead Sea Scrolls*, pp. 114-120; William S. LaSor, *The Dead Sea Scrolls and the New Testament*, pp. 89-92.

In Isaiah 11:1-9, the triumphant sweep of "knowledge" follows the destruction of the wicked by the Messianic king (vv. 4, 9). Similarly, in Test. Levi 18:5, it is declared that after the Messianic priest-king has shone forth as the sun, dispelling all darkness, then "the knowledge of the Lord shall be poured forth upon the earth, as the water of the seas." By analogy, one might challenge the above restorations of x,16f. and suggest rather a reference to Messianic judgment in the missing text. One might reinforce this by allowing that the "Man of Lies" is the prototype for the "man of lawlessness" (of "man of sin") who is to be slain by the Messiah in II Thess. 2:3-12. However, in light of the parallels in CDC, the judgment described at the bottom of col. x was most probably that of a theophany. According to 1Q M, this coming of God in a blaze of glory brings the final victory of the sons of light over the sons of darkness. See *Meaning*, pp. 124f.; "Jesus and Qumran," in *Jesus and the Historian*, p. 68; "Anthropology and Soteriology," pp. 237-40. If the present restoration is correct, II Thess. 2:3-12 may be viewed as not so much predicting a messianic judgment by the Christ through "the breath of his mouth" (vs. 8, cf. Isa. 11:4), as it depicts the consequence of his theophany (cf. II Thess. 1:9f.). The originally separate motifs of messiah and divine manifestation have been merged in the expectation of the return of Jesus the Christ. Accordingly, there may indeed be a kinship between Paul's "man of lawlessness" and the Qumrân "Man of Lies"—with the notable difference that the figure in the Habakkuk *pēšer* is historical, whereas that in II Thessalonians is non-historical, belonging to apocalyptic.

Interesting historical problems arise; for "the Man of Lies" must be presumed either to survive until the theophanic judgment or to be resurrected to face that fearsome ordeal. The former alternative would imply that he is a still living contemporary of the author of the *pēšer*; and, hence it could be claimed that "the Man of Lies" cannot be separated in time from the Kittim who then held sway. This would exclude any of the Hasmonean rulers prior to Hyrcanus II and Aristobulus II from being considered the "Prophet [or, Man] of Lies"—if one is to follow most scholars in identifying the Kittim with the Romans. On the other hand, it is entirely possible that in this pericope there is preserved a pre-Roman *pēšer* (perhaps even from the Righteous Teacher himself); but, after the demise of the "Man of Lies" and at the time of the present composition, it would be necessary to infer that his theophanic destruction must follow his resurrection for judgment. See here ¶28. Still another alternative would be to place the composition of the whole commentary in pre-Roman times, with the Romans either not referred to, or mentioned only in genuine prediction.

THE MIDRASH PESHER OF HABAKKUK

¶31 (xi, 2-8)

הוֹי מַשְׁקֶה רֵעֵיהוּ מְסַפֵּחַ 2

חֲמָתוֹ אַף שַׁכֵּר לְמַעַן הַבֵּט אֶל מוֹעֲדֵיהֶם 3

פִּשְׁרוֹ עַל הַכּוֹהֵן הָרָשָׁע אֲשֶׁר 4

רָדַף אַחַר מוֹרֶה הַצֶּדֶק לְבַלְּעוֹ בְּכַעַם 5

חֲמָתוֹ אַבֵּית גָּלוּתוֹ וּבְקֵץ מוֹעֵד מְנוּחַת 6

יוֹם הַכִּפּוּרִים הוֹפִיעַ אֲלֵיהֶם לְבַלְּעָם 7

וְלַכְשִׁילָם בְּיוֹם צוֹם שַׁבַּת מְנוּחָתָם 8

(Translation A)

2 (2:15) Alas for him who makes his neighbor drink,
3   putting (to him) / his wrath —
yea makes him drunk,
     so as to gloat at their festivals. /

(Translation B)

2 (2:15) Alas for him who makes his neighbors drink
3   the outpouring of / his wrath, year strong drink,
     so as to gloat over their stumblers. /

4-5   Its prophetic meaning concerns the Wicked Priest who / pursued
the Righteous Teacher in order to make him reel, through the vexation of
6 / his wrath, at his house of exile. It was at the time of the festival of the
7 resting of / the Day of Atonement that he manifested himself to them, in
8 order to make them reel / and to trip them on the day of fasting, the
sabbath of their resting.

179

¶31 *Exposition*

xi,2f. For the variants of 2:15, see *Text*, §§113-118. Two translations are required of the Biblical verse in order to bring out all the various meanings read into the text. Translation A applies to the Righteous Teacher, and Translation B fits his associates.

"Makes his neighbor drink." To find a correlation between this text, I once translated (*BA*, XIV, 1951, p. 67): "Woe to him who makes one drink his neighbor." This assumed that one should render בלע of li. 7 as "swallow," not "reel." See however the discussion below. The word רעיהו is either singular or plural. Read as a singular, the *Yôd* is simply a vowel letter. Cf. *lĕ-rēᶜekhā* at II Sam. 12:11. The singular reading was that of *BASOR*, 112, p. 15; and it has been followed by: Dupont-Sommer, *RHR*, p. 138; *Essene Writings*, p. 266; van der Ploeg, *Bi. Or.*, VIII, p. 9; Delcor, p. 27; Lambert, p. 295; Michel, p. 16; Edelkoort, p. 61; Bruce, *Biblical Exegesis*, p. 13; Sutcliffe, *Monks*, p. 177; Carmignac, *Textes*, p. 112; J. G. Harris, p. 33. The plural was read by: Molin, p. 15; Bardtke, p. 130; Vermès, *Discovery*, p. 131; *DSSE*, p. 241; del Medico, *Riddle*, p. 256; Elliger; van der Woude, *Bijbelcommentaren*, p. 38; with insistence ("Mehrzahl! Vgl. Mas.") in *Die Messianischen Vorstellungen*, p. 162; and Maier, I, p. 155.

xi,3. "Yea makes him drunk" follows the Massoretic vocalization. "Yea strong drink" vocalizes *ŠKR* as *šekher*. The verb was read by: Brownlee; Lambert; Reicke, *Handskrifterna*, p. 38; Edelkoort; Michel; Molin; Burrows, p. 370; Vermès; del Medico; Gaster, p. 255; Elliger; Bruce; van der Woude; Lohse; Maier; and Dupont-Sommer, *Essene Writings*; the noun, by: Dupont-Sommer, *RHR*; van der Ploeg; Delcor; Bardtke; Carmignac; Driver; and Harris. Driver (*Judaean Scrolls*, p. 128) renders: "that poureth out his fiery wine, even strong drink"—citing his earlier article, "On *Ḥēmāh* 'Hot Anger, Fury' and also 'Fiery Wine,'" *ThZ*, XIV, 1958, pp. 133-35. However, his discussion concerns the original sense of the verse, and not necessarily that of the *pēšer*.

"So as to gloat." *Webster's New Collegiate Dictionary* defines "gloat" as: "to look steadfastly; esp. to gaze with malignant satisfaction, ardent desire, lust, or avarice."

"At their *festivals*" (for the MT "pudenda") is required by lis. 6-8; but at the same time li. 8 favors a secondary sense "their stumblers." Thus the word might be read as *qal* active participle, although this form of the verb is unattested in the MT; but cf. the reading suggested by G. Beer for Prov. 25:19 in *Biblia Hebraica*. Vermès (*Discovery*) translated alternatively, "to look on their feasts ([their] stumbling)." This was amplified still more by del Medico: "So as to gaze on their celebrations (or, on their staggerings; or, on their nakedness)."

xi,5. "Who pursued the Righteous Teacher." Here it is a matter of "putting (to him) his wrath." Cf. the KJV: "putting his bottle to him." This derives the

Massoretic reading *mĕsappēaḥ* from √ *SPḤ* I. Gaster translates "that pours out his flask," using *SPḤ* II.

Silberman ("Riddle," pp. 355f.) relates the interpretation by a derivation of *mašqēh* from √ *NŠQ* II "which is connected with the noun נֶשֶׁק/נֵשֶׁק, 'equipment, armoury,' and seems to have a meaning of hostile encounter." For this derivation, however, the participial form should be spelled without the *Hē*. Jastrow (*Dictionary*, pp. 941bf.) lists for the *qal* and *piᶜēl* the meaning "to arm, equip"—the denominative of the noun *nešeq*, a meaning which is wholly unsuitable. The *hifᶜîl* alone provides an appropriate meaning: "bring into close contact." Since this last is the meaning of *SPḤ* I, nothing would be gained except a secondary verbal play, which would say: "Do not read *mašqēh*, but *maššîq*." Since this is not the actual reading, however, we should not translate the Habakkuk text in this manner. As regards *MSPḤ*, Silberman has still another suggestion. The verb *SPḤ* was punned as from the √ *SPG*, which in Rabbinic Hebrew means "to swallow." Hence *mĕsappēaḥ* was interpreted as *lĕ-ballĕᶜô*. Though an aspirated *Gimmel* sounds similar to a *Ḥêt*, the suggestion is unnecessary, since the association of *BLᶜ* with drunkenness is well attested in the Hebrew Scriptures.

"In order to make him reel" interprets Translation A, "yea makes him drunk." This meaning is attributed to the √*BLᶜ* III by Köhler-Baumgartner (p. 129b). Cf. Isa. 3:12; 19:3; 28:7; Ps. 107:27. One could also derive the verb from the √ *BLᶜ* I, "in order to swallow him up" (*BASOR*, 112, p. 15). The existence of these separate roots has sometimes been disputed. See Driver (*ZAW*, LII, 1934, p. 52), who argues for a *BLᶜ* II meaning "strike down." This also would be relevant, but he translated 1Q p Hab with "swallow up." Vermès (in *ETL*, 1951, pp. 74f., n. 46) argues not for a distinction in the roots, but for an evolved meaning, so that "pour le faire tituber" is amply justified as a translation. Van der Ploeg recognized the existence of the different roots, but he preferred √ BLᶜ I, out of consistency with Hab. 1:13*b* (1Q p Hab v,8). Barthélemy (*RB*, LIX, 1952, p. 208), however, argues that context determines the meaning. That an attacker might be thought of as swallowing his opponent may be defended on the basis of Jer. 51:34. Cf. also Test. Judah 21:7: "For the kings shall be as sea-monsters. They shall swallow men like fishes." The action of the Wicked Priest, if understood as a military attack, did intend to destroy the Righteous Teacher, and in that sense "to swallow him up;" but the primary sense, according to context, relates to the figure of drunkenness, not only here, but also in ¶32 (li. 15).

The meaning *tituber* ("reel") is well argued by Lambert and Vermès in *NRTh*, 1951, p. 390. They stressed the parallelism of this verb with *kāšal* in lis. 7f. The verb "reel" is used in English of both mental and physical confusion, also of the retreat of men in battle. It is stronger than the word "confuse," which does suit some passages (Isa. 9:15; 19:3; 28:7; Ps. 55:10 ᵓ=55:9]). Probably, however, the theoretical distinction between the roots was unknown to the ancient commentator, the same word having more than one meaning. Hence, the idea of "swallowing up, destroying" was probably not entirely absent from the mind of the ancient commentator.

xi,5f. "Through the vexation of his wrath" (bĕ-khaᶜas ḥᵃmātô) interprets MSPḤ ḤMTW as mispaḥ ḥᵃmātô, "the outpouring of his wrath" (Translation B), construed as a second object of the verb mašqēh. The Targum interprets here "and pours out in hot anger." (Cf. the use of mišpāḥ from √SPḤ II, according to BDB, p. 705b, in Isa. 5:7). The following phrase is appositional as "yea strong drink." Alternatively, one might read either ᵓaf šakkēr (with the meaning "the anger which makes drunk") or, ᵓafšēkhār ("the anger of intoxicating liquor"). But anger is present in the Biblial text without finding this in ᵓaf.

The phrase kaᶜas ḥᵃmātô may be compared also with kôs ḥᵃmātô ("his cup of wrath") in Isa. 51:17, 22. Cf. Jer. 25:15, as also 1Q p Hab xi, 14f. The Aramaic word for "cup" is kās, which at Qumrân with its weak gutturals may have sounded very similar to kaᶜas (a single long vowel compensating for the weakened ᶜAyin ?). Allegro posits a text of Hab. 2:15a (reading mis-saf): "to make him swallow from his cup of poison." See his book, The Treasure of the Copper Scroll, 1960, p. 147. The meaning "poison" for ḥᵃmātô is well supported by Deut. 32:24; but nothing in the present context favors the idea of any attempt to poison the Teacher. Curiously, the noun may be derived also from ḥēmet (or ḥemet) meaning "skin bottle" (as in KJV and Gaster). Cf. Gen. 21:14, 15, 19. Hence it may be this term which suggested the word kôs/kās, punned as kaᶜas.

xi,6. "At his house of exile" (ᵓab-bêt gālûtô). The first word was read initially as ᵓᵃvôt, the qal infinitive of ᵓBH, so as to obtain the sense "intending him to go into exile" (BASOR, 112, p. 15). R. de Vaux (in RB, LVIII, 1951, p. 440) observed that this could be a case of the infinitive absolute (which omits the prefixed Lāmed), and that in the case of Lāmed Hē verbs the infinitive absolute may borrow the form of the infinitive construct (as in Isa. 22:13; 42:20; Hab. 3:13). Dupont-Sommer's initial reading was ᵓāvîtā ("you wished") which he took to be an apostrophe to the Wicked Priest, with the meaning "Tu as osé," i.e., "You dared!" For this one would expect the plene spelling, ᵓBYTH, also the conjunction W—as argued by Vermès (in ETL, 1951, p. 75). The reading ᵓab-bêt or ᵓeb-bêt corresponds to bĕ-vêt or ᵓel bêt. This reading, proposed by Yalon (in KS, XXVII, p. 175) on the basis of Rabbinic Hebrew, was quickly followed by: Habermann, ᵓEdah, p. 54; Megilloth, p. 48; M. H. Segal, JBL, LXX, 1951, p. 135, n. 16; Reicke (regarding this, however, as a scribal error); Frank M. Cross, "The Essenes and Their Master," CC, LXXII, Aug. 17, 1955, p. 945. Any hesitation about this was largley dispelled by the discovery of the same idiom in the Beth Mashko document from Wady Murrabbaᶜât (Mur. 42, li. 4; RB, LX, 1953, pp. 270f.; DJD, II, p. 156). Hence de Vaux revised his earlier translation, "et a voulu son exil (ou le dénuder)" (RB, 1951, p. 441) to "dans la maison, dans le lieu de son exil." This has convinced nearly everyone; but it was rejected by

Elliger and Rabinowitz, in *VT*, VIII, 1958, pp. 394f., n.4. The former regarded the phrase as too far removed from *rādaf* with which it had been connected. Yet there is the nearer verb *lĕvallēᶜô* which has not this difficulty. The latter objected that the Qumrân Scrolls are not written in "the language and style of the Murabbaᶜât letter." However, the Hebrew of Qumrân is not pure, classical Hebrew, so that this spelling may show the influence of popular Rabbinic Hebrew.

GLWTW has been read in the following ways: (1) *gêlôtô* (*qal* inf.), (2) *gallôtô* (*piᶜēl* inf.), (3) *gālûtô* (a noun). No. 1 was used in *BASOR*, 112 ("intending him to go into exile"); but it was quickly abandoned for No. 2 in *BASOR*, 114, p. 9 ("wishing to uncover him"), with the qualification that "both ideas may have been intended in the midrashic play on words." The latter rendering would reflect acquaintance with the Massoretic reading מעוריהם ('their pudenda') of Hab. 2:15, despite the citation of the form מועדיהם ('their festivals')." Dupont-Sommer conjectured that this uncovering of the Teacher was a stripping for crucifixion; and thereby he stirred up a great controversy as to whether the supposed crucifixion of the Teacher was both an historical and a theological prototype of the crucifixion of Jesus. Though Lambert and Vermès in their article adopted this reading, they argued that there was no allusion here to crucifixion, but simply to a stripping naked as an act of disgrace (as in Hos. 2:12 [= 2:10]). Others who have seen an allusion to stripping are: Vermès, *CH*, March, 1951, p. 8; R. Tamisier; and van't Land.

No. 3, when translated "wishing his exile," has the same import as No. 1. This reading was proposed by de Vaux (*RB*, 1951, p. 440), though it is possible that the commentator played upon both senses. The nominal reading was embraced by Delcor in *RB*, LVIII, 1951, p. 524. Already Yalon had proposed this as part of the revised reading of the whole phrase ᵓab-bêt gālûtô. But does this mean "at" or "to his house of exile?" Scholars giving the meaning "at" (or, "in") are: Yalon; Habermann; de Vaux, *RB*, 1953, pp. 270f.; M. Wallenstein, *VT*, V, 1955, p. 279, n. 3; Vermès, *Discovery*; van der Woude, *Die Messianischen Vorstellungen; Bijbelcommentaren*; Driver, *Judaean Scrolls*; Maier; Carmignac; Lohse; Baer, p. 28; LaSor, p. 107. Scholars translating "to" are: Segal; Vermès, *DSSE*; del Medico, *Riddle*, p. 256; Gaster; Sutcliffe; Driver, *JTS*, IX, 1958, p. 348; Bruce; S. Talmon, *Sh*, IV, 1958, p. 167; Ringgren, *The Faith of Qumran*, p. 34, n. 88; and Harris. In most cases, "at [or in] the house [or place] of exile" interprets ᵓ*BYT* as equivalent to *BBYT* rather than ᵓ*L BYT*. Yet Maier was uncertain as to which equivalence to suppose, and Lohse chose the latter. The preposition ᵓ*el*, however, goes better with "*to* his house of exile."

To read ᵓ*eb-bêt* as a case of assimilated *Lāmed* would be similar phonetically with the assimilation of the *Lām* of the article in colloquial Arabic. In that case, we would not expect this kind of pronunciation to be limited to a single letter or word. The evidence would be more widespread. Interpreted as a phonetic spelling of *BBYT*, the prefixed ᵓ*Ālef* appears to be an effort to preserve the hard B-sound where the rule of aspirated letters would require the pronunciation bĕ-vêth. Bayit(h) and its construct bêt(h) with an initial hard B occurred so frequently that the popular pronunciation disliked its softening into a V-sound. Severel times a day one might well speak of someone or something as being bab-bayit(h), and the pronunciation of the construct may have been a modification of this as ab-bêt(h), the ʾĀlef having no consonantal quality. For the vowel, cf. also hab-bayit(h), a word which was constantly on one's lips. Therefore, we should probably vocalize the word as ʾab-bêt (= ab-bêth in actual pronunciation). The analogy of the Beth Maskho letter also favors the equivalence with BBYT.

Maier, followed by Lohse, begins a new sentence with ʾab-bêt: "At the place of his exile and at the time of the rest of the day of atonement, he appeared. . . ." This punctuation is entirely possible, and even attractive by reason of the suggested parallelism between the adverbial phrases of place and time. Yet one may prefer taking the reference to place as the conclusion of the preceding sentence, judging that the following sentence was written to emphasize one point only, the occasion at which all this happened. Thus the final sentence begins and ends with a stress on the time of the occurrence. The preceding sentence describes more fully the event, its perpetrator, and its purpose; yet something of this is carried forward into the subsequent sentence.

G. R. Driver (Judaean Scrolls, p. 272) has argued that ʾab-bêt gālûtô means "in the place of his discovery," and so translates "at the place where he was discovered." Driver's vocalization gᵉlôtô, however, evidently reads this as the infinitive construct with a nominal meaning. For the sense required one would expect, however, the nifᶜal stem. Similarly, Silberman has wished to interpret the phrase as "in the House of His revelation," by making this refer to the temple at Jerusalem to which the Wicked Priest pursued the Teacher. The Rabbinic expression bêt galyāʾ, which Jastrow (Dictionary, p. 248 b) interprets as "place or temple for oracles" is not the same expression as found in 1Q p Hab; and their equivalence is not an easy assumption. Hence any allusion to the Jewish temple seems improbable; and there is no need to infer this from the Biblical text by reading LMᶜ N as lam-māᶜôn, "to the temple." In that case one would expect the plene spelling LMᶜ WN.

Sukenik (Megillot Genuzot, II, p. 32) saw a parallel between the present line and 1Q H iv,8f.: "They drive me from my land as a bird from its nest; and all my friends and intimates are driven from me." If one agrees that the Teacher wrote the hymn, then this may well refer to the same unnamed place of exile. If this "house of exile" is Qumrân, then one naturally thinks of Stratum IA. Yet the allusion may rather be to "the Land of Damascus" mentioned in CDC vi,5,19 (= 8:6, 15); viii,21; xix,34; xx,12 (= 9:28,37). Robert North (PEQ, LXXXVI, 1955, pp. 1-14) has argued that Qumrân is the "Land of Damascus." But according to CDC vi,5, the "penitents of Israel . . . went forth out of the land of Judah and sojourned in the land of Damascus," whereas from the Biblical standpoint the "wilderness" where Qumrân is located belongs to the "Wilderness of Judah" (Josh. 15:61f.; Jud. 1:16; Ps. 63: 1). To get outside the "Land of Judah" one would need to go east of the Jordan. Also "Damascus" is located in the "land of the North" (CDC vii,12-19 [=9:4-8]), but Qumrân is east of Jerusalem! See *Meaning*, pp. 133-137; "Anthropology and Soteriology," pp. 224f.

During the whole heated controversy concerning the meaning of $^{\circ}BYT$ *GLWTW*, Dupont-Sommer showed himself linguistically flexible, while at the same time maintaining the same historical reference. When a number of scholars insisted on the infinitive reading $^{\circ}BWT$ (either inf. ab., as de Vaux; or inf. con., as Henri Michaud in *VT*, II, 1952, pp. 83-85), Dupont-Sommer (VT, I, 1951, pp. 210 f.; *VT*, II, 1952, pp. 276-278) adopted the infinitive absolute, which he rendered "On a voulu le dévêtir." This left the text wholly in the 3rd person, avoiding the previous radical shift from the 3rd to the 2nd person. After the discovery of the Beth Mashko letter, he was able to translate "engloutit le Maître . . . en sa résidence d'exil." (*VT*, V, 1955, p. 126). Thus in *Essene Writings*, he translates: "swallowing him up in the anger of his fury in his place of exile."

xi,6b. "It was at the time of the festival." This is an emphatic reference, not only by reason of its initial position in the sentence, but also by the lengthy elaboration of it. On *qēṣ* in the significance of "time," cf. above at vii,7 (¶ 21). In December, 1948, H. L. Ginsberg urged in private conversation, that *qēṣ* should be translated "time." This was done in *BASOR*, 114, p. 10. N. Wieder (*JJS*, V. 1954, pp. 22-31) has argued similarly, citing as an example the phrase *bĕ-qēṣ pesaḥ* in a Medieval Jewish hymn as meaning "at the time of the Passover." Sukenik (*Megillot Genuzot*, I, p. 22) has sought to establish this meaning even for many Scriptural passages. However, his examples appear sufficiently ambiguous that his claim seems inconclusive. In any case, the Qumrân usage is clear; and the Wicked Priest would surely have timed his attack so as to disrupt the rival observance of the Day of Atonement more effectively than an appearance at the end of the festival would have done.

"The Day of Atonement." By reason of sect's difference of dating this occasion, it was possible for the Wicked Priest to be absent from Jerusalem without neglecting his own duties there. This is well argued by S. Talmon in *Biblica*, XXXII, 1951, pp. 549-563; and in *Aspects of the Dead Sea Scrolls*, *SH*, IV, 1958, p. 167. Nothing in the context supports the continuing view of Dupont-Sommer that this refers to the taking of Jerusalem by the Romans in 63 B.C., since the manuscript makes no allusion here to either Jerusalem or the Kittim.

xi,7. "He manifested himself to them." In *BASOR*, 112, I translated "he appeared in splendor unto them," supposing that this referred to a rival observance by the Teacher in the temple itself, with the Wicked Priest launching his attack, dressed in the splendor of his highpriestly robes. Cf. Sirach 50: 5-11. Bardtke (p. 130) and Edelkoort (p. 61) translated similarly. Harris's expansive translation makes this even clearer: "showed himself in full regalia." Schoeps (*ZRG*, 1951, p. 324, n. 9) stated that "the verb probably designates the glistening white clothes of the High Priest on the Day of Atonement (M. Yoma III, 6)." Dupont-Sommer, stressing the use of the verb *hôfîaᶜ* in connection with theophanies (eg., Deut. 33:2; Pss. 50:2; 80:2; 94:1), interpreted the present passage to refer to an apparition of the Righteous Teacher over Jerusalem. Accordingly, he translated Hab. 2:15: "So that God [ᵓēlᶜ] might look upon their festivals." Hence, also, he inferred that ᵓēl = *môrēh haṣ-ṣedeq*, whose apparition was a veritable theophany! These interpretations, when combined with the reference to "his body of flesh"(ix,2) were the basis of his inference of a doctrine of the Teacher as a divine incarnation, not unlike the Incarnation of Christ! He even compared the apparition of the Teacher in judgment upon Jerusalem in 63 B.C. with the fall of Jerusalem in 70 A.D. However, there is no alleged theophany of Christ over Jerusalem in connection with the latter, though the fall of the city was to be an omen of his coming (Matth. 24; Mark 13; Luke 21). Meanwhile Dupont-Sommer has changed his reading of the texts, and so no longer holds to the divinity of the Righteous Teacher. He has taken a less radical position (*The Jewish Sect of Qumran and the Essenes*, 1954, p. 34):

> If I am not mistaken, the idea that there should be a supernatural apparition of the Teacher of Righteousness, coming personally to wreak vengeance, seems to them [critics] monstrous. It presupposes, in fact, that after the Teacher's tragic and ignominious death his followers considered that God had granted him an exceptional exaltation and a celestial after-life.

What seemed "monstrous" in his first translation was in part theological, but it also involved serious questions of grammar. A priori, there is no impossibility but that the great Teacher could have been awarded by God "an exceptional exaltation" after death; but what would there be in this to suggest his return in judgment? As for heavenly warriors, only Michael or Melchizedek was expected. Thus nothing in Qumrân messianic conceptions supports the idea of the Righteous Teacher as a celestial warrior. A priori, one would not expect a change of subject from the Wicked Priest to the Righteous Teacher without a clear indication in the text. The Biblical verse has pronounced a woe upon the one "who swallows up his neighbors." This person has already been identified with the Wicked Priest. The possibility of an antithetical conjunction *W* is tenuous ground for a reapplication of the text to the Teacher. What woe is now due him?

Despite Dupont-Sommer's present avoidance of a change of person in the verb (no longer reading ᵓāvîtā, but ᵓab-bêt), some of the old objections still stand as regards his present translation: "But at the time of the feast of the rest of the Day of Atonement he appeared before them to swallow them up." Nothing in the context suggests an attack upon Jerusalem by the Romans. See here Carmignac, *Christ and the Teacher*, pp. 35-37.

The possibility was always open that any theophany would refer to God

Himself, not the Teacher. However, God did not seem to be mentioned in the context; but Silberman's view remedies this by a heightened sense of the divine in the Biblical verse through a mentioning of the "temple" as "the House of *His*" revelation." Consistent with this, he joins the initial translation of Dupont-Sommer of li. 3b, "God looks upon their festivals." Silberman regarded this as referring to some obscure event in the history of Jerusalem at the time of the official observance of the Day of Atonement.

The verb *hôfia^c* is used in the Scrolls not only for the appearance of God (CDC xx,25 [9:49]; 1Q M i,16; xviii,9; 1Q H iv,6,23; ix,26,31) or His truth (xi,26). In 1Q M xii,2, Jerusalem is the subject. In CDC xx,3,6 (=9:31,33), the reference is to wicked deeds. In the Hebrew of Ben Sira (Ecclus. 12:15), the subject is the wicked. Thus context alone determines any allusion to theophany. So rightly has argued Delcor, *Midrash*, pp. 36f. Cross translated: "he (the Priest) confronted them suddenly," which may overly nuance the verb, but gives the correct historical understanding.

"In order to make *them* reel." The plural application here, in contrast with the singular at li.5, may interpret *rē^{c}ehû* of the Biblical text (li. 2) as a plural, "his neighbors." It may likewise reflect the phrase "to make *them* drunk also" (li. 3) and correlate with the pl. suff. of *mô$^{c a}$dêhem*. Likewise, the previously mentioned *gālût* may have a collective meaning. Just as "the exile of King Jehoiachin" (Ezek. 1:2) included others (33:21; 40:1), so that of the Teacher included his devotees.

xi,8. "To trip them" (or, "to make them stumble"). *Lakhšîlām* is the *hif^{c}îl* infinitive, with an elided *Hē*. See Segert, §§688-691. This interprets "to gloat over their *stumblers*" (Translation B). *Mô$^{c a}$dêhem* is here interpreted as the *qal* plural participle of the verb *M^{c}D*, plus the pronominal suffix. This is a clear case of double meaning in the interpretation, for there is an equally clear reference to "their *festivals*" in li. 6 (Translation A). This is the stumbling of drunkenness; but it was applied figuratively. It may mean that the Wicked Priest intended that they "stumble" in the physical sense of their being overthrown or subdued by force; or, again, it may have the cultic meaning of their being forced to fight or to flee on the Day of Atonement, against their scruples. For a similar concern, see the insertion of "or on a Sabbath" (RSV) in Matth. 24:20, a phrase which is lacking in Mark 13:18. Thus Segal states that the purpose of the Wicked Priest's intrusion was to occasion a breach of the Law; and Talmon translates (*SH*, IV): "He appeared unto them to confound them and to cause them to *transgress* on the day of fasting, the sabbath of their rest." Sutcliffe interpreted the literal "stumble" as "to act wrongly." The Wicked Priest, being a secular ruler, probably appeared with a contingent of his army, both to kill the celebrants and to disrupt their celebration. The bloody character of this persecution is well attested by ¶¶27 and 33. See the reserved treatment of Cross, *Ancient Library*, pp. 157f.

A probable allusion to Hab. 2:15, in the reading of 1Q p Hab, appears in 1Q H iv,11f. as Dupont-Sommer noted (*RHR*, p. 149):

> They withheld the drink of knowledge from the thirsty,
>   and for their thirst they *made them drink* vinegar,
> in order *to gaze upon* their error,
>   that they might behave insanely at *their festivals,*
>   to be trapped in their snares.

There is no need here to imitate Dupont-Sommer by reading ᵓ*L* as ᵓ*ēl,* "pour que *Dieu* regarde leur égarement." In the "anthological" character of these Hymns, the psalmist constantly alludes to Biblical passages by scattered words and phrases. Thus "the thirsty" who are "made to drink vinegar" echoes Ps. 69:22 (=69:21). To "behave insanely" (*lĕ-hithōlēl*) may reflect Jer. 51:7. The words "to gaze upon . . . their festivals" comes from Hab. 2:15, in the reading of 1Q p Hab. The verb "made them drink" coincides also with the text of Habakkuk. Perhaps the drunkenness of Hab. 2:15 is interpreted here as "staggering" (or "their straying," *tāᶜûtām*), and as "insane" behavior "at their festivals"—even though some of this language comes from other Biblical passages. "Their error" may also allude to "their stumblers" as a second meaning of *môᶜᵃdêhem.* There is possibly another pun on the word in *mĕṣûdôtām* ("their snares"), the similarity being more visual than auditory, since ᶜ*Ayin* and *Ṣādê* resemble one another in appearance. Both texts complement the verb *habbēt* with the preposition ᵓ*el* rather than ᶜ*al.* Yet in both cases, Dupont-Sommer read ᵓ*ēl* ("God"), though neither passage requires this. The *pēšer*-type of exegesis certainly underlies many passages in the Hymns; but the allusions are less demonstrable and more speculative than in a *pēšer* proper with its direct quotations. Hence, it is possible to doubt (as does Delcor, pp. 36f.) that there is any allusion to Hab. 2:15 in 1Q H iv,11f. In any case, the Hymn is not dealing with an historical event, but with the stumbling caused by false teaching. Therefore, the passages are not fully synonymous as claimed by Baer, p. 29.

"On the day of fasting, the Sabbath of their resting," or, "on the day of the fast of the Sabbath of their resting." Cf. the construct chain of five words in lis. 6f. A. S. van der Woude (*Die Messianischen Vorstellungen,* pp. 162f., n. 6) would interpret the preposition of *bĕ-yôm* as instrumental (*durch*), as in Mal. 2:8. A variation of this explanation would not be strictly instrumental (by means of), but causal (by reason of). Certainly, by reason of the sacred festival, no matter what one did he would "stumble" in some sense. If he fought or fled, he would be violating the requirement of solemn rest. If he did neither, he would "stumble through the sword" (Dan. 11:33). However, if one interprets this as a temporal reference, this is no mere redundancy, for as an inclusion, it introduces a new element, the necessity of fasting and rest.

That the Day of Atonement should be referred to as a Sabbath fits the prescription of Lev. 23:27-32. The day is to be a time in which "to afflict oneself" (or, as in the new JPSA version, "to practice self-denial") with allusion to fasting. It is also to be a *šabbat šabbātôn* in which no work is to be done.

Max Radin (*The Jews Among the Greeks and Romans*, 1915, p. 400) noted that this festival, unlike others, had originally no individual name and that *yôm hak-kippûrîm* "seems rather a descriptive term than a proper name." For Josephus the designation was ἡ τῆς νηστείας ἡμέρα ("the day of fasting"). In the Talmud it was *yômā⁾* ("the Day"), *ṣômā⁾ rabbā⁾* ("the Great Fast"), and *yômā⁾ rabbā⁾* ("the Great Day"). In Acts 27:9, it is called ἡ νηστεία ("the Fast"). Radin believed that among the Egyptian Jews *šabbat šabbātôn* was the proper designation; for, though in connection with the weekly Sabbath (Ex. 31:15; 35:2; Lev. 23:3) the LXX translated the phrase as σάββατα ἀνάπαυσις ("a sabbath, a rest"), in connection with the Day of Atonement it transliterated the Hebrew as σάββατα σαββάτων. "Similarly," he observed, "in Philo, *De Septenario*, all the festivals have names except this, which is referred to simply as 'the Fast.'" Now *šabbat měnûḥātām* in 1Q p Hab is an apparent equivalent to *šabbat šabbâtôn* translated as σάββατα ἀνάπαυσις.

The new element in the paraphrase of the expression is the pronominal suffix, "the Sabbath of *their* resting." This could be explained in two ways: (1) It was *their* resting, i.e., according to *their* calendar. (2) It was a time of such solemn rest that *they* (unlike the Wicked Priest) could not fight, even in self-defence. Actually, it was probably a matter of both. According to I Maccabees, some of the early Hasidim suffered martyrdom rather than fight on the Sabbath day (2:29-38); but later on they concluded that they could fight in self-defence (2:39-41). II Maccabees 6:11 does not record this compromise; nor does it relate any fighting ever taking place during a Sabbatical Year, a matter which seems not to have bothered the author of I Maccabees. See "Books of Maccabees," *IDB*, Vol. K-Q, esp. pp. 204 *a*, 209. Fighting during Sabbatical Years is avoided in the War of the Sons of Light against the Sons of Darkness.

It may be that Josephus understood the fall of Jerusalem to Pompey in 63 B.C. as occurring on the Day of Atonement, an occasion when Jews could not fight. Even so, Josephus may have misunderstood one of his sources, as some scholars believe. See M.B. Dagut in *Biblica*, XXXII, 1951, pp. 542-548.

THE MIDRASH PESHER OF HABAKKUK

¶ 32 (xi, 8-17)

שֶׁבַעְתָּ   8

קָלוֹן מִ[כָּ]בוֹד שְׁתֵה גַם אַתָּה וְהֵרָעֵל   9

תִּסּוֹב עָלֶיךָ כּוֹס יְמִין יהוה וְקִיקָלוֹן   10

עַל כְּבוֹדְךָ   11

פִּשְׁרוֹ עַל הַכּוֹהֵן אֲשֶׁר גָּבַר קְלוֹנוֹ מִכְּבוֹדוֹ   12

כִּיא לוֹא מָל אֶת עוּרְלַת לִבּוֹ וַיֵּלֶךְ בְּדַרְכֵי   13

הָרְוָיָה לְמַעַן סְפוֹת הַצִּמְאָה וְכוֹס חֲמַת   14

[אֵ]ל תְּבַלְּעֶנּוּ לוֹסִי[ף] עָ[לָ]יו קִי קְ[ל]וֹ[נ]וֹ וּמַכְאוֹב   15

[חֳ]ל[יֳ]יו [ֳ]ל[   ]ל[   ]   16

[   ]   17

8-9 (2:16)   Thou art more full of / shame than of glory;
            Drink, thou too, and stagger. /

10   The cup of the LORD's right hand shall come round to thee,

11   and disgrace will be / upon they glory. /

12   Its prophetic meaning concerns the priest whose

13   shame surpassed his glory; / for he did not circumcise
the foreskin of his heart, but he walked in the ways of /

14   satiation in order to quench (his) thirst; but the cup

15   of the wrath of / [Go]d will make him reel, so as to
hea[p upo]n [him the vomit of his sha]m[e] and the

16-17   pain of / [his sic]k[ness] . . . / . . . .

190

¶32 *Exposition*

xi,8-11. For the textual variants of Hab. 2:16, see *Text*, §§119-122.

xi,9f. "Thou art full of shame." Many have translated "Thou hast filled (or, sated) thyself." One does not know whether any have read the *pi^{c}ēl, šibba^{c}tāh* instead of the *qal, šāva^{c}tāh*.

xi,9. Two interpretations of the text are possible both in the scroll and in the Bible: "instead of glory" and "more than glory." "Instead of" was the reading in *BASOR*, 112, p. 15; van der Ploeg, *Bi. Or.*, VIII, p. 9; Molin, p. 16; Edelkoort, p. 62; Bardtke, p. 130; Vermès, *Discovery*, p. 131; van't Land; Burrows, p. 370; Gaster, p. 255; Bruce, *Biblical Exegesis*, p. 12; Sutcliffe, *Monks*, p. 177; Lohse; Driver, *Judaean Scrolls*, p. 129. "More than" is the rendering of: Dupont-Sommer, *RHR*, p. 138; *Essene Writings*, p. 267; Lambert, p. 296; M. H. Segal, *JBL*, LXX, 1951, p. 138; Brownlee, *BA*, 1951, p. 68; Delcor, p. 27; Elliger; Michel, p. 17; del Medico, *Riddle*, p. 257; van der Woude, *Bijbelcommentaren*, p. 38; Maier, I, p. 155; Vermès, *DSSE*, p. 242; Carmignac, *Textes*, p. 114; J. G. Harris, p. 41.

The *Kaf* of מכבוד is really present. The *Mêm* was at first omitted. When it was inserted later, it was carelessly entered as a correction of the *Kaf* (*Text*, ¶119a). In the French edition of his book, del Medico (*L'énigme des manuscrits de la Mer Morte*, p. 116) translated: "Tu es rassasié de la nonte des mensonges?" ("Are you sated with shame from lies?"). Apparently he read *MBYD*, with which one may compare the Rabbinic *bîdā$^\circ$* and *bîdû*. However, in the English edition of his book (*Riddle*), he rendered: "Thou art filled with shame more than glory!" M. Martin (*Scribal Character*, II, §40, pp. 667f.) suggests that the corrector may have intended to produce the word מבור ("than purity") but he neglected to correct the last letter. However, li. 12 interprets this with the word כבוד ("glory").

xi,12. "Concerns the priest." The absence of the qualification "wicked" may or may not be significant. Cf. viii,16; xii, 8.

"Whose shame surpassed his glory." This interprets the Scriptural citation of li. 9: "More full of shame than glory." However, the same interpretation might also be deduced from li. 11, by assigning to ^{c}*al* the force of the comparative: "Disgrace will be above [or, more than] thy glory." So, Driver. Popularly this priest had achieved great "glory." This is, conceded, but his glory was overshadowed by his ignominious behavior. Cf., after Driver, I Macc. 1:40.

xi,13. "For he did not circumcise the foreskin of his heart." On spiritual circumcision, cf. Lev. 26:41; Deut. 10:16; 30:6; Jer. 4:4; Ezek. 44:9. In 1Q S v,5, the sectaries have the duty *lā-mûl bĕ-yaḥad ^{c}orlat yēṣer wĕ-^{c}ôref qāšeh* ("to circumcise in community the foreskin of impulse and of the stiff neck"). This statement of the text may allude to the textual reading *H^{c}RL* ("and appear uncircumcised") of the MT, as interpreted in *BA*, XIV, 1951, pp. 68f. C. Rabin (*VT*, V, 1955, pp. 158f.) classified this as an example of

"simultaneous interpretation of two variant readings." See the discussion of
"Dual Readings," in *Text* pp. 118-123. H. L. Ginsberg (cited in *Text*, pp. 77f.)
saw in this a simple verbal play, as also Silberman ("Riddle," p. 361) would
interpret. In view of the subsequent allusion to Deut. 29:18 (=29:19), the
midrashist may have had in mind the statement of the wicked recorded there,
"though I walk in the stubbornness of my heart." So, Silberman.

Curiously, ^cWRLT(^corlat, foreskin) was written as two words: $^cWR\ LT$.
Nothing in the appearance of the manuscript would suggest any roughness
which the scribe might try to avoid. Could this be a purely accidental spacing?
Yet, since the first three letters can be read as "skin," this may be a case of
verbal play.

xi,13f. "But he walked in the ways of satiation in order to quench (his)
thirst." *Hā-rěwāyāh* ("satiation") interprets the verbs *śāva^ctāh* and *šětēh*
("thou are full . . . drink thou"). It also draws upon Deut. 29:18 (=29:19):

> It will come to pass when he hears the word of this oath, he will bless himself in his heart,
> saying, "I shall be safe, though I walk in the stubbornness of my heart"—in order to
> destroy the moist with the dry.

The final clause has been variously interpreted: "to add drunkenness to thirst"
(KJV), "to destroy the moist with the dry" (ASV), "That would mean the
destruction of the moist grass with the dry" (Moffatt), "as though to sweep
away both the watered soil with the parched ground" (NAB), "much water
drives away thirst" (Jerusalem Bible, which includes this within the
quotation). The clause is generally taken as a proverbial expression. The
rendering of the New English Bible ("but this will bring everything to ruin")
takes this as simply an idiom for total destruction. The LXX interpreted this
to mean: ἵνα μὴ συναπολέσῃ ὁ ἁμαρτωλὸς τὸν ἀναμάρτητον "lest the sinner
bring also the destruction of the sinless"). With this interpretation, the New
American Bible agrees in its note: "Apparently a proverb signifying that such
an unfaithful Israelite will cause God to punish the good with the wicked, to
root out the good plants growing in irrigated soil, together with the worthless
plants growing in the dry ground." Silberman (p. 362) cites the evidence of
both the Targum of Onkelos and the Targum of Jonathan for the meaning:
"adding inadvertent sins to those of presumption." The idea of inadvertence,
according to Rashi, was derived from the behavior of the drunken man, who
acts without thinking. Silberman believes that the Bible has the opposite
meaning: "Sins of presumption are to be added to inadvertent sins, for the
declaration of the speaker in the verse is, 'I shall be safe, though I walk in the
stubbornness of my heart.'"

The basic question is whether *sěfôt* means "to add" or "to destroy." My
initial translation took this as grim irony: "but he walked in the ways of hard
drinking—only to add to his thirst!" This understanding appears also in the
translations of: van der Ploeg; Segal; and Reicke, *Handskrifterna*, p. 39. For
the meaning "add" see Num. 32:14; Isa. 30:1. In *BASOR*, 114, 1949, p. 10, I
gave recognition to the meaning "destroy," and used this rendering in *BA*,

XIV, 1951, p. 68. By then one knew the meaning "destroy" in 1Q S ii,12ff., in its warning to the backslider:

> It will come to pass when he hears the terms of this covenant, that he will bless himself in his heart, saying: 'Let me be safe, though I walk in the stubbornness of my heart!' But *his spirit will be destroyed, the thirst together with the satiation,* with no forgiveness! God's anger and His jealous judgments will burn upon him for eternal destruction.

The application of this to the human spirit suggests that the Manual of Discipline interprets Deuteronomy to mean: "But his spirit will be destroyed, the *lust* together with its *satisfaction*." Cf. I Cor. 6:13: "'Food is meant for the stomach and the stomach for food'—and God will destroy both one and the other." The following have interpreted *sĕfôt* in 1Q p Hab as "add:" van der Ploeg, Segal and Reicke. Others take the meaning "destroy," and appropriately to the context choose some such word as "quench" or "slake." Notice should be also taken of the √ *SP* ᵓ ("to feed"), from which the noun *mispô*ᵓ ("fodder") is derived (Gen. 24:25; 42:27; 43:24; Jud. 19:19). In Rabbinic Hebrew the roots have fallen together, so that *SPY / SPH* may mean either "to feed" or "to destroy." In the present case, one seeks to destroy the thirst by feeding it.

xi,14f. "The cup of the wrath of G[od]" echoes Isa. 51:17,22. Yalon (*KS*, XXVII, p. 175) would restore [רע]ל as the first word of xi,15, rather than [ל]א. Despite his claims, there is insufficient space for this. "Wrath" favors a personal reference.

xi,15. "Will make him reel." On this meaning of the *piᶜēl* stem of *BL*ᶜ, cf. xi,5f. (¶31). The present passage confirms that meaning, since the verb interprets *wĕ-hērāᶜēl* of 2:16 (xi,9), as C. Rabin observed. The sudden employment of the imperfect verb contrasts with the use of the perfect in lis. 12-14. This points either to a doom which is eschatological or to a prediction (real or alleged) of the death of a contemporary priest.

"So as to hea[p upo]n [him the vomit of his sh]a[me]." The restoration is suggested by the fact that at this point we should find an interpretation of the word *qîqālôn* which would have some sort of affinity with the following reference to "pain" (*makh*ᵓ*ôv*). Most scholars have followed the first translation by restoring: לוס[י]ף עליו את קלון] ("so as to bring upon him shame"). Possible restorations are shown in the following display:

The display was made by cutting out xeroxed copies of the photographs and by pasting the words into their appropriate places. For clarity some letters have been retouched. The *Lāmeds* of the large, central lacuna were made to align exactly with those showing beneath li. 14. Otherwise, there would have been room to spell qî³ with its ³*Ālef.* One would expect the spelling of ᶜ*ālāw* as ᶜ*LYW*, as in viii,12; but ᶜ*LW* is attested at viii,7. One could seek to fill the space where *QY* has been inserted by writing ᶜ*LYHW*, but this orthography is not found in 1Q p Hab. The parallel construction of viii,12 omits the sign of the accusative. The interpretation of *QYQLWN* as *QY QLWN* is supported by six manuscripts listed by B. Kennicott, namely: Mss. 1, 30, 150, 155, 225, and 227. M. Stenzel (*VT*, III, 1953, p. 97) noted that the Vulgate version divided the word in its translation as "vomitus ignominiae." This indicates a tradition of interpretation, to be compared with the implied division of ᶜ*avţîţ* as ᶜ*av ţîţ* at viii,12f. Though ³*Ālef* could have been elided as quiescent, its omission could reflect the knowledge of a variant reading of the text.

An allusion to "vomit" is particularly pertinent in the context of drunkenness (Isa. 19:14; 28:8; Jer. 48:26) and satiation (Prov. 25:16). This idea served to open up the subject of the priest's sickness and suffering. The compound expression "the vomit of his shame" may be compared with "the guilt of transgression" following the same verb in the same sentence structure in viii,12.

Other restorations of li. 15 are now to be considered. Ratzaby (*JQR*, XLI, p. 157) restored only the first word of the large lacuna, giving [רו]לְיַקָ. Vermès (*Discovery*) translated this: "through cha[stising him]." Segal restored: [ן]קלו עליו יף[לוס; but the preserved letter at the end is *Wāw.* Elliger has rightly insisted upon this letter. Habermann (ᶜ*Edah,* p. 54; *Megilloth,* p. 48) restored: [לוס]יף קלון וקיקלו[ן—a restoration followed by Gaster and Bruce. The required space is about right. Baer (p. 30) has restored לוס]יף יגו[ן which is not only too brief, but it contains no *Lāmed* (of which the tips of two appear below li. 14) and it too ends with the wrong letter.

xi,15f. "And the pain of [his sickness]." For *ḥolyô,* see Isa. 38:9; Eccles. 5:16; II Chron. 16:12; 21:19; I Kings 17:17; II Kings 13:14; Hos. 5:13. In Isa. 53:3f., *makh³ōv* and *ḥōlî* are parallel terms. The translation of *BASOR,* 112, "and causing pain," implied the participial reading *ū-makh³îv.* This was followed by Edelkoort and del Medico, the latter giving it the nominal sense and "he who has caused suffering." It may well be that the phrase "and the pain of his sickness" begins a new sentence exactly as "and ways of abomination" does at viii,12f. One may suggest: "And the pain of his sickness *will wear him out* ([*yĕba*]*ll*[*ēh* ³*ôtô*])." Cf. ix,11.

Is the priest's vomiting and sickness literal and so connected with the actual history of a dissolute chief priest? If so, then we must ask, why is not the priest's illness attributed directly to his excessive drinking instead of to the "cup of the wrath of God"? The answer to this inquiry is explained by the fact that consequences of violating both the natural and the moral law were anciently interpreted as an act of divine intervention. An analogy to this theology is the case of Ptolemy Philopater in III Maccabees. (See *IDB*, Vol. K-Q, pp. 210-212.)

Schoeps (*ZRG*, 1951, p. 30) has argued for a figurative interpretation, citing as a parallel to 1Q p Hab the Pss. of Sol. 8:15:

> Therefore God mingled for them a spirit of wandering;
> and gave them to drink a cup of undiluted wine,
>   that they might become drunken.

"Verses 15-19," he noted, "agree with Josephus' account of Pompey's march and Aristobulus' meeting of him; and in spite of the plural, Aristobulus is meant." Barthélemy (*RB*, 1952, p. 210) also argued that the allusions are not to literal drunkenness. Reicke thought the literal interpretation more probable.

Understood as literal history, this priest's heavy drinking and illness have suggested to a number of scholars his identity with Alexander Jannaeus. I suggested this (orally) as one possibility in 1948. It was formally advanced by Segal, and accepted by: Reicke; Delcor, pp. 61f.; and Carmignac, pp. 108f., n. 2; 115, n. 16. I accepted this in *BASOR*, 126, 1952, p. 15. The death of Jannaeus is described by Josephus in these terms:

> But after these conquests King Alexander fell ill from heavy drinking and for three years he was afflicted with a quartan fever, but still he did not give up campaigning until, being exhausted from his labors, he met death in the territory of the Gerasenes while besieging Ragaba, a fortress across the Jordan.
>
> (*JA*, XIII, xv,5 [§398])

Cross (*Ancient Library*, p. 152) asserts: "The comment admirably fits Simon's drunken demise," referring to I Macc. 16:16:

> When Simon and his sons were drunk, Ptolemy and his men rose up, took their weapons, and rushed in against Simon in the banquet hall, and they killed him and his two sons and some of his servants.

Whatever identification one makes of "the Priest," it is important to note that any distinction between this man and the Wicked Priest would thereby exclude him from being considered the Wicked Priest *par excellence*.

THE MIDRASH PESHER OF HABAKKUK

¶ 33 (xi, 17-xii, 10)

17 ‏[כִּיא חֲמַס לְבָנוֹן יְכַסֶּכָה וְשֹׁד בְּהֵמוֹת]

xii,1 ‏יַחְתֶּה מדמי אָדָם וַחֲמַס אֶרֶץ קִרְיָה וְכָל־יוֹשְׁבֵי בָּה

2 ‏פֵּשֶׁר הַדָּבָר עַל הַכּוֹהֵן הָרָשָׁע לְשַׁלֵּם לוֹ אֶת

3 ‏גְּמוּלוֹ אֲשֶׁר גָּמַל עַל אֶבְיוֹנִים כִּיא הַלְּבָנוֹן הוּא

4 ‏עֲצַת הַיַּחַד וְהַבְּהֵמוֹת הֵמָּה פְּתָאֵי יְהוּדָה עוֹשֵׂה

5 ‏הַתּוֹרָה אֲשֶׁר יְשׁוֹפְטֶנּוּ אֵל לְכָלָה

6 ‏כַּאֲשֶׁר זָמַם לְכַלּוֹת אֶבְיוֹנִים וַאֲשֶׁר אָמַר מִדְּמֵי

7 ‏קִרְיָה וַחֲמַס אֶרֶץ פִּשְׁרוֹ הַקִּרְיָה הִיא יְרוּשָׁלַ ם ‏חֲרָשָׁע

8 ‏אֲשֶׁר פָּעַל בָּה הַכּוֹהֵן מַעֲשֵׂי תוֹעֵבוֹת וַיְטַמֵּא אֶת

9 ‏מִקְדַּשׁ אֵל וַחֲמַס אֶרֶץ הֵמָּה עָרֵי יְהוּדָה אֲשֶׁר

10 ‏גָּזַל הוֹן אֶבְיוֹנִים

(Translation A)

xi,17 (2:17) [For (your) violence to Lebanon will overwhelm you,
and (your) ravaging of the livestock.] /

xii,1 A schemer would snatch away lowly men.

(Translation B)

xi,17 [For (your) pillage of Lebanon will overwhelm you.

xii,1 A ravager] / will snatch away *[livestock]*
by (shedding) the lowly man's blood,
amid pillages of the land,
the city's (blood)
as of all its inhabitants. /

2   The prophetic fulfillment of the passage concerns the Wicked Priest,
3   by heaping upon him / the same recompense which he heaped upon the
4   poor—for "Lebanon" is / the Council of the Community; and the
5   "livestock" are the simple of Judah / the Law *Doer*—for God will
6   condemn him to destruction, / in as much as he plotted to destroy the
    poor. And as for that which He said,

7   By / the city's *blood*
        amid the pillages of the land,

8   its prophetic meaning is: The "city" is Jerusalem / wherein the (Wicked
9   Priest wrought works of abomination and defiled / the sanctuary of God;
10 and the "pillages of the land" are the towns of Judah where he robbed the
    possessions of the poor.

196

¶33 *Exposition*

xi,17-xii,1. For the textual variants, see *Text*, §§123-125. One item not discussed there was the restoration of xi,17. Despite the use of the article in the words *hal-lĕvānôn* and *hab-bĕhēmôt* as cited at xii,3f., without further evidence one should not so restore the text in xi,17. Note that when Hab. 2:17*b* is quoted a second time at xi,7 *qiryāh* still lacks the article. The following interpretation inserts the article, which is only natural. "The" in each case means "the one referred to in the text." Two-thirds of the time in the Old Testament, *lĕvānôn* receives the article. Of the nineteen times in which the article is omitted, only one is in prose, II Chron. 2:7*b* (*=2:8b*), in what may have been a familiar expression "trees of Lebanon." Yet the possibility of a variant of this kind in xi, 17 is illustrated by 1Q Isa*a* at Isa. 14:8, which contains the article where it is lacking in the MT.

The variant *yaḥteh* at xii,1 (for the obscure reading *yĕḥîtan*) has until now not been understood. Preoccupation with what would make sense in the original context has led to the common emendation of *YḤTH* to *YḤTKH* (*yĕḥittekhāh*), an excellent parallel to the preceding verb *yĕkhassekhā(h)*. However, since this scroll often contains improbable readings upon which the *pēšer* builds, we should look for appropriate subject and object in the context, through new grammatical constructions. In translation A, the subject is found in the word *MDMY* interpreted as *mĕdammê*, the *pi*ᶜ*ēl* participle of *DMY* / *DMH* (a Rabbinic word meaning "schemer"); and the object of *yaḥteh* is *ʾādām*. This reading is inferred from li. 6: "He *plotted* to destroy the poor." Translation B is presented as an additional interpretation. It finds a subject for *yaḥteh* in the noun *šôd* of xi,17 and an object in *bĕhēmôt*. This takes *šôd* concretely, in the sense of *šôdēd* as in Isa. 16:4. With this second construction, one now interprets MDMY with the MT as *mid-dĕmê*. In view of the double readings, this word was left unpointed in the presentation of the text. Thus, in both ways, one finds an appropriate subject and object for *yaḥteh*. In Prov. 6:27; 25:22; and Isa. 30:14, the verb *ḤTH* is used for the gathering up of hot coals of fire; but in Ps. 52:7 (=52:5), it is used of the snuffing out of life:

> But God will break you down for ever;
> He will *snatch* and tear you from your tent;
> He will uproot you from the land of the living.

This latter is the meaning required by 1Q p Hab. Nothing contextually supports the rendering of Dupont-Sommer "attisera (le feu)" (*RHR*, p. 139), which became in Del Medico (*Riddle*, p. 258): "the fury of beasts *will blaze forth.*"

xii,1. "*By (shedding)* the blood of lowly men." This, rather than "*because of* the blood," is required by the punctuation of Translation B. Here the phrase refers to bloodshed—not primarily as the reason for the judgment overtaking the oppressor, but as a description of the violence of which he is guilty.

ʾĀdām was not treated as the generic for men, but as a designation of persons in low station, "lowly men." Thus in Pss. 49:3 and 62:10, the bĕnê ʾîš are contrasted with the bĕnê ʾādām as men in high station and in low station, respectively. Ezek. 34:31 identifies Yahweh's flock as ʾādām—hence, these are His "livestock."

xii,2. "The prophetic fulfillment . . . concerns the Wicked Priest by heaping upon him . . ." This is strikingly different from other introductions, in which it is "the Wicked Priest who did such and such." The present wording implies that the pēšer of the passage itself brings the recompense. This strongly supports the carefully argued case of Isaac Rabinowitz (RQ, No. 30, 1973, pp. 219-232) that the original and basic meaning of pēšer is "presage," and that sometimes it refers to "the reality presaged." See my discussion in the Introduction. Thus in the strictest sense the pēšer of a passage is not any meaning attributed to it or deduced from it, but an ascertainment of the history which it presages. The event presaged inheres in the text itself, although by all but the Teacher it is undetected. The text's presage brings into being the event which it forbodes. Thus Hab. 2:17 not only foretells the doom of the Wicked Priest, but it also effects it. Cf. the personified word of Yahweh in Isa. 55:10f.

xii,2f. "By heaping upon him the same recompense which he heaped." The verb gāmal is used not only of recompensing, but also of the bestowal of divine favor, as in 1Q S ii,1: "He has heaped upon us His gracious mercy from of old."

xii,3. "The poor" is one of the many self-designations of the Qumrân Community. Cf. the fuller designation ᶜadat hā-ʾevyônîm ("the Congregation of the Poor") in 4Q Pssᵃ ii,9 (¶7); iii,10 (¶16). The same should probably be restored in iii,15f. (¶17) of 4Q p Pssᵃ: "Its prophetic meaning concerns the priest, the [Righteous] Teacher, [whom] God [ch]ose to take office [and whom] He appointed to build for Him the Congregation of [the Poor]." One might restore the last lacuna with "His chosen" as in ii,5; iii,5; or with "the Community" as in iv,19. However, to read אביונים allows for a fitting pun on אבנים—this "congregation" being built of "poor" instead of "stones." The Righteous Teacher, its builder, refers to himself as ʾevyôn in the Hymns (1Q H ii,32; iii,25; v, 15f., 18). (Cf. Delcor, RB, 1951, pp. 533f.). The Sons of Light are called ʾevyônîm in 1Q M xi,9,18; xiii,13f. Most striking is 1Q H v,22: "to bring up . . . communally all the devoted poor (ʾevyônē ḥesed)." For an excellent study of the whole subject, see Leander E. Keck, "The Poor among the Saints in Jewish Christianity and Qumran," ZNW, LVII, 1966, pp. 54-78.

The use of ʾevyôn and its synonym ᶜānî for the devout poor goes back to the Psalmists, who as persons in humble circumstances often felt themselves to be oppressed. Cf. Pss. 37:14; 40:18 (=40:17), 70:6 (=70:5), 86:1; 102:1. Parts of the Bible condemn the oppression of the poor, because they were weak and helpless. In some of these passages the sect saw their own persecution foreshadowed. Yet Schoeps (*ZRG*, III, 1951, p. 322) noted that of twenty-six occurrences of *ᵓevyôn* in the Old Testament there is no hint of a sectarian meaning. Hence more proof is required than the present passage to establish "the poor" as a name of "a pre-Christian group which despised riches as the Essenes or the Damascus Community." J. L. Teicher has sought to identify the sectaries with the Ebionites. See the bibliography. For refutation, see the incisive criticisms of J. A. Fitzmyer in *ThS*, XVI, 1955, pp. 335-372 (*Essays*, pp. 435-480); and L. E. Keck, "The Poor among the Saints in the New Testament," *ZNW*, LVI, 1965, pp. 100-129.

Elliger opposed recognizing *ᵓevyônîm* as a technical expression in 1Q p Hab, since it is used here without the article. In this he may be right, and yet one must not forget that when a definite noun becomes a proper noun the article may be elimintaed, as in *śāṭān* (I Chron. 21:1). Cf. the anarthrous *nāvîᵓ* at 1Q S ix,11. Although the article occurs with *ᵓevyônîm* in 4Q p Pssᵃ, Keck (*ZNW*, 1966, p. 76) rightly cautions that since this *pēšer* treats Ps. 37 (whose vs. 14 speaks of the "poor and needy"), "it does not prove that 'the Poor' was a regular, technical, self-chosen, self-applied name of the Qumrân community." In other words, it may be in this case only an *ad hoc* self-designation, intended to identify the sectaries with the poor mentioned in this Psalm. Yet such a coined expression could only be understood against the ancient historical concept of the pious poor and the previous practice of the sect to apply such terminology to themselves in at least a descriptive sense. Once such an appellation was coined, its usage would not likely be restricted to the commentary. Among Qumrân coinages were "the Council of the Community" (each part separately, and in other combinations) and "the sons of light." Terms like "Israel," "Judah," "the Congregation of God," and "the holy ones" were inherited expressions given a restricted meaning in the community.

xii,3f. "For 'Lebanon' is the Council of the Community," which suffered persecution. This shows that *ᶜēṣāh* means "council" as well as "counsel," as often in 1Q S. The evidence for this meaning in the Old Testament is at best ambiguous; but see: Roland Bergmeier, "Zum Ausdruck in Ps. 1.1, Hi. 10.3, 21.16 and 22.18," *ZAW. LXXIX*, 1967, pp. 229-232.

Since Lebanon was famous for its *ᶜēṣîm* ("trees"), it is attractive to see in this a reason for the use of *ᶜēṣāh* in the present passage. In Jer. 6:6, *ᶜēṣāh* appears as a collective noun meaning "trees"—as noted by my former student William R. Murdock, so that the passage may also be understood to say: "Lebanon is the forest of the Community." The allegorizing of *ᶜēṣîm* is witnessed to by the targumic interpretation of I Kings 5:13 (=4:33): "He spoke of trees, from the cedar that is in Lebanon to the hyssop that grows out of the wall." This is allegorized by the Targum of Jonathan to mean: "He prophesied of the kings of the house of David that were destined to reign both in this age and in the age of the messiah." It may be an irrelevance to note in this connection the curious democratization in the statement of CDC vii,16f (=9:7): "The king is the congregation."

The Community itself was allegorized as a planting of trees in 1Q H viii,4-12, 22, 25, in a hymn which has in mind the concept of the eschatological society of the people of God as the New Garden of Eden. Note the identical conception in Pss. Sol. 14:2f.:

> The pious of the Lord shall live for ever;
> the Lord's paradise, the trees of life, are His pious ones.
> Their planting is rooted for ever;
> they shall not be plucked up all the days of heaven.

Behind this concept lies Third Isaiah:

> Your people shall all be righteous;
> they shall possess the land for ever,
> the shoot of My planting, the work of My hands,
> that I may be glorified.
>
> (Isa. 60:21)
> That they may be called oaks of righteousness,
> the planting of the LORD, that He may be glorified
> (61:3f-g)

This divine planting recalls Gen. 2:8: "The LORD God planted a garden in Eden." Second Isaiah foretold God's purpose of planting luxurious vegetation in the wilderness (Isa. 35:1f.; 41:19), of making Zion's wilderness "like Eden . . . like the garden of the LORD" (51:3). In fact, the various trees are to be planted "together (*yaḥdāw*), according to 41:19; and the *ᶜaṣat hay-yaḥad* has its establishment in the Wilderness of Judea.

Dupont-Sommer has suggested that the term Essene has derived from the noun *ᶜēṣāh* (*The Jewish Sect of Qumran*, p. 63); but this noun does not seem to be a term capable of receiving a gentilic form which is congruent with "Essene." However, in the light of Murdock's observation, it becomes more credible since the actual term from which "Essene" derives could conceivably be *ᶜēṣîm* / *ᶜēṣîn*. (Rabbinic Hebrew often used the *Nûn* termination for the plural.) This would satisfy the Greek spelling Ἐσσηνοί, the double plural being like the barbarous "cherubims" of the King James Version of the Bible. However, the alternative spelling Ἐσσαῖοι requires the Aramaic plural termination *ayyāʾ*; but the Aramaic equivalent of *ᶜēṣ* is *ʾāᶜ*, and the cognate term for *ᶜēṣāh* is *ʾaᶜah* (as in the Targum to Jer. 6:6). The most popular etymology derives the term Essene from Aramaic *ḥᵃsēʾ* = Hebrew *ḥāsîd*. This attractive derivation is certainly better suited to explain the spelling Ἐσσαῖοι. One difficulty with it is that it is better attested in Syriac than in Aramaic. In fact, the Targum regularly uses the cognate term rather than translate *ḥᵃsēʾ*. This could be explained, however, by a desire to avoid any suggestion of identity between the Essenes and the Hasidim.

According to the Targum of Jonathan, "Lebanon" refers to the temple at Jerusalem. Since 1Q p Hab contains several parallels to the Targum, I suggested already in 1953, that the people of Qumrân appropriated this equation by applying it to their Community, since they themselves constituted a spiritual temple. (See *JJS*, VII, 1956, pp. 174f.). References to the sect as temple lay implicit in *The Dead Sea Manual of Discipline*, p. 21, n. 20; p. 32; p. 35, n. 10. It remained for Bertil Gärtner (*The Temple and the Community in Qumran and the New Testament*, 1965) to exploit fully this important interpretation. The long tradition of interpreting Lebanon as the temple has been fully explored by Vermès in the following writings: "The Symbolical Interpretation of Lebanon in the Targums: The Origin and Development of an Exegetical Tradition," *JThS*, IX, 1958, pp. 1-12; *Scripture and Tradition in Judaism*, 1961, pp. 26-39. See also A. Finkel, p. 366.

The identification of Lebanon with the temple in the Targum correlates well with the Qumrân Community whether as temple or as trees, for the temple of Solomon was built of cedars of Lebanon and "the glory of Lebanon" with all its trees are destined to beautify the place of God's future sanctuary (Isa. 60:13). Cf. Ps. 92:13f. (=92:12f.):

> The righteous flourish like the palm tree,
> and grow like a cedar in Lebanon
> They are planted in the house of the LORD,
> they flourish in the courts of our God.

Isa. 35:2 would be susceptible to sectarian interpretation with its promise that "the glory of Lebanon" will be bestowed upon the Wilderness of Judea.

Gaster, p. 269, n. 45, has suggested that "Lebanon" was interpreted as referring to the Qumrân sect through the root meaning of the word as "white"—and Essenes according to Josephus were clothed in white (*JW*, II, viii,3 [§123]). At present, these white robes are unattested at Qumrân. More probably white was for the Essenes a symbol of moral purity (Isa. 1:18; Ps. 51:9 [=51:7]) and for the perfection of those who had been refined through martyrdom (Dan. 11:35). Cf. Rev. 3:4; 7:13f. The whiteness of the garments attributed to the Essenes probably represented such purity, but the robes themselves would be secondary to this concept.

xii,4. "The livestock are the simple." *Bĕhēmôt* (pl. of *bĕhēmāh*) designates animals in general in the Old Testament, whether wild or domestic. There is no evidence, despite some translations, that the domestic animals referred to were ever limited to cattle (bovines). Gaster has interpreted the *bĕhēmôt* of 1Q p Hab as "wild beasts," but with better reason Teicher has interpreted them as domestic animals. These "livestock" are like the ox and the ass of Isa. 1:3, since they own Yahweh as their Lord. Unlike wild animals, they are humble, submissive, and obedient to their Master. In the Targum of Jonathan "the livestock" are interpreted as "its [the sanctuary's] people." Thus, exactly as 1Q p Hab, it links closely temple and people. This interpretation appears anterior to Qumrân, and not vice versa; for the equations "Lebanon" = "the sanctuary" and livestock" = "its people" seem logically prior to the equations: "Lebanon" = "Council of the Community" (which is also temple), and "livestock" = "the simple of Judah" (who are the people of the santuary). So was it argued rightly by G. Vermès, *JThS*, IX, p. 7 and G. R. Driver, *Judean Scrolls*, p. 459; contrast Rabin, *VT*, V, 1955, pp. 157f. Thus, rather than with Rabin to argue "that the whole equation arose in sectarian circles," one reasons rather that the people of Qumrân reapplied in a sectarian manner certain inherited interpretations. Ringgren (*The Faith of Qumran*, p. 10) thought it tenable that in some cases the Habakkuk *pēšer* is dependent upon the targum, but in this case he allowed that the dependancy is just the opposite! Neither Rabin nor Ringgren noted in this connection the concept of the Community as a spiritual temple.

xii,4f. "The simple of Judah the Law Doer." The "simple" like "the livestock" connote something good as in one definition of *Webster's New Collegiate Dictionary:* "devoid of ostentation; unaffected; natural." More than this, however, the Hebrew word means "open to instruction, teachable," and hence may probably mean "disciple." In the area of learning, "simple" in English means "ignorant, not wise," and "lacking sense, foolish." These last meanings belong to *petî* in some Hebrew passages in the Old Testament, such as Ezek. 45:20, Prov. 1:22, 32; 8:5; 14:18; 22:3; 27:12. (Cf. also Job 18:3 where to be "counted as beasts" is to be "stupid in your sight.") The simple were generally not beyond hope; but they were appealed to as prospective learners (Prov. 8:5). Their simplicity may be due to their youth and lack of education (1:4). Yet sometimes chastisement was required before they could (or would) grasp wisdom (19:25; 21:11). They are not only open-minded, but naive and inclined to be gullible (14:15), and they are easily misled (7:7). Since their character is not fixed, Lady Wisdom may appeal to them with the same language as employed by Dame Folly (9:4, 16). Among the simple, therefore, the sage seeks his disciples (1:4). From the Torah they gain understanding and insight (Pss. 19:8 [=19:7]; 119:130; and they are the objects of God's special care.

Teicher argues, by analogy with the Arabic, that the word means "children." At most, however, "youth" (not "child") is the meaning of *petî* in Hebrew (Prov. 1:22, 7:7). Still, it is their quality of being teachable which is the precise point that Jesus had in mind in insisting that His disciples must "turn and become as little children" (Matt 18:1-4). According to 10:42, "one of these little ones" is "a disciple." The author of 1QH thought that he himself was to be a source of "prudence for the simple" (1QH ii,9), having the obligation "to give the simple insight into the might of Thy strength" (Frg. 15, li. 4). According to Jer. 20:7f., the Lord has "deceived" *(pittîtanî)* the prophet and subjected him to "violence and destruction" *(ḥāmās wā-šōd)*. The text may be given a favorable sense by interpreting the verb denominatively: "O

LORD, Thou hast discipled me and I am become a disciple." Thus it could have influenced the interpretation of Hab. 2:17.

These "simple ones" belong to "Judah the Law Doer," a phrase which, by 1952, I recognized to be a designation of the Righteous Teacher. The words *ᶜôseh hat-tôrāh* are orthographically "the doer of the Law," and not "the doers of the Law." It is not (as most scholars believe) that we find here a misspelling of *Hē* for *Yôd*; nor is it (as Teicher has argued) that an original *Hē* has been corrected by a deformation of the righthand side of the letter in order to convert it into a *Yôd*. Rather, it is, as Martin (II, §45) has observed, that an original *Yôd* has been converted into a *Hē*! This is confirmed by the fact that none of the strokes by which the letter was made into a *Hē* are characteristic of the normal *Hē* of the original scribe. It may be that this scribe himself made the correction, but the strokes which make it a *Hē* are clearly additional. As viii,1 shows, there could be no possible objection to the plural ᶜ*WSY*, if the intended reference were to the Community of Qumrân. The correction can be explained only by the intention of insisting upon a real singular. An important parallel to the initial scribal error is to be seen in the writing of *môrēh haṣ-ṣedeq* in 1Q p Mic, which spells the first word as *MWRY*. The passage also offers a very significant interpretative parallel to the present passage, as J. T. Milik noted in *RB*, LXIX, pp. 412-418. The key section is an interpretation of Mic. 1:5c (the restoration of which will be discussed in our next projected volume):

> [Now what is Ja]cob's [rebellion],
>   is it not / [Samaria?
> And what are the heights of Judah,
>   are they not Jer]us[alem?
> I will reduce Samaria /
>   to a ruin in the fields,
>   to plantings of a vineyard.]

> Its prophetic meaning concerns the Prophet of Lies [who is the beguiler of the] simple. "And what are the heights of Judah, [are they not Jerusalem?" its prophetic meaning con]cerns the Teacher of Right who is [an interpreter of knowledge to] his [Council] and to a[l]l who volunteer to join the elect of [God, the doers of the Law] in the Council of the Community, who will be deliver[ed] from the Day of [Judgment].

This *pēšer* is exceedingly interesting in that it interprets "Jacob" as an epithet of the "Prophet of Lies" and "Judah" as designating the Righteous Teacher (or here, for the sake of antithesis, the Teacher of Right). Neither of these figures stands in isolation from his community. The "rebellion" of the Prophet of Lies is his seduction of "the simple," who together constitute "Samaria," i.e., apostate Israel. The "heights" of the Teacher of Right are the men of his Council, who constitute "Jerusalem," i.e., the true Israel. These "doers of the Law in the Council of the Community who will be delivered from the day of judgment" (if correctly restored) are similarly described in 4Q p Pss*ᵃ* ii,14 (¶8) and in 1Q p Hab viii,1f. (¶24). At issue in the Micah *pēšer* is the reading *môrê haṣ-ṣedeq*, spelled as if a plural. Gaster, in the first edition of his book (pp. 239, 262, n.2), interpreted this as a plural; and he defended this reading in his second edition (p. 31) on the basis that it interprets the plural *bāmôt* of Mic. 1:5. The plural "teachers" is excluded by the following words *ʾăšer hûʾāh* ("who *is*" or "who *was*"). The use of the singular pronoun as the copula proves that *môrê* = *môrēh*, the words being phonetically indistinguishable. Already Milik had recognized that the *bāmôt* like the *běhēmôt* of Hab. 2:17 were interpreted as the Teacher's disciples, the former being understood as an abbreviated spelling of the latter.

The Micah *pēšer* has an important bearing upon the Teacher's name. The interpretation of "Jacob" as the Prophet of Lies is solely an exegetical equation, for as yet we know of no text which employs this as his name. If the real person referred to is John Hyrcanus as Barthélemy (*RB*, LXIX, 1952, pp. 214-216) and I (*BASOR*, 126, 1952, pp. 17-19) proposed independently, one can see why he was identified with "Jacob," since this patriarch was known as the supplanter of Esau, and it was Hyrcanus who repeated this history by crushing Idumea and Judaizing it. In 1Q p Mic, the equation of "Judah" with the Teacher is likewise exegetical, but in 1Q p Hab xii,4, it is used in the interpretation itself as a designation of the Teacher. From this one cannot be sure whether Judah was the Teacher's real name or whether it was only his sobriquet derived from the Scriptures. It could be that by a felicitous coincidence his real name made it possible for one to claim that he was actually named in prophecy.

At the end of the discussion of ¶17, we discussed the identity of the Righteous Teacher and the Man of Lies. If the latter can be none other than John Hyrcanus, then the Teacher who rebuked him could have borne the real name Eleazar (following Josephus) and still be identified with Judas the Essene, by interpreting Judah as only his assumed name. Or supposing Josephus to have erred as to the rebuker of Hyrcanus, his proper name being Judah son of Jedidiah (following the Rabbinic account), then this same man could also be Judas the Essene. Already we have examined in ¶24 the possibility that the term Essene (esp., when spelled with an *O*) may have been derived from the Hebrew word *ʿôśîn* ("doers"). If this uncertain hypothesis could be accepted, then "Judah the Law Doer" and "Judas the Essene" would be linguistically synonymous, the latter appellation translating the former. On the other hand, these persons might be identified with each other, even if "the Essene" and "the Law Doer" are unrelated epithets. (Note that two other possible etymologies of Essene have already been discussed in this present section.)

Naturally, if one supposes that the Teacher's name was Judah, many other Judahs could be considered. Thus Isaac Rabinowitz (*VT*, VIII, 1958, pp. 402ff.) considered Judas Maccabeus as one of the persons referred to as *môrēh haṣ-ṣedeq*. H. E. Del Medico, however, thought this name alluded to the zealot leader Judas the Galilean (*Riddle*, pp. 252, 258). In this he has been followed by Cecil Roth (*The Historical Background of the Dead Sea Scrolls*, 1959, p. 54) and G. R. Driver (*Judean Scrolls*, pp. 306, 458). Each of these scholars allowed that there were also other Righteous Teachers.

xii,5f. "*For* God will condemn him to destruction, in as much as he plotted to destroy the poor." The word ᵓᵃšer is more easily read as a conjunction than as a relative, in view of the distance from the previous reference to the Wicked Priest. It gives an explication of the previous statement of li. 3 that the Wicked Priest "heaped upon the Poor" some sort of recompense. In both places we have a tit-for-tat description of the retribution to be visted upon him through the use of cognate nouns and verbs: *gĕmûlô* / *gāmal*, *lĕ-khālāh* / *lĕ-khallôt*. This is in full accord with the sense of Hab. 2:17 itself. Cf. the similar sort of statement at ix,1f, also Jud. 9:24.

"He plotted to destroy the poor." In the use of the verb *zāmam*, there may have been some influence from Ps. 37. In vs. 7, the evil-doer is characterized as one who "carries out plots" (ᶜōśeh mĕzimmôt). The intention, according to vs. 14 is "to bring down the poor and needy;" but, according to vs. 12 (as interpreted by 4Q p Pssᵃ ii, 13, 15 [¶8]), the plot was not entirely successful. (The passage is cited above at viii,1 [¶24].)

xii,7. "By the city's blood." The fact that this can be quoted without including the previous verb *yaḥteh* indicates a new construction of the text in this fresh quotation. It is this which justifies Translation B of the text in this *pēšer*. In the requotation "the *city's* blood" replaces "*the lowly man's* blood." However, there is an ellipsis in connection with the final stich (or colon) of the verse. In the writing of the prophet the understood noun was probably *ḥāmās* ("violence"):

> Because of man's (shed) blood and violence to the land,
> (to) the city and (to) all its inhabitants.

However, the midrashist chose to interpret the ellipsis as carrying forward the earlier reference to "man's shed blood." The intervening words would need to be taken parenthetically, and this was done by interpreting the phrase *wa-ḥᵃmas* ᵓereṣ as circumstantial ("amid pillages of the land"). The dislocation of this to a position after the mention of the city's blood indicates this construction. This is only one of many indications that the ancient interpreter applied his ingenuity to new ways of interpreting the syntax and not just to verbal play. Thus one must not entertain the unimaginative view of Habermann (ᶜEdah, p. 55) that this variant quotation arose from a lapse of memory on the part of the scribe. Rather, it is a reshaped text for the sake of indicating a syntactical interpretation. See *Text*, pp. 119f. The concern of the interpreter was to connect the bloodshed with the city and the pillaging with the land. The explanation of Hab. 2:17b is quite different from that given to the same language in Hab. 2:8b at ix,8-12 (¶27). The commentator would probably reason that the Biblical repetition was not superflous, but had a special meaning of its own.

"The city is Jerusalem." The pronoun hi° is used as the copulative verb. The city is also identified with Jerusalem in the Targum of Jonathan.

xii,9. "The Wicked Priest wrought works of abomination and defiled the sanctuary of God." In the accusation against Sodom and her dependencies that they did not assist the poor (Ezek. 16:49f.) there was also the further charge that "they wrought abomination." Especially important is Ezek. 22:1-12, which describes Jerusalem as "the bloody city." Here, where the prophet was commanded to make known to Jerusalem "all her abominations," there is a prominent place given to murder, but also to other defiling sins, including lying with one's wife at the time of her issue of blood. The fact that the midrashist in his interpretation of the syntax was so eager to connect "blood" with the "city" makes it appear probable that his "works of abomination" included bloody crimes. Consequently, the suggestion that the non-mention of the word "blood" in the explicit interpretation indicates that nothing was made of the reference to "blood" is probably erroneous. The Scriptures indicated that bloodshed defiled the Holy Land (Num. 35:33). Child sacrifice was especially defiling of both the worshipper (Ps. 106:35-39) and the sanctuary (Lev. 20:3; Ezek. 23:39). To enter the temple in a state of impurity was also to defile the sanctuary of the Lord (Num. 19:20). Therefore, even if one's hands were defiled with blood (Isa. 59:3) which had been spilled elsewhere, this too would defile the sanctuary. Yet one could well imagine some Essene seeking to reinforce this interpretation at Qumrân by the clever reasoning: "Do not read *mĕdammê* ('schemer'), but *mĕṭammē*ʾ ('He defiles the city')." The reference to blood, however, is sufficient to justify the reference to defilement.

There is no need to limit the defiling blood in this reference to bloodshed. It may also include the menstrual blood, as in CDC v,6f. (=7:8f.): "And they also defile the sanctuary since they separate not according to the Law, and lie with her who sees the blood of her issue." This alludes to laws of ritual cleanness set forth in Lev. 12 and 15:31. Cf. also Pss. Sol. 8:13 (or 8:12):

> They trode the altar of the Lord,
>> (coming straight) from all manner of uncleanness;
> And with menstrual blood they defiled the sacrifices,
>> as (though they were) common flesh.

For defilement of the sanctuary in general, cf. CDC iv,18 (=6:11); Pss. Sol. 2:3; Assumption of Moses 5:4; 6:1. However, it would be a mistake to press the evidence of such passages in such a way as to exclude the crime of murder. Bloodshed by the Wicked Priest anywhere, as when he attacked the Righteous Teacher and his associates at their place of exile (¶31), would render him unclean, so that upon entering the temple he would defile it. There is also the possibility that among the Wicked Priest's works of abomination were acts of murder committed in Jerusalem itself. This best explains the reference to "the city's blood." The text does not say explicitly whether any of these abominations were committed in the temple, however, nor does it exclude it. The most dramatic event to which it could refer would be Jannaeus' slaughter of 6,000 Jews at the celebration of the Feast of Tabernacles, as proposed by M. H. Segal, *JBL*, LXX, 1951, pp. 136, 139. See Josephus, *JA*, XIII, xiii,5 (§§372-374).

xii,9f. "The 'pillages of the land' are towns of Judah where he robbed the possessions of the poor." The translation of *ḥāmās* as "pillage" accords with the context of the commentary, and it is supported by the targum's rendering *ḥᵃṭôf*. The plural "pillages" is required in English by the copulative pronoun *hēmmāh*, which indicates that *ḥᵃmas ʾereṣ* is to be interpreted as a collective. Cf. the collective interpretation of "Amon" (ʾ*MWN*) in 4Q p Nah iii,9 (¶12).

The idea of "pillage" is to be found not only in the Biblical word *ḥāmās*, but also in *šôd*, a word which means either "destruction" or "plunder." The English words "ravage" and "ravager" include in their meaning both destruction and plunder, and hence the use of these words in the translation. In Ob. 5, the *šôdĕdê layĕlāh* are parallel to *gannāvîm*, and so the former was rendered appropriately in the KJV as "robbers by night" and the latter as "thieves". The RSV uses the words "plunderers by night" in parallelism with "thieves." The two versions agree on "robbers" for *šôdĕdîm* in Job 12:6. In Isa. 16:4, the KJV rendered appropriately both *šôdēd* and *šôd* as "spoiler," where the RSV uses the words "destroyer" and "destruction." Amos 3:10 accuses the Israelites of "storing up *ḥāmās* and *šôd* in their palaces," where both nouns stand for that which was acquired by extortion or robbery. Thus, since both words occur in Hab. 2:17, the ancient midrashist was doubly justified in his interpretation of the verse as referring to robbery.

The interpretation of the "land" as "towns" explains ʾ*ereṣ* as referring to the whole country outside Jerusalem, where most of the people lived in towns or villages. This interpretation could have been suggested by Jer. 48:8: "And the spoiler shall come upon every city and no city shall escape" (KJV)—even though in context this should refer to Moab. That such robbery and bloodshed refers particularly to Judah may have been inferred from Joel 4:19 (=3:19):

> Egypt will become a desolation,
>   and Edom a desolate wilderness,
> because of (their) *ḥāmās* to the sons of Judah,
>   for they shed innocent blood in their land.

The Targum of Jonathan interprets *ḥāmās* also here as *ḥᵃṭôf* ("robbery").

The "towns of Judah" which were robbed may be Essene settlements where the Wicked Priest tried to suppress the sect by confiscation of their property. J. van der Ploeg has discussed these towns as follows (*Excavations at Qumran*, p. 70):

> Philo says that the Essenes avoided cities on account of the corrupt morals of such places.

They lived, he says, 'in villages' (literally, in village fashion) [κωμηδὸν οἰκοῦσι]. This must mean that they lived not inside but outside the walls of the towns, or in little villages in the country. More easily than in a town, they could find there a place where they could live in community and keep themselves ritually pure as far as possible. . . . If such a spot was walled in ancient times, it could be called a city in Greek; if it was open, a village. The lack of any essential difference between city and village makes it possible for Josephus to say that the Essenes had no 'city' of their own, but that there were colonies of them in various 'cities.' Obviously, he does not distinguish between city and village, and so does not necessarily contradict Philo.

For Philo, see *Every Good Man is Free*, xii (§76). For Josephus, see *JW*, II, viii,4 (§124). Eusebius, *Preparation of the Gospel*, VIII, 11 quotes Philo as having also said of the Essenes: "And they inhabit [οἰ]κοῦσι many cities [πόλεις] of Judea, and many villages [κώμας] and great and populous communities [ὁμίλους]."

In view of the apparent use of "Judah" earlier as a name or sobriquet of the Righteous Teacher, "the cities of Judah" may refer especially to settlements of the Teacher's votaries. If, however, the term "towns of Judah" refers to all villages of the land, then one must think of robbery in the form of burdensome taxation. That "the poor" were particularly the victims suggests a sectarian reference.

THE MIDRASH PESHER OF HABAKKUK

¶34 (xii, 10-14)

מָה הוֹעִיל פֶּסֶל כִּיא פְּסָל פֶּסֶל יָצְרוּ׃ 10

מַסִּיכָה וּמְרִי שֶׁקֶר כִּיא בָטַח יֹצֵר יִצְרָיו עָלֵיהוּ 11

לַעֲשׂוֹת אֱלִילִים אִלְּמִים פֵּשֶׁר הַדָּבָר עַל כּוּל 12

פְּסָלֵי הַגּוֹיִם אֲשֶׁר יְצָרוּם לְעָובְדָם וְלִשְׁתַּחֲוֹת 13

לָהֵמָּה וְהֵמָּה לוֹא יַצִּילוּם בְּיוֹם הַמִּשְׁפָּט 14

10 (2:18)　　What help is a carved image,
　　　　　　　when they have shaped the carving? /
11　　　　　　　or a libation and fatling of falsehood?
　　　　　For he who shapes his idol trusts in it, /
12　　　　　　　though making a dumb dummy!
13　　The prophetic meaning of the passage concerns all / the carved
images of the nations which they have shaped in order to worship them
14　and to prostrate themselves / before them; but these will not deliver them
on the Day of Judgment.

¶34 *Exposition*

xii,10f. For the variants, see *Text*, §§126-131.

xii,10. "When they have shaped the carving." Other constructions are possible, as discussed in *Text*, §127. The reading chosen here calls for no defective spellings, and the verb agrees in number with the plural of xii,13.

xii,11. "Or a libation and fatling of falsehood?" The *massêkhāh* is generally taken as "molten image"; but the sense "libation" is supported by Isa. 30:1 (MT) and 65:11 (1Q Isa*a*), as argued in *Meaning*, pp. 177f. The erasure of the *Yôd* of *MSYKH*, which is clearly visible in the photographs, was probably motivated by the desire to prevent the misreading of the word as *MSWKH* (*měsûkhāh*), "hedge," as Dupont-Sommer (*RHR*, p. 15) correctly observed.

The word *MRY* for the Massoretic reading *MWRH* (*môreh*) could be interpreted as a purely orthographical variant, a mixture of defective spelling (omission of the *Wāw*) and phonetic spelling (the *Yôd* for the *Ṣērê*), by reading the construct form. This would preserve the original sense "false teacher." A variant of this interpretation would be to read *marê* = *marʾēh* ("vision"). This too would lie close to the original sense of the passage. In either case, it is strange that the midrashist did not exploit it for another condemnation of the Prophet of Lies. The reference to idolatry could have been correlated with this, by interpreting the idolatry as metaphorical (as in 4Q p Hos ii,6 [¶5]).

MRY could also be interpreted simply as a derogatory term for an idol, among which the following have been proposed: *marê* ("bitter things") and *měrî* (interpreted as "rebelliousness"). All the above readings have been discussed in *Text*, §129. Any specific term of contempt would be sufficiently neutral that one would not expect it to be reflected in the commentary, since in any case idolatry is condemned.

Two suggestions for interpreting *MRY* suit the idea of false worship. "Myrrhs" was suggested as an alternative reading by Dupont-Sommer (*RHR*, p. 151) in 1950; but he never adopted it in any of his translations. In my article "The Composition of Habakkuk," p. 271, n. 2, I rendered the phrase "myrrhs of false worship." However, the defective spelling of a presumed *môrê* (or *murê*) does not favor the reading, neither does the lack of attestation for the use of this word in the plural. Better is the rendering of Vermès (*DSSE*, p. 242), "a fatling of lies." This interprets *měrî* as *měrîʾ*—the words being phonetically and orthographically confusable. After the mention of "a libation," the "fatling" must denote a sacrificial victim. Yet it would also connote "rebelliousness," all worship of idols being an affront to the true God. Here is the *Ansatzpunkt*, the absence of which was noted by Elliger. *Šeqer* as used here means either "false god" (an idol) or "false worship" (idolatry).

"For he who shapes his idol." *Kîʾ* might be rendered "yet," rather than "for," since it is sometimes a contraction of *kî ʾim*. However, each of the other woes of this chapter is concluded with a *kî* which really means "for" (2:8a, 11, 14, 17a). The noun *yĕṣārâw* ("his own idol") is plural in form; but it is singular in meaning as is shown by the following *ʿālêhû*. The plural of majesty was anciently used more widely than in the MT. For 1Q Isa*ᵃ*, see *Meaning*, pp. 170f. Not noted there is the scroll's reading at 14:27: *wĕ-yādâw han-nĕṭūyāh* ("As for His stretched out *hand*, who will turn it back?"). In 49:2, the word for "quiver" is plural, because it is God's quiver. Thus the accouterments of the divine were also accorded this reverential form.

xii,12. "Though making a dumb dummy." The Hebrew is plural, but in the light of the preceding clause it is to be interpreted as singular in meaning. The translation represents in English the Hebrew pun: *ʾĕlîlîm ʾillĕmîm*. Both words parody the divine name *ʾĕlōhîm*, which is thereby withheld.

xii,13. "The carved images of the nations." The passage is applied to gentiles only, and not to Jews, as it could have been appropriately applied during the time of Antiochus Epiphanes. This may well argue for a much later period of composition for this *pēšer*.

"Which they have shaped." At this point a second hand takes over and completes the scroll. See Del Medico, *Riddle*, p. 48. The detailed arguments which convincingly prove the change of hand are given with the word *ʾŠR* by Elliger, pp. 78-81. The concluding scribe sometimes erred as to the use of medial and final letters. Thus in li,14 he wrote להמה, giving us also the sole example of this longer spelling for להם. In li. 15, there is a medial *Ṣādê* in final position and in xiii,2 a medial *Mêm* in final position.

xii,13f. "To worship them and to prostrate themselves before them." These references to the worship of false gods are drawn from the special reading "libation and fatling" (li. 11). The infinitive *lištaḥᵃwôt* contracts *lĕ-hištaḥᵃwôt*, as correctly noted by O. H. Lehmann, *PEQ*, LXXXIII, 1951, p. 51.

xii,14. "These will not deliver them on the Day of Judgment." This explains the "help" concerning which question was raised in the text and it indicates that for which one "trusts" when fashioning an idol. This is reminiscent of Isa. 41, where God summons the nations to judgment (vs. 1), who for their part hastily manufacture idols out of fear of the approaching doom (vss. 5-7). The denial that the idols can deliver them contrasts with what the true God will do for His own people. 1Q p Mic, if properly restored, speaks of "the elect of [God . . .] in the Council of the Community, who will be deliver[ed] from the Day of [Judgment]." (See the full citation, as given above at p. 203.

The theme of the Day of Judgment prepares for the next pericope, which is here anticipated, for this idea was derived from 2:20. This linking of Vs. 18 with the following verses is correct, since Vss. 18-20 as the final woe of the chapter constitutes a literary unit. The interpretations in 1Q p Hab do not always ignore contexts. Even the eschatological interpretation of the passage is not in error. See *Meaning*, pp. 66-69.

THE MIDRASH PESHER OF HABAKKUK

¶35 (xii, 14-xiii, 4)

הוֹי 14

הָ[אוֹמְרִים] לָעֵץ הָקִיצָה [עוּרִי] לְ[אֶבֶ]ן דּוּמָם 15

[הוּא יוֹרֶה הִנֵּה הוּא תָּפוּשׁ זָהָב וָכֶסֶף וְכָל־ 16

רוּחַ אֵין בְּקִרְבּוֹ וַיהוה בְּהֵיכַל־קָדְשׁוֹ] 17

הַס מִלְּפָנָיו כּוֹל־הָאָרֶץ פִּשְׁרוֹ עַל כָּוֹל־הַגּוֹיִם xiii,1

אֲשֶׁר עָבְדוּ אֶת הָאֶבֶן וְאֶת הָעֵץ וּבְיוֹם 2

הַמִּשְׁפָּט יְכַלֶּה אֵל אֶת כָּוֹל עוֹבְדֵי הָעֲצַבִּים 3

וְאֶת הָרְשָׁעִים מִן הָאָרֶץ 4

14   (2:19)   Alas /
15   for [those who say] to wood, "Wake up!"
             "[Bestir!"] to dumb [sto]ne — /
             [it will teach!?
16   Though indeed it be plated with gold and silver,
17   there is no / spirit at all within it!
   (2:20)   But the LORD is in His holy palace;] /
             hush all earth, at His presence!
xiii,1   Its prophetic meaning concerns all the nations / who worship
2   "stone" and "wood"; but, on the Day of / Judgment, God will
3   eradicate all the idolaters / and the wicked from the earth.

¶35 *Exposition*

xii,14–xiii,1. For the variants, see *Text*, §§ 132-135. At li. 15, the plural *hā-*
ʾômĕrîm, "those who say" is restored by reason of space. This reading was
suggested by Martin, II, §23, and by *Text*, §132. Both in ᶜ*Edah* (p. 56) and in
Megilloth (p. 48), Habermann restores with a dittograph of *hôi*. This is a real
possibility. "To wood," or "to a tree"; but in the commentary ᶜ*ēṣ* is regarded as
merely the material of which idols are made.

At the end of li. 15 I first read *RWMH* ("To the *lofty* stone, 'Arise!'"),
BASOR, 112, p. 16. However, after reexamining the manuscript itself in 1949,
I concluded that the final letter was a *Mêm*, whose lower horizontal stroke
had been peeled off. Trever's colored photograph also reveals that we do not
have here a straight break, but one which cuts through on an angle, peeling off
part of the surface of the skin, bringing some damage even to the lower
horizontal of the medial *Mêm*. The stance of the letter and its strokes have
been discussed in *Text*, §132a. There, I have also argued that the first letter of
the word is a *Dālet* rather than a *Rêsh*. This conclusion might still be
questioned, but one needs to compare this letter not with the characteristic
*Dālet*s of the scroll but with those of the new scribe who completed the
manuscript, beginning with the third word of li. 13. The upper right corner of
his *Rêš* does not rise to a point level with the upper tip of the left hook of the
letter. The left hook may rise above the ruled line from which the letter is
hung, but the right corner remains below the line. In *DWMM*, both the upper
right and the upper left tips of the letter rise above the line. The short
horizontal stroke, which unfortunately is eroded, once joined the right
vertical stroke at a point flush with the bottom of the ruled line. Admittedly,
the upper right tip did not rise much above this horizontal stroke; but in all
probability the letter is a *Dālet*.

xii,16f. The distribution of the lines given here differs from that of
Habermann, Lohse, and Elliger by placing *wĕ-kol* at the end of li. 16, not at
the beginning of li. 17. Habermann and Lohse forgot that the
Tetragrammaton would require more space on li. 17 when written in paleo-
Hebrew letters. Elliger seems to have noted this, since he located *qodšô* at the
beginning of li. 18! Because the citation of the Biblical text is continuous, there
must have been full lines at this point. As restored here, li. 16 calls for thirty-
five letters and spaces and li. 17 for thirty-three (counting seven spaces for the
Tetragrammaton as at x,14, when compared with the line above it). Li. 2 of the
present column has only thirty-three letters and spaces, and li. 12 has thirty-
four. It is the present column which establishes the measurement of seventeen
lines per column. See *BASOR*, 118, 1950, pp. 7-9. Elliger's insistence on the
need for eighteen lines per column seems arbitrary.

On "though indeed" as a translation of *hinnēh*, see "The Composition of
Habukkuk," p. 265, n. 2.

xii,17. "No spirit at all within it;" or "no breath." This denial is directed against the pagan claim that the spirit of a god inhabited its image. Yehezkel Kaufmann (*The Religion of Israel*, 1963) makes the frequent claim (but see esp., pp. 17-20) that to the Biblical authors the condemnation of idolatry was "mere fetishism." The prophets did not bother to deny the existence of gods themselves, since their Hebrew audience was unfamiliar with the pagan understanding of idolatry. The present passage, according to him (p.399), "is directed for the first time to pagan ears."

"But the LORD is in His holy palace [or, temple]." If applied to the earthly temple (as in the Targum of Jonathan), the prophet would be saying that in contrast with pagan idols which contain no divine spirit within them, the LORD is actually present in the temple at Jerusalem. He would thereby claim for the temple what the pagan claimed for his idol! However, parallels with other passages indicate that in this verse the Lord is thought of as present in His heavenly temple, or palace. Note the synonomous statements of Ps. 11:4: "The LORD is in His holy palace, the LORD's throne is in heaven." Other relevant passages will be quoted below.

xiii,1. We have *HRṢ* instead of *H°RṢ*. This probably indicates that in popular pronunciation *hā-°āreṣ* was first of all pronounced with a quiescent *°Ālef*, as *hā-āreṣ*, and it was then further contracted to *hāreṣ*. Even with the most contracted pronunciation, the classical orthography was normally retained, especially since the *°Ālef* could be reinterpreted as a *Qāmeṣ*. However, we cannot be certain that at all times and among all members the full contraction prevailed at Qumrân. An awareness of the classical pronunciation may have prevented some scribes from succumbing to the vulgar. Even on the part of an individual scribe, *hāreṣ* may have come to expression through a mere slip of the tongue. Moreover, the scribe who wrote this word is not the main scribe of the manuscript. For this reason, the misspelling here was not accepted as sufficient evidence for vocalizing the word everywhere as הָאָרֶץ. For further discussion, see *Text*, §135. Note, however, that 1Q Isa^b reads °*RṢ* and not *HRṢ* at Isa. 49:6 for the MT *H°RṢ*.

"Hush, all earth, *at His presence*;" or "*from before Him.*" This is not the silence of worshipers in reverential awe, but it is the deathly fear of men when confronted personally by the divine Judge whom they have affronted through idolatry. God is thought of as emerging from His heavenly palace and making His presence felt upon the earth where He wreaks judgment. Cf. the following Scriptures:

> Hear, you peoples, all of you;
>   hearken, O earth, and all that is in it;
> and let the Lord GOD be a witness against you,
>   the LORD from His holy palace.
> For behold, the LORD is coming out of His place,
>   and will come down and tread
>   upon the high places of the earth.
>   (Mic. 1:2 f.)

> Hush, all flesh, before the LORD;
> for He has bestirred himself from His holy dwelling.
>   (Zech. 2:17 = 2:13)

The latter is of particular interest here, because of both the interjection "hush" and the verb "bestir." The idolater in Hab. 2:19 had addressed his idol with the imperative $^c\hat{u}r\hat{\imath}$, but only Yahweh has "bestirred Himself" ($n\bar{e}^c\hat{o}r$), and so He is about to come in judgment from His heavenly temple.

xiii,2f. "All the nations who worship '*stone*' and '*wood*'." The commentator quotes from vs. 19, thereby showing (as against Gaster, p. 256, who followed Habermann's $^c Edah$) that there is no missing commentary at the bottom of the preceding column, the quotation there being continuous with vs. 20. Idolatry is attributed only to the "nations," as at xii,13. Yet the worship of "wood" and "stone" is attributed to Judean imitators of the nations in Jer. 2:26-28; Ezek. 20:32.

xiii,3f. "But on the Day of Judgment." The reference to "judgment" recalls Ps. 76:9f. (=76:8f.):

> From heaven you will sound the sentence,
>   the earth will shudder and fall still;
> When you arise for the judgment, O God,
>   to save all the meek of the earth.
>   (Dahood, *Anchor Bible*, II, p. 217)

Characteristically, Habakkuk, as probably also the Psalm, was interpreted eschatologically. "The Day of Judgment" has already been mentioned in the preceding pericope, at xii,14. It is probably alluded to also in ¶¶23 and 28. The phrase occurs with variations in Jub. 24:30; I Enoch 10:6, 12; 16:1; 19:1; 22:4, 13; 62:13; 84:4; 94:9; 98:10; 99:15; 104:5; Matt 10:15; 11:22, 24; 12:36; II Peter 2:9; 3:7; I John 4:17. Cf. Acts 17:31; Jude 6; Rev. 20:11-15.

"God will eradicate all the idolaters and the wicked from the earth." The verb "eradicate" is employed in the translation, rather than "destroy," in order to link the verb closely with the final phrase, and to indicate clearly that both "the idolaters and the wicked" are not only to be destroyed, but eliminated from the earth. Alternatively, one could rearrange the phrasing in translation: "God will *destroy from off* the earth all the idolaters and the wicked." This, however, would remove the final phrase from its climactic position at the very end and would conclude the scroll with a less impressive sentence.

The first translation (*BASOR*, 112, p. 13) produced the well balanced statement: "God will destroy in the sea all the worshippers of 'wood'; and from off the earth, the wicked!" The unpublished palaeographic justification for the reading of $^c S\ BYM$ for $^c \d{S}BYM$ was that the scribe had used a medial $\d{S}\bar{a}d\hat{e}$ in final position in xii,15, and that he was crowding the words at this point, running them together—a feature later mentioned by Elliger, pp. 73f. Also influential, of course, was the fact that the word "wood" occurs in the Biblical text and that the commentary sometimes finds expression in parallelistic phrases. For this strange motif of the destruction of idolaters "in the sea," I appealed to the fact that the Kittim came "from the isles of the sea" according to iii,11. And hence, I observed (p. 18, n. 84): "The author's sense of justice might condemn them to destruction in the sea." However, nothing anywhere in the extensive literature of Qumrân, as so far published, supports such an idea.

The idea of destruction was inferred by the ancient commentator from the interjection *has* ("be silent"). The same interpretation is given in the Targum of Jonathan: *yĕsûfûn qŏdāmôhî kol daḥᵃlat ᵓarᶜāᵓ* ("Let them destroy before Him every idol of the earth," i.e., "Let every idol *be destroyed*"). A similar interpretation of *has* is given by the Targum at Zeph. 1:7: *sāfû kol rašîᶜayyāᵓ* ("All the wicked have come to an end"). Although in the scroll it is the idolaters, and not just the idols, who are to be destroyed, the similarity of interpretation to that of the Targum is striking, and was noted by Solomon Zeitlin, *JQR*, XLIII, 1952, p. 150. The attribution of this meaning to *has* could have arisen by equating it with its synonym *dāmam*, which in its various stems often carries this meaning. One might even read the word *DWMM* of li. 15 as *dômēm* rather than *dûmâm*, in order to make 2:19a read: "'Bestir!' to stone. *Perishing* is he who teaches (such)." However, in view of the tradition associated with *has*, we need not derive the idea of destruction from *DWMM*.

In *BA*, 1951, p. 75, I suggested that the word *BHYKL* may have been interpreted as *B[YWM] H[MŠPṬ] YKL[H]* ("on the Day of Judgment He will destroy"). However, in a paper issued to select scholars on Feb. 2, 1953 (*The Dead Sea Habakkuk Midrash and the Targum of Jonathan*, pp. 10f.), I stated:

> The discovery of a traditional basis behind some of the interpretations of DSH calls for but slight modification of the hermeneutical analysis of DSH in the *Biblical Archaeologist*, Sept. 1951, where the author listed thirteen hermeneutical principles in DSH. Since the interpretations of two passages of DSH explained on the basis of *notarikon* are now seen to rest upon tradition (DSH vi,2ff.; xiii,2f.), there is no necessity any more to resort to this explanation ("H.P. 12"). Since this is but one of the principles previously discussed, the midrashic character of interpretation in DSH is practially unimpaired.

John V. Chamberlain (*An Ancient Sectarian Interpretation*, pp. 115f.) has used here my Hermeneutic Principle 9, which was as follows:

> Sometimes the prophet veiled his message by writing one word instead of another, the interpreter being able to recover the prophet's meaning by *a rearrangement of the letters in a word*.

Thus Chamberlain argued that היכל was interpreted in the commentary as יכלה, and that there may even be here a cryptic prophecy of the destruction of the earthly temple (Cf. Test. Levi 15). It is, indeed, true that the temple as temple does not figure in the interpretation and that there is no explicit reference to destruction in Hab. 2:19f. Nevertheless, the Targum and the parallel Scriptures cited above are sufficient to suggest the interpretation of the present passage.

"The wicked" is probably intended to include Jews as well as gentiles. Hence, according to x,4 (¶28), the Wicked Priest is to be raised up "for the Judgment." According to vii,14ff. the godless Jews will not be pardoned when they are judged, again perhaps referring to their appearance before God's own tribunal. V,5 (¶16) speaks of "the wicked of His people," whose judgment God has committed to His elect. This "judgment" is probably not that of the Day of Judgment, but it refers to that meted out by the Children of Light upon the Children of Darkness (1Q M) during their forty-year warfare. It is only at the conclusion of the wars that the final victory is achieved by the luminous manifestations of God Himself. Only the latter should be thought of as the Day of Judgment.

Despite the dread character of the announcement, the elimination of both idolaters and wicked *from the earth* makes the scroll end with a happy note; for from then on there will be no more fierce, trampling Kittim, no persecuting Wicked Priest, and no Prophet of Lies or smooth interpreters to misinterpret the Torah. Similarly Ps. 104 (which celebrates the grandeur of God's creation) concludes with the longing: "Let sinners be consumed from the earth, and let the wicked be no more!"—as if to say, "Only one thing mars the beauty of God's creation, the wicked." According to Zeph. 1:2f., one might expect the elimination of all mankind from the earth; but 1:4-6 suggests a doom directed primarily against idolaters. The coming of Elijah, according to Mal. 3:23f. (=4:5f.) is to bring about a wholeness to Jewish society which will prevent Yahweh from imposing a *herem* upon the whole earth when He comes. According to 1Q p Mic, it might appear that the Righteous Teacher performs the work of Elijah, since his adherents "will be delivered from the Day of [Judgment]." (See above, at xii,14 [¶34]). According to 1Q p Hab v,3, "God will not destroy His people by means of the nations."

That the wicked are to be destroyed from off the earth appears repeatedly in Jubilees and Enoch: Jub. 22:21; 30:22; I Enoch 1:1; 10:16,20,22; 38:1,3; 45:6; 53:2; 62:2; 69:27ff.; 84:6. Some of these passages relate to the Flood rather than to the Day of Judgment, but the former seems often to be a type of the latter. In most of these citations it is clear that the removal of the wicked makes possible the flourishing life of the righteous.

So also in Ps. 37:10f., the wicked are to be eliminated from the earth, whereas the humble are to flourish there. Their contrastive destinies are depicted in 4Q p Pss^a ii,5-11 (¶¶6-7). The interpretation of vs. 10 is of special interest here:

> The prophetic meaning of the passage concerns all wicked society at the end of forty years, when they will be consumed and no wicked man will be found upon the earth.

This recalls the forty years of warring in the Military Manual, with the final victory of the Sons of Light over the Sons of Darkness being achieved not merely by the dispatch of Michael (1Q M xvii,6f.), but also by the epiphany of God Himself (i,16f.; xviii,1,9). So likewise, in CDC xx,13-27 (9:39-49), a forty-year period follows the death of the Righteous Teacher, during which "all the men of war" are destroyed. There too "the glory of God shines forth to Israel" to "cut off . . . all those of Judah who do wickedly." Herein, it would seem, is the Day of Judgment, marked by the theophany to which a reference once stood at 1Q p Hab x,16f. (¶30).

According to a manuscript of Mt. Athos, the patriarch Levi prayed:

> καὶ τὴν ἀνομίαν ἐξάλειψον
> ὑπὸ κάτοθεν τοῦ οὐρανοῦ
> καὶ συντελέσαι τὴν ἀνομίαν
> ἀπὸ πρώπου τῆς γῆς.

And wipe out lawlessness from beneath the sky,
    and abolish lawlessness from the face of the earth.
(Cited by J. T. Milik, "The Testament of Lévi in Araméen," *RB*, LXII, 1955, pp. 398-406, esp. pp. 401f.)

The day of Judgment will bring the fulfilment of Levi's prayer. According to 4Q Ps^f ix,4-14, the removal of the wicked will result in paradisal conditions on earth:

> They will praise the name of the LORD,
>   for He comes to judge every w[or]k,
> to make the wicked vanish from the earth,
>   [that] perverse [men] may not be found [there].
> The sky [will yield] its dew,
>   and no [wasting will be in] their [bor]ders;
> but the land [will yield] its fruit in its season,
>   and its produce will not disappoint.
> Fruit trees [will yield abundantly],
>   and its [springs] will not fail.
> The meek will eat and be satisfied;
>   those who fear the LORD [will never hunger].

(See J. Starcky in *RB*, LXXIII, 1966, pp. 356f., 366 ff., and Pl. XIII.)

Just as the prophet's message at Hab. 2:20 ended with "the earth," so does the commentary itself; for it will be purged so as to become a fit place where those of God's own planting may take root and thrive, living from the abundance of the fertile earth.

Excursus on the Omission of Chapter Three

Chapter Three of Habakkuk was placed here in the tradition lying back of the canonical book, in order to provide a description of the theophany which was hinted at in 2:20. Or, if the original conclusion of the woes of Chap. 2 was at vs. 17 and Chap. 3 was a disconnected composition, then it may be an editorial process which introduced vs. 20 to prepare for the following theophany, as suggested in "The Composition of Habakkuk," pp. 271, 273. This theophanic understanding of 2:20 accords well with the interest of the author of 1Q p Hab, who interpreted the "glory of the LORD" in vs. 14 as a manifestation of God in judgment. (See ¶30.).

In view of all this, it seems curious that the *pēšer* of Habakkuk should not have presented us with an interpretation of Chap. 3. One explanation would be that the document was never finished. The primary scribe (Hand A) did stop at the end of the second word of xii,13 and leave to a second hand (B) the completion of the scroll, as noted above. However, this latter hand carefully corrected the entire manuscript, according to Malachi Martin, so that the document must have been completed by it.

One early explanation for the omission of Chap. 3 from the commentary was that it was passed over because it was a psalm. This has been disproved, since we now know that the Qumrân Community did have *pěšārîm* on the Psalms. (See my discussion on *Text*, §135a.) Neither is the suggestion that this passage was somehow too sacred (since it contained a depiction of a divine appearance), for 4Q p Nah treats the theophany of Nah. 1. There is, however, the clear evidence of selectivity in a number of the *pěšārîm*, so that it cannot now be claimed that the absence of Chap. 3 proves that Qumrân knew Habakkuk only without its concluding psalm. One factor in the selectivity, as in Isaiah and the Psalms, was undoubtedly the size of the books and the desire to limit each *pēšer* to a modest sized manuscript. The very fact that the theophany of Nahum was handled in one midrashic work would be reason for not treating Hab. 3. Curiously, the surviving fragments of 4Q p Nah seem to allegorize and historicize the text of Nah. 1; but, in working at the problem of restoring the missing text, I have become convinced that it once contained also some references to God's manifestation in judgment—but by a strange coincidence they are all lost in the lacunae! For the evidence, we must await the publication of a subsequent volume.

INDEX TO COMMENTARY

Pericope	1Q p Hab	Habakkuk Text	Page
¶ 1	i,1-5	1:1-2	37
¶ 2	i,5-6	1:3a	39
¶ 3	i,7-10	1:3b	41
¶ 4	i,10-11	1:4a	43
¶ 5	i,12-14	1:4a-4b	45
¶ 6	i,14-16	1:4b	51
¶ 7	i,16–ii,10	1:5	53
¶ 8	ii,10-16	1:6a	59
¶ 9	ii,16–iii,2	1:6b	63
¶10	iii,2-6	1:7	66
¶11	iii,6-14	1:8-9	68
¶12	iii,14-17	1:9c	72
¶13	iii,17–iv,2	1:10a	74
¶14	iv,3-9	1:10b	77
¶15	iv,9-16	1:11	80
¶16	iv,16–v,8	1:12-13a	84
¶17	v,8-12	1:13b	91
¶18	v,12–vi,8	1:14-16	99
¶19	vi,8-12	1:17	104
¶20	vi,12–vii,5	2:1-2	107
¶21	vii,5-8	2:3a	114
¶22	vii,9-14	2:3b	118
¶23	vii,14-17	2:4a	122
¶24	vii,17–viii,3	2:4b	125
¶25	viii,3-13	2:5-6	131
¶26	viii,13–ix,7	2:7-8a	145
¶27	ix,8-12	2:8b	153
¶28	ix,12–x,5	2:9-11	158
¶29	x,5-13	2:12-13	167
¶30	x,14–xi,2	2:14	174
¶31	xi,2-8	2:15	179
¶32	xi,8-17	2:16	190
¶33	xi,17–xii,10	2:17	196
¶34	xii,10-14	2:18	209
¶35	xii,14–xiii,4	2:19-20	212

Reviews

M. P. Horgan, CBQ 43/3 (1981) 440-442

PAUL D. SANSONE, O.F.M.
10 - II - 82   3.12